Little Book of Fixed Stars

Expanded
Second Edition

By Elizabeth Hazel

Cover image credit: Eagle Nebula M16 by Jimmy Walker, October 15, 2015
in Hubble Palette. ESA/Hubble, NASA.gov, available under
the Creative Commons Attribution 4.0 International license.

Quotes from "The Drunken Boat" and from "Vision Letters" from
Arthur Rimbaud: Complete Works translated from the French by Paul Schmidt.
©1967,1970,1971,1972,1975 by Paul Schmidt.
Used by permission of HarperCollins Publishers.

FEED THE AUTHORS!

Authors are not rolling in cash. Most make less than
$10K a year. Please don't plagiarize text or images
from this book! Be polite and request permission before sharing
any of this material in any way. Reader's reviews on Amazon are the best way
to tell an author "thank you." If a book has over 50 reviews, Amazon will list
it in newsletters and other promotions. Reviews can be
short. "I liked it" is fine! It's the number of reviews that matters
the most. And giving the book 4 or 5 stars helps the book, too,
in addition to being a great ego stroke for the author.

KOZMIC KITCHEN PRESS

Little Book of Fixed Stars
Expanded Second Edition

Table of Contents

Part IV Chart Delineations

Introduction to the Expanded Second Edition

Credit for this book goes to Ananke, the Goddess of Necessity and the mother of invention. I needed a star list with current positions in zodiacal order. The stars don't move much, but they *do* move, and there wasn't a printable list available anywhere. The first incarnation of **Little Book of Fixed Stars** was a handout with about seventy stars generated for "Fixed Stars: Lights of Destiny," a presentation first given to members of the SMARRT- Ann Arbor chapter of NCGR in August 2017 and again as a webinar for Kepler College in February 2018. Attendees were enthusiastic to receive the star list.

The second incarnation of the book came into being when I expanded the handout into the first edition of **Little Book of Fixed Stars** during the autumn of 2017. Formatting the astrological glyphs and little Greek letters was a horrible task. Persistence paid off and the book was in production by early 2018. There have been several printings of this home-grown first edition. Every time I ran out of copies, I went to the local copy shop and printed another batch.

The idea of producing a subsequent incarnation as a print-on-demand book was floating around in my brain, but the Borg Queen (my computer at the time) was uncooperative and unreliable. The POD book idea got shelved for happier times. In the meantime, I produced a series of short articles about individual constellations for the NCGR *E-News*. Writing these was an opportunity to study the star lore attached to non-zodiacal constellations.

The Goddess of Fate finally intervened! I moved to a new house during the sweltering summer of 2018. It was like starting my life over again. A new computer arrived in the spring of 2019 and the Borg Queen was retired at last, although that wasn't as exciting as blowing her out of the air lock. Resistance is *not* futile!

Work on the expanded second edition of *LBFS* began in earnest in September 2019. Michael Munkasey was very supportive. He provided a list of star positions for January 2020 and we eventually agreed to include brief meanings from his massive research project on fixed stars. This expanded edition contains 102 additional stars.

I was also pleased to execute original pen-and-ink drawings to supplement the constellation essays and chart samples in Parts III and IV. Seeing where the stars are placed is easier than trying to imagine them. Seeing a portrait helps one get a sense of the individual. Drawing the portraits was a lot of fun. The constellation images were another story.

Copyrighted constellation images were out of the question and were insufficient in any case. Available images were either astronomical star maps, figure drawings without precision, outlines with star names but no figure or sky grid, or the old "God's eye view" illustrations from the 1600-1700s that, while beautifully rendered, are utterly confusing because they're backwards and don't indicate star names or letters. There were no images that incorporated astronomically precise star positions, the sky grid, full figure illustrations, star names *and* Greek letters. I followed IAU star maps for precise positioning, sketched the figures around the stars and let the devil take the hindmost. Chris Hemsworth wasn't available for life drawings, much to my sorrow, and using accurate star positions resulted in distorted body shapes. Poor Orion and Auriga ended up with long torsos and stubby legs! It wasn't all bad, though; the buff-and-studly Boötes was a revelation that exemplifies the constellation's heroic distant past history so much more than a scruffy mountain man.

Allow me to convey a few heartfelt acknowledgements: I'd like to thank my parents for their continued and generous support, and the friends who kindly feed me and thereby save me from my own horrible cooking. More thanks to the SMARRT board and group members who have been constantly enthusiastic about my presentations and literary efforts.

I hope that this book proves to be useful, enlightening, and inspires more research into fixed stars. If this is your first book on fixed stars, I'm honored. As the ancient Romans used to say, *per aspera ad astra* – the road to the stars is rough. That phrase can be understood in various ways. In the esoteric realm of soul transmigration, moving from one lifetime to the next through the Gates of Life and Death to the path of the stars blazed by the Milky Way and then returning for the next incarnation is a difficult journey. Learning to understand oneself and becoming familiar with the destiny plotted by one's natal planets and stars is the job of a lifetime. I like to think that a hidden meaning of the phrase is a red flag for astrologers – that understanding the fixed stars and their role in astrology is a rocky road, but one imminently worthy of one's efforts.

May the light of the stars and the songs of the spheres guide you along the way!

Elizabeth Hazel
May 15, 2020

Michael Munkasey's Star Position Calculations and Star Meanings

I was exceptionally grateful to have the aid and assistance of Michael Munkasey when expanding the fixed star list for the second edition. He also contributed brief star meanings to most of the entries. These are denoted by [**MM**:] in the text. These meanings are derived from his massive fixed star research project. Michael is comparing the influence of planet-star contacts on nearly 1,000 AA-rated charts and looking for consistencies.

Michael also calculated the star positions for January 1, 2020. I asked him to explain how he performed these calculations, which differ somewhat from other sources. This is his answer in his own words:

I started with the formal German Astronomical FK3 (Fundamental Catalog 3) back in the 1970s. FK3 had (with German precision) about 1500 bodies included - along with the numbers needed to move those bodies over time. I think they are presently on FK6, maybe FK7. In FK3 they gave math equations showing how to move stars over time.

I went through FK3, extracted the math, and wrote computer programs to assist me in moving the bodies I had selected over time. I was working for WMATA (The Washington Metropolitan Area Transportation Authority) in their computer department and had access to IBM 360 and Hewlett Packard computer equipment. I did all of this on my own time, staying after work hours - and also on weekends.

Then I discovered the Yale Catalog of Bright Stars that lists about 9,300 bodies, along with the information necessary to move stars over time. Wrote a computer program for that.

The head astronomer at the Naval Observatory who gave me an article published in the 1940s on moving star bodies over time. It uses Vectors with a Precession Matrix. Each of the three methods I had for moving stars over time gave the same results - almost to the second of arc. The equations and data I use account for both precessional as well as a body's proper movement in space. Precession accounts for 99% of a body's movement. Precession moves a body backwards in the Zodiac about one degree every 72 years. A body's proper motion is almost negligible - but since I can include it in my work, why not?

In the 1980s I obtained the data in the Yale Catalog in a computer readable form. This saved copying all of those numbers by hand. That data is what I use now. The data in the Yale Catalog of Bright Stars from the Yale University Astronomy Department is accurate enough for astrological work. With the computer programs I have (written in BASIC and now on my Macintosh laptop - originally I did the work in FORTRAN) I can take any the Yale 9300+ entries and generate the data to produce a multi-century star position list.

So that is how I do it. I ran maybe 1000 bodies using the Yale data, and from these I extracted the 360 I use. Are my star positions accurate? As accurate as the Yale (or German) source data. Where do Solar Fire, etc., get their positions? I don't know. But they certainly are not as accurate as what I have produced. I have noted slight position and star name errors in the Solar Fire, etc., data too. I was more meticulous.

It's an honor to include an early glimpse of Michael's star meanings in this text. His full-length star meanings will be printed in his forthcoming fixed star book. Michael's meanings sometimes contrast with the traditional star meanings. Others confirm the ancient lore. Enjoy!

The Greek Alphabet

Form	Name	Latin
A α	alpha	A a
B β	beta	B b
Γ γ	gamma	G g, ng
Δ δ	delta	D d
E ε	epsilon	E e
Z ζ	zeta	Z z
H η	eta	E e
Θ θ	theta	Th th
I ι	iota	I I
K κ	kappa	K k, C c
Λ λ	lambda	L l
M μ	mu	M m
N ν	nu	N n
Ξ ξ	xi	X x
O o	omicron	O o
Π π	pi	P p
P ρ	rho	Rh rh, r
Σ σ ς	sigma	S s
T τ	tau	T t
Y υ	upsilon	Y, y, u
Φ φ	phi	Ph ph
X χ	chi	Ch ch (k)
Ψ ψ	psi	Ps ps
Ω ω	omega	O o

Part I

The
Fixed Stars
In
Zodiacal
Order

List of Fixed Stars in Zodiacal Order
247 stars and 20 celestial points with positions calculated for January 2020

Aries

Intersection of the Ecliptic and Earth's Equator 0♈00. Sun at 0° North/South, conjunct ecliptic. Spring Equinox or Aries Ingress.

Scheat 0♈00/+28.21 (beta Pegasus, Mag 2.6 variable, ♂☿) from *Al Said*, the shoulder of the left leg. Free-thinker, creative, logical, intellectual, fast, dare to do the impossible; impulsive, headstrong, rash, prone to fantasizing. Gain and lose friends; forced to relocate. With difficult planets, troubles and losses, danger of accidents, prison, and sudden death. Mundane events include dangers from floods, mudslides, collapsing buildings, serious accidents, riots, droughts, contaminated or poisoned water, especially on ASC or MC.

Super Galactic Anti-Center 1♈08/-13. Located a bit north of beta Cetus.

Kerb 1♈19/+23.50 (*tau Pegasus*, Mag 4.6, ♂☿) Adventures, risk-taking, potential for accidents.

Deneb Kaitos 2♈52/-17.43 (*beta Cetus*, Mag 2.04, ♄) aka **Difda**. From *Al Dhanab al Kaitos al Janubiyy*, the Tail of the Whale toward the South. Inhibitions, restraints. Brutality, forced or compulsory changes, misfortunes, recklessness and speculation that leads to own undoing. MM: Reconsideration, review, responses to criticism, raises issues from the past.

Heaven's Sewer 6♈10/-10.21 (*phi 1 Cetus*, Mag 4.7, ♃♄) Misfortunes with no control.

Algenib 9♈26/+15.27 (*gamma Pegasus*, Mag 2.8, ♂☿) from *Al Janb*, the side. Wing tip. Penetrating mind, strong will, determination. Good speaker. Distinctive career may end in notoriety, misfortune, poverty. MM: Develop mannerisms, needs to be noticed, seeks public attention. Simple lifestyle, willing to undertake controversial assignments.

Alderamin 13♈03/+62.48 (*alpha Cepheus*, Mag 2.6, ♄♃) from *Al Dhira al Yamin*, the right arm. Marks the shoulder of the king. Cepheus is an inconspicuous but highly regarded constellation, with one foot on the celestial north pole and the other on the solstitial colure. This star will become the north star in 7500 CE. Authority, sobriety, judgments, hard lessons in life. MM: Sets personal standards for achievement; practice, motivated to improve, inspiring confident manner.

Alpheratz 14♈35/+29.21 (*alpha Andromeda*, Mag 2, ♃♀) from *Al Surrat al Faras*, the horse's navel; the lucky star shared by Pegasus and Andromeda. Marks her hair. Honor, independence, wealth, good mind. MM: Weigh alternatives, appraise and evaluate opportunities before making choices.

Revati 20♈09/+7.50 (*zeta 1 Pisces*, Mag 5.24, ♃♀) Fortunate star in the Fish, name from the Hindu nakshatra. MM: Shapes opinions, confronts needs, communicates views and opinions, speak through action.

Baten Kaitos 22♈14/-10.06 (*zeta Cetus*, Mag 3.7, ♄) from *Al Batn al Kaitos*, the Whale's belly. Forced emigration, accidents, bad luck. Shipwrecks and rescues, falls and blows. MM: Must respond and take responsibility for decisions; faces hard choices.

Acamar 23♈33/-40.07 (*theta 1 Eridanus*, Mag 3.4, ♄) The former terminal star of the River, later replaced with Achernar. MM: Visionary, idealist, productive, creative, marketing savvy, understands promotion.

Cassiopeia A 26♈42/+58. Radio galaxy with strongest known source of radio emissions.

Al Pherg 27♈06/+15.36 (*eta Pisces*, Mag 3.6, ♄♃) Preparedness, steady and determined efforts lead to eventual success.

Local Galactic Group Center 27♈11/+41. Near gamma Andromeda. MM: Faces and resolves dilemmas and confrontations, challenges views of others, ends up in situations with more than one interpretation.

Vertex 28♈07/+41.32 (*NGC0224* or *M31 Andromeda*, Mag 3.4, ♂☽) The Queen of the Nebulae. Family quarrels, separations, emotional turbulence. A major source of X-ray and radio emissions.

Northern Intersection of the Local System and Galactic Equators 28♈30/+60. [MM] Versatility, sees and adapts to different perspectives, makes selections from range of choices, creates new approaches

Al Resha 29♈40/+2.6 (*alpha 2 Pisces*, Mag 4.3, ♂☿) from Babylonian Riksu, The Cord. Lucida star of Pisces, marks the knot of the cord between the two fishes. Fortunate, prosperous, good friends. MM: Learns emotional control and to control reactions; becomes aware of postures and gestures that can intimidate.

Taurus

Mirach 0♉41/+35.53 (*beta Andromeda*, Mag 2, ♀) from *Mi'zar*, the Girdle. Beauty & brains, fame, fortune. Artistic skills. Love affairs, possibly scandalous. Sexual desirability and attraction. If badly aspected, excessive desire for sex or other temptations, infidelities, using beauty or sex to manipulate others, and indolence. MM: Need for attention and self promotion, urge to make contributions.

Stella Mira 1♉48/-2.46 (*omicron Cetus*, Mag-highly variable, ♄) The Whale's neck. A flushed yellow star that varies in magnitude from 1.7 to 9.5 over 331 days. Gains and losses, inconsistent stability or poverty. Maritime or naval careers. Marks the south pole of the Milky Way. MM: Acquire flexibility, make adjustments to plans or intentions.

Angetenar 2♉54/-22.55 (*tau Eridanus*, Mag 4.8, ♄) Marks a bend in the River, a stream of golden tears for Apollo's son Phaëthon. Accidents, sorrows, and losses, maritime professions, voyages of discovery that lead to skills and wisdom gained through experience. Out-of-body or near-death experiences, powerful dreams, contact with alternate dimensions, spirits and ghosts. Interest in the passage of time, history, and antiquities.

Mesarthim 3♉27/+19.03 (*gamma Aries*, Mag 4.8, ♂♄) May be from Hebrew word for "ministers." Risk, impulsive nature, a daredevil. Heights. Head injuries.

Sheratan 4♉15/+21.02 (*beta Aries*, Mag 2.6, ♂♄) from *Al Sharatain*, the Signs [of the opening year] from name of lunar mansion with Mesarthim, a protective pair. Hindu Ashwini, the horsemen and healers. Similar meanings – impulsive, daredevil, head injuries. Head-butting, bullying, strong opinions, forceful nature, strong will power. MM: Acquiring and retaining dogmatic views, the idea that one is correct.

Caph 5♉23/+59.25 (*beta Cassiopeia*, Mag 2.2, ♄♀) Upper right corner of queen's throne. Called "the Guest Star" or Pilgrim star, considered a temporary abode of souls between earth and the afterlife. MM: Seeks answers to the who-what-how-why-when of situations.

Alphirk 5♉49/+70.47 (*beta Cepheus*, Mag 3.2, ♄♃) Authority, sobriety, judgments, hard lessons in life. MM: Desires prominence, acts out, shows of display.

Hamal 7♉57/+23.41 (*alpha Aries*, Mag 2, ♂♄) from *Al Ras al Hamal*, head of the sheep. Forehead or horn of the Ram. Babylonian Si-Mal, the Horn star, and I-ku, the Prince or

Leading One. First of ten Akkadian King stars on ecliptic. Brutish, headstrong, violent. May mingle with Schedir: overly influenced by spouse, unable to get away from bad spouse, or spousal abandonment. MM: curiosity, need to forge ahead or investigate for satisfaction.

Schedir 8♉04/+56.48 (*alpha Cassiopeia*, Mag 2.2, ♄♀) from *al Sadr*, the breast. Queen chained to a throne. Gentle, decent, diplomatic, but also intrigue, power games. Possible marital problems, difficult or scandalous divorces. MM: May face disappointments, challenges, unlucky breaks and must work through them.

Azha 9♉01/-8.49 (*eta Eridanus*, Mag 4.9, ♄) Accidents, sorrows, and losses, maritime professions, voyages of discovery that lead to skills and wisdom gained through experience. Out-of-body or near-death experiences, powerful dreams, contact with alternate dimensions, spirits and ghosts. Interest in the passage of time, history, and antiquities.

Achird 10♉31/+58.04 (*eta Cassiopeia*, Mag 3.4, ♀☿) Beauty and talent. MM: Efforts to maintain stability and achieve balance through conflicts.

Alamaak or Almach 14♉30/+42.33 (*gamma 1 Andromeda*, Mag 2.2 binary, ♀☿) from *Al 'Anak al 'Ard*, a badger-like creature. Marks left foot. Fame, artistic skills, honor, eminence. Love affairs, artistic skills, and the likelihood of scandalous love affairs. Sexual desirability and attraction. If badly aspected, excessive desire for sex or other temptations, infidelities; using beauty or sex to manipulate others, and indolence. MM: Increases drive and motivation to move beyond difficulties and obstacles.

Menkar 14♉36/+4.16 (*alpha Cetus*, Mag 2.53, ♄) aka **Mekab**, the Monster's mouth. Unexpected events and situations that impact the person for good or evil. Injury, loss, evil legacy, confinement. A tyrant to others. MM: Arouses sympathy to the misfortunes and needs of people in bad situations.

Ruchbah 18♉12/+60.29 (*delta Cassiopeia*, Mag 2.68, ♄♀) MM: Encounters difficulties that prevent achieving the fulfillment of goals.

Botein 21♉07/+19.47 (*delta Aries*, Mag 4.5, ♀) Fertile, productive star of Aries.

Zaurak 24♉09/-13.23 (*gamma Eridanus*, Mag 3, ♄) Accidents, sorrows, and losses, maritime professions, voyages of discovery that lead to skills and wisdom gained through experience. Out-of-body or near-death experiences, powerful dreams, contact with alternate dimensions, spirits and ghosts. Interest in the passage of time, history, and antiquities. MM: Helps with visualization, conceptualization, building on dreams.

Capulus 24♉28/+57.22 (*NGC 0869* or *33Hvi Perseus*, Mag 5.2, ♂☿) Nebula in Sword of Perseus. Turbulent mind and powerful passions, brute strength, forceful. Can focus on good or be ruthless and violent. Use of weapons. Strong sexual energies/libido.

Caput Algol 26♉27/+41.08 (*beta Perseus*, Mag 2.1 variable binary, ♄♃) Latin *Caput* [head] and Arabic *Al Ghul*, the demon or ghoul. Medusa's head. Misfortune, bad death, victory over others. Work with metal, mining, jewels or jewelry. Strong protective properties in talismanic magic, assoc with diamonds. Mundane—mass fatalities. MM: Must work through difficult situations or in demanding environments.

Miram 28♉59/+56.05 (*eta Perseus*, Mag 3.7, ♂♄) Strength, courage, honor. Competitive challenges, daring. MM: Driven to make a lasting impression, leaves enduring contributions.

Beid 29♉42/-6.47 (*omicron Eridanus*, Mag 4.1, ♄) cluster of small stars at the bend of the River. Accidents, sorrows, and losses, maritime professions, adventures that lead to skills and wisdom. Out-of-body or near-death experiences, powerful dreams, contact with alternate dimensions, spirits and ghosts. Interest in the passage of time, history, and antiquities.

Northern Intersection of Galactic and Super Galactic Equators 29♉28/+59. Miram [*eta Perseus*] is the closest star to the northern intersection.

Gemini

Beemim and Theemim 0♊09/-30.31 (*upsilon Eridanus 1, 2, 3, and 4*, Mag 3.9, ♄). A small cluster of stars at a curve in the River, rarely used in natal astrology.

Pleiades 29♉34 to 0♊40/+24 (*eta Taurus*, Mag 3.0 cluster, Alcyone -☽♃. The whole cluster - ♂☽) Seven daughters of Atlas and Pleione: Alcyone [brightest star at 00♊16, called *Al Jauz*, the walnut; Sanskrit Amba, the mother], Maia [first born, mother of Hermes], Electra, Taygete, Celaeno, Sterope, and Merope [wife of Sisyphus, the missing sister who hid in shame]. Omar Khayyam called them Parwin the Begetters, beginning of all things. Rosette of diamonds or pearls, seal of immortality. Flock of doves that carried ambrosia to infant Zeus. Assyrian Kimtu or Kimmatu, a family group that influence the fate of humanity. Travel, intellect. Love, fame; mothering, foster children, accidents to face, fevers. Family separations, restrictions, banishment; odd-eyed or eye problems. Hindu – Krittikas, the wives of the Seven Rishis or Sages (Ursa Major), mothers to Muruga (Mars). MM: Alcyone gives resourcefulness to find satisfaction in life.

Keid 0♊26/-7.37 (*omicron 2 Eridanus*, Mag 4.5, ♄) Minor star in the River.

Marfak 2♊22/+50.01 (*alpha Perseus*, Mag 1.7, ♃♄) aka **Mirfak**, Arabic for The Elbow. Strength, courage, honor. Competitive challenges, daring. MM: Driven to overcome limitations and move beyond impediments.

Hyades 6♊05/+15.44 (*gamma Taurus*, Mag 3.6, ♄☿) Group of sisters named for their lost brother Hyas. Daughters of Atlas and Aethra. Half sisters of Pleiades, the nurses of Bacchus. Anglo-Saxon Raedgastran. Cluster of six stars marks the forehead of the bull. Tears and grieving, sudden changes, wounds. Changes of fortune. With ASC/MC – military leaders, fortunes of war, loot, impetuosity. Connected to rain, storms, tempests. MM: Desire to shape opinion, efforts to gain recognition for achievements.

Ain 8♊45/+19.17 (*epsilon Taurus*, Mag 3.5, ♀☽) MM: Ability to devise multiple approaches to a situation or encounter.

Aldebaran 10♊04 /+16.36 (*alpha Taurus*, Mag .85, ♂ *or* ♃♂) from *Al Dabaran*, the Follower (of the Pleiades) or *'Ain al Thaur*, the Bull's Eye. Stella Dominatrix, drives Pleiades before it. Royal Watcher star Taschetar, the creator spirit that brings rain. Popularity, power, wealth, intelligence, eloquence, integrity. Success doesn't last; possible disease, violent death. An intense infrared source. MM: Able to manage various opposing elements and things that demand attention.

Tabit 12♊12/+7.02 (*pi 3 Orion*, Mag 3.1, ♂☿) Fist that holds the shield. MM: Motivated to save others from themselves. May have strong opinions.

Witch Head Nebula 15♊12/-7.1 (*IC2118 Eridanus*, Mag 13, ♃☽) Strange unexplainable events, synchronicity. MM: Careful examination of the implications of proposals and preparations.

Kursa or Cursa 15♊33/-5.02 (*beta Eridanus*, Mag 2.7, ♄) from *Al Kursiyy al Jauzah*, the chair/footstool of the Central One. Supports Rigel (Orion's left foot). The star at the whirlpool. Involvement in emerging trends, fashions, arts and culture, medical and technological developments. Information, news, and discoveries that spread quickly through society. MM:

Seeks to appease conflicts that arise, adjust circumstances to reduce discontentment.

Al Kab or Hasselah 16♊54/+33.11 (*iota Auriga*, Mag 2.9, ♂☿) Star in Auriga's left knee. Potential injuries to knees and legs, lack of mobility. Alternate means of locomotion. Survival conditions that necessitate invention and creativity.

Rigel 17♊07/-8.09 (*beta Orion*, Mag 0.12, ♃♂) from *Rijl Jauzah al Yusza*, the left leg of Jauzah. In early Arabic lore, Al Jauzah was the term for a black sheep with a white spot at mid-body. Designates the Central One of the Sky, the large sky figure that straddles the ecliptic. The foot in river. Shares knowledge, educator, mass communications, vanguard of trends, zeitgeist, disperses information to improve society. MM: Gives focus, intensity, persistence; the need to evaluate situations with care.

Sadaltoni 18♊54/+41.06 (*Hoedus 1-zeta Auriga*, Mag 3.8 variable, ♂☿) from *Al Said al Thani*, the second arm. An orange star. Hoedus 1 and 2 mark the pair of kids/baby goats held beneath the Nanny Goat star Capella in the arm of Auriga. Greek *Eriphoi*. A frivolous attitude, lust and promiscuity, criminality, and bad habits. Ungrateful children or bad seeds. Custodial relationships to children, groups, flocks.

Hoedus II 19♊43/+41.10 (*eta Auriga*, Mag 3.3, ♂☿) Frivolous, fickle. Sports, lust-driven. Lies, doesn't fulfill promises. Disgrace and possible ruin from excesses. Manilius writes of business, judicial, and governmental talents when the Hoedi are setting (7th/8th houses).

Ensis 20♊26/-2.22 (*eta Orion*, Mag 3.3, ♂☿) Near M42. The star that marks the sword or genitals of Al Jauzah. Potency, legacy, potential to create a dynasty or found lasting institutions. MM: Address and nurture one's self-image, persist in spite of pressures or setbacks.

Bellatrix 21♊14/+6.23 (*gamma Orion*, Mag 1.6, ♂☿-☽) The Amazon star, Latin for female warrior. *Al Najid*, the Conqueror, or *Al Murzim al Najid*, the roaring conqueror that announces the rising of Rigel. Also *Al Mankib*, the left shoulder. Success after long struggles, fleeting honors, wealth, help through high status friends, harsh voice. MM: Develop flexibility and adaptability to meet and confront change.

Capella 22♊08/+46.02 (*alpha Auriga*, Mag .08, ♂☿) Latin for Little She Goat; aka **Albajoth**. Other names are Capra, Hircus, and Amalthea. The Horn of Plenty. India – Brahma Ridaya, the Heart of Brahma. Akkadian Dil-gan I-ku, Messenger of Light, the Leader, the Star of Marduk. Northernmost Mag 1 star. Military honors, wealth, fame, curiosity, knowledgeable, aid from helpful friends. May be timid but curious. MM: Gives motivation to achieve fame, recognition and celebrity.

Phact 22♊27/-34.03 (*alpha Columba*, Mag 2.6, ♀☿) Right wing of dove. Generous, lucky. Adventures, seeking knowledge. Going into the unknown, uncharted, unexplored zones. MM: An adventurer, risk-taker, willing to push the limits of exploration.

El Nath 22♊51/+28.38 (*beta Taurus*, Mag 1.6, ♂) from *Al Natih*, the Butting One. Shared star: tip of the north horn of the Bull and also Auriga's left foot. Assoc with Hindu fire god Agni and Hutabhuj, devourer of the sacrifice. Fortune and high status. Neutral party. Interest in religion or sciences. Problems with partners. Wounds, accidents, foot injuries. Close to the galactic anti-center. MM: Encourages development of a social conscience, likely to be rebellious and outspoken.

Hatsya 23♊16/-5.56 (*iota Orion*, Mag 2.9, ♄☿) Star in Orion's sword, meanings similar to Ensis (20♊).

The Great Nebula 23♊18/-5.26 (*NGC1976* or *M42 Orion*, Mag 4 nebula, ♂☽) In Sword of Orion near Ensis. Vision problems, illnesses, violent death. May start a dynasty with great or notable progeny. MM: The ability to concentrate, focus on important matters at hand.

Orion's Belt: The Belt has been called *Al Nijad* or *Al Nasak* (the Line); *Al Alkat* (golden grains, nuts or spangles). In Latin Balteus (belt). In Scandinavia - Frigge Rok (Freya's distaff). The three kings or the three Marys. Sometimes associated with measurements as Elwand, the yardstick. The three stars of the belt signify good fortune, strength, energy, organizational skills, lasting fortune, good memory, legacies, influential friends, and gifts. Sometimes scandals from love affairs.

    Mintaka 22♊30/+0.16 (*delta 2 Orion*, Mag 2.2 binary, ♄☿ or ♃♄) from *Al Mintakah*, the belt. MM: A desire to nurture and develop talents, ideas, creations.

    Alnilam 23♊45/-1.11 (*epsilon Orion*, Mag 1.7, ♄☿ or ♃♄) from *Al Nilam*, string of pearls, the central star of the belt. MM: Develop marks of personal distinction, uniqueness, personal trademarks.

    Alnitak 24♊58/-1.56 (*zeta Orion*, Mag 2, ♄☿ or ♃♄) The Girdle, from *Al Nusak*, a line. MM: The ability to develop insightful, innovative approaches and new ways forward.

Crab Nebula 24♊22/+22.02 (*NGC1952* or *M1 Taurus*, Mag 8.4, ♂☽)

Meissa 23♊58/+9.54 (*lambda Orion*, Mag 3.7, ♃♄) From *Al Maisan*, the head. Also *Ras al Jauzah*, head of the Central One. Confident and honorable but foolish, impious, inconstant. Orion has brilliant body stars with dim head stars, isn't always wise or shrewd.

Al Hecka 25♊04/+21.10 (*zeta Taurus*, Mag 3, ♂ [☿♄]) South horn. Scholarly, strategic thinker, bad habits and low friends. Ambushes and accidents.

Wezn 26♊34/-35.45 (*beta Columba*, Mag 3.12, ♀☿) Like Phact - generous, lucky. Adventures, seeking knowledge. Going into the unknown, uncharted, unexplored zones.

Saiph 26♊40/-09.41 (*kappa Orion*, Mag 2.2 triple star, ♃♄) From *Saif al Jabbar*, sword of the giant. Right foot of the Central One. Relentless pursuit of goals, crush obstacles underfoot. MM: Honoring personal convictions, relentless pursuit of goals and missions.

Galactic Anti-Center (GAC) 27♊07/+29. Astronomical point opposite to the Galactic Center. Nearby star is El Nath (*beta Taurus*) and Taurus T-4, a stellar T-association with clouds of interstellar dust and variable young stars near a dark nebula. It is a strong infrared emitter, a property associated with messages received in the subconscious mind.

Polaris 28♊51/+89.05 (*alpha Ursa Minor*, Mag 2.1, ♄♀) from *Stella Polaris*, the Pole Star. Aka *Stella Maris*, Phoenice, the Lode Star, Anglo-Saxon Seip-steorra, the ship star. India – Grahadhara, the pivot of the planets, seat of god Dhruva. Semetic *Mismar*, needle or nail; Arabic *Al Katb al Shamaliyy*, the North Axle or spindle; *Al Katb*, the Pin; *Al Fass*, the Hole (in which Earth's axle has its bearing). Tramontana, peak of Mons Coelius. Hindu - Mount Meru, Norse – Himinbiorg, home of Heimdal the guardian; the seat of the gods. Exact at the celestial north pole on March 24, 2100. Navigational star. Finding the direction, a leader who shows the way for others, but not for self. Can augur violence, harm, difficulties in life. Losses, evil legacies. MM: Motivated to develop a personal perspective and a comprehensive world-view to aid in understanding situations.

Betelgeuze 29♊02/+7.24 (*alpha Orion*, Mag .05 variable, ♂♀) From *Ibt al Jauzah*, the armpit of the Central One or *Ied Algeuze*, the right hand. Right shoulder, a red-orange giant. Fortune, military honor, wealth and kingly attributes. Blessings, success without complications. Ingenuity and high status. An intense infrared source. MM: Devotion to personal development and the ability to remain adaptable to life's changes.

Cancer

Celestial North Pole 0♋00/+90. Greatest separation of Sun from ecliptic at 23°26' North. Near chi 2 Orion and Tejat Prior [*eta Gemini*].

Menkalinan 0♋11/+44.56 (*beta Auriga*, Mag 1.9 variable, ♂☿) from *Al Mankib dhi'l Inan*, the shoulder of the Rein Holder (right shoulder). Burdens, responsibilities, struggle with parenting or attaining high professional goals. Disgrace, danger, ruin. Inherited family traits, both strengths and weaknesses. MM: Exploring potentials and new possibilities, desire for expansion.

Propus or Tejat Prior 3♋43/+22.29 (*eta Gemini*, Mag 3.2 variable spectroscopic double, ☿♀) Star in Castor's foot. Very close to the intersection of the ecliptic and galactic equator. Charm, talent, share inspiration with others, influential. MM: Ability to make adjustments, rework/retool, proceed with necessary alterations.

Tejat Secunda 5♋35/+22.28 (*mu Gemini*, Mag 2.8, ☿♀) Charm, talent, share inspiration with others, influential. MM: Able to manage complexities, entanglements; sees life as a form to be molded.

Mirzam 7♋28/-17.59 (*beta Canis Major*, Mag 1.9, ♃♂) from *Al Murzim*, the Announcer. Right fore-paw of the dog. Makes a statement, carries a message, brings new ideas to the world; physical feats. May be all potential but no outcome. MM: Develops personal style, flair, lively, attracted to fresh ideas and novelties.

Alhena 10♋13/+16.21 (*gamma Gemini*, Mag 1.9, ☿♀) from *Al Han'ah*, name of lunar mansion, the foot of Pollux; aka *Al Misan*, the Proudly Marching One. A sign of importance or physical marks, determined to achieve goals, forward momentum**.** Indelible evidence of events or achievements. MM: Motivated to address and resolve unexpected complications and sudden demands.

Mebsuta 9♋56/+25.04 (*epsilon Gemini*, Mag 2.9, ☿♀) Another Twin foot star – charm and talent. MM: Develop an individual style, personal interests, create a unique self-identity.

Dolones or Stimulus 8 to 10♋/+40 to +52 (*psi 1 to 10 Auriga*) The Goads or Whip stars. A mean streak, ruthlessness, cruelty. Demagogues whipping the masses into a frenzy.

Sirius 14♋21/-16.48 (*alpha Canis Major*, Mag -1.4, ♃♂) The nose of the dog. The Scorcher or The Shining One. Also *Elseiri* from Greek, Arabic *Al Shi'ra*, brightly shining one; possibly related to Sanskrit *Surya*, the shining one, Chaldean *Kakkab Lik-ku*, star of the dog, and Assyrian *Kab-bu-Samas*, Dog of the Sun. Early Egyptian Isis-Sepdet, late Egyptian -Greek *Sothis*. Arabic *Barakish* for 1,000 colors. African *Yoonir*. Mixed meanings: Benefic in ancient Egypt as its rising coincided with rise of the Nile. Difficult star in other cultures associated with fevers, plagues and disease, summer heat and drought. Power over the weather. Wealth and renown. Injects charisma into the planet; small actions that have large consequences. Dog pays attention to Orion but watches for the Hare (Lepus). Both protective and dangerous. Lengthy observation and written records led to discovery of precession, written about by Hipparchus. Position very close to Super Galactic South Pole. MM: Recognize one's personal destiny, strive to achieve recognition and success.

Canopus 15♋14/-52.44 (*alpha Carinae/Argo*, Mag -0.7, ♄♃) Egyptian patron god of pilots and voyagers, also name of the pilot of the Argonauts. Rudder or oar of the ship. Egyptian *Karbana*, Coptic *Kahi Nub*, the Golden Earth. Arabic *Suhail* or *Al Sahl* - brilliant, glorious, wise. Able to transform evil into good. Knowledgeable from travels, spiritual and occult interests; associated with precious stones and immunity from disease. Path finder, possible memories of past lives. Writers and actors. Strongly associated with water and maritime activities. Rose at autumn equinox in 6500 BCE. MM: Creative, industrious, inventive, spearheads innovative new projects.

Super Galactic South Pole 16♋20/-15. Nearest stars are alpha and gamma Canis Major.

Wasat 18♋48/+21.53 (*delta Gemini*, Mag 3.5, ♄) from *Al Wasat*, the middle; on the ecliptic. Star at the waist or elbow of Pollux. Mastery of skills and abilities, gain expertise and mastery but prone to sorrows, loss of position, exile, legal problems. Uranus discovered near this star in 1781. MM: Develops talents and goals to a higher level. Exaggerates ambitions.

Castor 20♋31/+31.46 (*alpha 2 Gemini*, Mag 1.9 binary, ☿) aka *Eques*, the Horseman. North Twin. The mortal son of Tyndarus and Leda. Horses, intellectual, writing and law, success and creativity that flows easily, unobstructed. Travel, fame, morals, refinement. Social critic, satirical. MM: Heightens communication skills, adds charisma through words, writings, and speeches.

Adhara 21♋02/-29.03 (*epsilon Canis Major*, Mag 1.5, ♃♂) Protective, charismatic, defensive. MM: Increases the desire for perfection, investigates details, devises successful approaches and solutions.

Gomeisa 22♋28/+8.11 (*beta Canis Minor*, Mag 2.9, ☿♂) Star in the smaller dog. Separation, sorrows. MM: Intense focus on inquiry, investigation, digging deeper for answers.

Muscida 23♋16/+60.39 (*omicron Ursa Major*, Mag 3.5, ♂) Tip of the Great Bear's nose. Strong instincts and senses. A nose for trouble, curiosity, urge for discovery. Dangers and disasters.

Wezen 23♋24/-26.23 (*delta Canis Major*, Mag 1.5, ♃♂) Swiftness, fleeting opportunities, may be jealous, stubborn, contrary. MM: Deal with consequences of contrasting viewpoints.

Pollux 23♋30/+27 (*beta Gemini*, Mag 1.2, ♂) South Twin. Immortal son of Zeus and Leda. Boxer, judge, can be cruel, tyrannical. Crafty and cunning, audacious. Eminence and renown; also a tormented artist, difficulties swamp efforts, constant struggles, deceived or tricked by others. Successes and losses. Gall bladder and stomach problems. May emigrate, travel for work or study. Brings hidden information to light; social critic. MM: Strength of purpose and direction, overcome indecision.

Procyon 26♋04/+5.05 (*alpha Canis Minor*, Mag 0.3 binary, ☿♂) from Greek *Procanis*, before the Great Dog. North of Canis Major. Arabic *Al Ghumaisa* – dim, weeping, sister left in tears when sister Suhail (Sirius) and Jauzah (Orion) fled south across the river [Milky Way]. Euphratean *Kakkab Paldara* – Star of the Crossing of the Water Dog. Hasty, jealous, stubborn. Sudden changes. Rapid but fleeting success. Advantages should be leveraged quickly. Mouthy, hot temper, illicit wealth, promotions. MM: Learn how to cope with situations that take unanticipated twists and turns.

Aludra 29♋49/-29.25 (*eta Canis Major*, Mag 2.4, ♃♂) Defensive, courageous, loyal, alert. MM: the need to communicate through actions, events, deeds, and personal efforts.

Leo

Tegmen 1♌37/+17.29 (*zeta 1 Cancer*, Mag 5.4, ☿♀) Charming, hospitable, talkative, social, enjoys gatherings.

Talitha 3♌04/+47.57 (*iota Ursa Major*, Mag 3.1, ♂) Star in fore-paw of the Great Bear.

Al Tarf 4♌32/+9.01 (*beta Cancer*, Mag 3.5, ☿♀) Charming, hospitable, talkative, social, enjoys gatherings. MM: Keen awareness, comprehension, understanding.

Praesepe 7♌40/+19.21 (M44 *epsilon Cancer*, cluster-nebula, Mag 6.3, ♂☽) from Latin for a manger or crib. The Crab Nebula or Beehive. The manger of the Aselli. Hard worker, diligent, orderly, fecund, entrepreneurial skills. Eye problems, infectious diseases, miscarriages; may speak with spirits. MM: Leadership skills, sharp focus on achieving goals.

Asellus Borealis 7♌49/+21.17 (*gamma Cancer*, Mag 4.6, ♂☉) The northern ass. Pair of mules near the manger (Praesepe) in the body of the Crab. Hospitable, protective, possible accidents, falls. MM: Heightens focus on self-image, promotes personal accomplishments, desire to be noticed.

Asellus Australis 9♌00/+17.57 (*delta Cancer*, Mag 3.9, ♂☉) The southern ass. Unfair accusations, oversensitive to criticism. Burns, fevers, fires, disgraces. Portent of violent death. MM: rash, impulsive, controversial, pushy.

Giansar 10♌36/+69.13 (*lambda Draco*, Mag 4.1, ♄♂) from Persian *Giauzar* or Arabic *Jauzahar*, the Poison Place. Also Nodus Secundus, the Second Knot. Central star of Draco.

Kochab 13♌36/+73.57 (*beta Ursa Minor*, Mag 2, ♄♀) aka **Alrucaba**, from Arabic *Al Kaukab al Shamaliyy*, the Star of the North, from Assyrian/Chaldean *Kakkab*, star. On the back of the small bear. Indifference, improvidence, troubles in life. MM: Attention on matters that require deep, thorough scrutiny.

Acubens 13♌55/+11.39 (*alpha Cancer*, Mag 4.2, ♄☿) aka **Sertan**; from *Al Zubanah*, the Claws. Marks south claw. Patient, heroic, worries about family problems. Endings. Social status. Magnetic and artistic. Imbalanced or jumpy nature. Ordeals and disappointments with difficult planets. MM: Need to be noticed, strong opinions and viewpoints.

Dubhe 15♌29/+61.28 (*alpha Ursa Major*, Mag 1.7, ♂) from *Thahr al Dubb al Akbar*, the back of the Greater Bear. Ursa Major depicted as a plow, a wagon (Karl, Thor, Odin, King Arthur) or funeral bier, with 3 handle stars as the daughters mourning their father. Thirst for vengeance. Slothful and lazy, from the slow turning of the constellation around the pole. The seven stars are also the Seven Rishis or Sages, wed to the Pleiades. Quiet, nurturing, patient and protective, but also suspicious, distrustful. Forceful and ferocious when roused, the forces of nature unleashed, excessively vengeful. Enduring; strength from position rather than actions. MM: Explores and develops new problem-solving methods.

Merak 19♌43/+56.06 (*beta Ursa Major*, Mag 2.2, ♂) A greenish white star; from *Al Marakk*, the bear's loin although the star occupies the Bear's chest. Love of command and domination. Power to improve circumstances in life. MM: Ambitious, driven to improve upon existing circumstances.

Tania Borealis 19♌49/+42.48 (*lambda Ursa Major*, Mag 3.5, ♂) One of a pair of stars in Bear's rear paw.

Algenubi or Ras Elased Australis 20♌59/+24.08 (*epsilon Leo*, Mag 3, ♄♂) from *Al Ras al Asad al Janubiyyah*, the south star in the Lion's head. Can be bold, cruel, destructive; fevers and accidents. Possibility of spiritual gifts in evolved individuals, put whole heart into work and efforts. MM: Analytical skills, makes deductions using large and varied sets of information.

Tania Australis 21♌30/+41.45 (*mu Ursa Major*, Mag 3.2, ♂) Star in Bear's rear paw.

Pherkad 21♌53/+71.45 (*gamma Ursa Minor*, Mag 3.1 double, ♄♀) from *Alifa al Farkadain*, the two calves. With Kochab (beta star) the Wardens of the Pole, called Guardas or guardians.

Owl Nebula 22♌56/+54.44 (*NGC3587 or M97 Ursa Major*, Mag 8.9) MM: Compelled to face serious events, react to and resolve difficulties.

Alphard 27♌33/-8.53 (*alpha Hydra,* Mag 1.98, ♄♀) from *Al Fard al Shuja,* the Solitary One in the Serpent; aka Cor Hydra, heart of the serpent. In Babylonian lore, was the source of the fountains of the deep. Wisdom and deep insights, cultured, passionate, unconventional, mystic. Capable of emotional outbursts, revolting deeds. Dangers from poisons and water, bites, suffocation. Poisonous hatred, toxic emotions. Manifestation greatly dependent on nature of planet and its chart connections. MM: Ability to cope with adversity, must overcome impediments and entrenched policies.

Adhafera 27♌51/+23.09 (*zeta Leo,* Mag 3.4, ♄☿) Star in Lion's mane. Confident and authoritative but may be impulsive, disingenuous or dishonest. MM: Tendency to be confrontational, outspoken, driven to make a point.

Al Jabhah 28♌11/+16.30 (*eta Leo,* Mag 3.5, ♄☿) White super-giant in Lion's mane/neck. Temperamental, low flash point for anger. Actions driven by impulse, pride creates dangerous situations. Adversaries block progress. Willfulness, dishonesty or covert motivations. May start well but behavior or conditions deteriorate. MM: Face opposition, struggles with getting agenda accepted, stagnant situations.

Algeiba 29♌54/+19.35 (*gamma 1 Leo,* Mag 2.6, Ven/Sun) Star in Lion's mane. Confident and authoritative but may be impulsive, disingenuous or dishonest. MM: Impetus to forge ahead with determination and test new grounds.

Virgo

Regulus 0♍06/+11.43 (*alpha Leo,* Mag 1.3 triple star, ♃♂) Latin diminutive of Rex. Akkadian *Sharru,* the king, Persian *Miyan,* the Center. Leader of the Royal Watcher Stars Venant, he who rules the affairs of heavens. Arabic *Al Kalb al Asad,* the lion's heart. Mythic links to Moon, Jove and Juno, Mithra, and Bacchus. Noble nature, courage, strong spirit, grand gestures, ambitious, power-hungry. May be born into or gain high status and power, or become acquainted with royalty and highly placed people. Gain wealth, a great name. Prone to a rise followed by a fall. Power lost, unhappy death. In mundane charts, revolutions, overthrows, protests, assassinations, historic events. MM: Review and adjust past mistakes, erroneous assumptions or approaches.

Phecda 0♍45/+53.25 (*gamma Ursa Major,* Mag 3.3, ♂) Topaz yellow star. Thigh of the bear. Strong libido, sexual drives. With malefics in mundane charts, blood baths, assassinations, riots.

Megrez 1♍20/+56.55 (*delta Ursa Major,* Mag 3.4, ♂) A pale yellow star; from *Al Maghrez,* root of the tail. The wise Rishi Atri who rules the other stars of the bear.

El Kophrah 3♍56/+47.40 (*chi Ursa Major,* Mag 3.8, ♂) beneath Phecda, the thigh of the Great Bear. Water accidents, capsizing, drowning.

Alkaid or Alula Borealis 6♍56/+32.59 (*eta Ursa Major,* Mag 3.7, ♂) star in lower rear paw of the Great Bear. MM: Set high standards for achievement, organization, improve existing conditions.

Alula Australis 7♍37/+31.25 (*xi Ursa Major,* Mag 3.9, ♂) star in lower rear paw of the Great Bear. Water accidents, capsizing, drowning.

Thuban 7♍44/+64.08 (*alpha Draconis,* Mag 3.6 eclipsing binary with a 51.4 day cycle and a 6 hr blink], ♄♂) from *Al Thuban,* the dragon. Persian *Azhdeha,* Akkadian *Tir-An-na,* the Life of Heaven. Euphratean peoples associated with the god Caga Gilgati, aka *Dayan Same*–judge of heaven, *Dayan Sidi*–the favorable judge, *Dayan Esira*–the prospering judge, the crown of heaven, *Dayan Shisha*–the judge directing (highest seat in heaven). North Star from 3000 to 1000 BCE; in 2787 BCE was 10' from celestial North Pole. Acts as pivot of whole constellation; some evidence its brilliance has faded to a lesser magnitude. Associated with danger and disease; comets here sprinkle poison over the world (Comet Negra's visit in 1347 CE coincided with the bubonic plague). Eternal vigilance, guardian of the heavens. Creating and fiercely guarding a treasure hoard, whether material or spiritual. MM: Review past issues or accomplishments with the intention of improving results.

Alioth 9♍13/+55.41 (*epsilon Ursa Major*, Mag 1.7, ♂) Tail of the bear. Unstable emotions, dangers to pregnancies, birth defects or troubles from birth. Professional disappointments, family troubles. May produce great achievements in spite of liabilities. MM: Strives for perfection, invents versatile approaches.

Al Suhail al Wazn 11♍28/-43.39 (*lambda Vela*, Mag 2.2, ♄♃) from Arabic, brightly shining or brilliant one at the center; in Argo's sails. Potential to attain greatness, shine brightly. Learning and mastery, travels and adventures, gain wisdom through experiences. MM: Faces frustrations from incomplete comprehension about situations; hopes thwarted.

Zosma 11♍36/+20.14 (*delta Leo*, Mag 2.2 triple star, ♄♀) from Greek for girdle. Arabic *Al Thahr al Asad*, the lion's back. Euphratean *Kakkab Kua*, the god of oracles – prophetic tendencies. Intelligent but melancholy. Diseases of intestines and reproductive organs. Constrictions or sorrows in life. If culminating, improves health, gain success through aid of superiors. Associated with victims of oppression and martyrs. MM: Leverage friendships, collaborate and network to achieve results.

Chort 13♍42/+15.09 (*theta Leo*, Mag 3.3, ♄♀) in body of Lion. MM: Desire to have contributions acknowledged; improve methodologies.

Mizar 15♍59/+54.40 (*zeta 1 Ursa Major*, Mag 2.2 binary, ♂) A white-emerald binary star in the tail of the Great Bear. In personal charts with good planets - artistic, creative and literary talents; otherwise troublesome. Mundane events - assoc with catastrophic fires and mass calamities. MM: Skill at developing opportunities, vision, focus, go straight to the goal.

Alcor 16♍09/+54.53 (*80 Ursa Major*, Mag 4.0, ♂) Star in the tail of the Great Bear. In personal charts with good planets - artistic, creative and literary talents; otherwise troublesome. Mundane events - assoc with catastrophic fires and mass calamities.

Chara 17♍59/+41.05 (*beta Canes Venatici*, Mag 4.2, ☿♂) the northern and smaller dog of Boötes named Chara. Loyal, love of hunting, run with the pack. Lesser status. MM: Able to realize potentials in situations.

Denebola 21♍54/+14.17 (*beta Leo*, Mag 2.2, ♄♀) from *Al Dhanab al Asad*, the lion's tail. Preferment and aid from superiors, but prone to losses and misfortunes. Quarrelsome and litigious. With difficult planets can be out of step with society, impulsive, unpredictable; a persecutor or vulnerable to persecution. Daring, generous, involved with other's affairs. Despair and regrets, possibly from children. Twitches and spasms. MM: Increases the need for appreciation and gaining notice for actions and performances.

Alkes 23♍58/-18.34 (*alpha Crater*, Mag 4.2, ♀☿ or ☉) The goblet of Apollo, aka *Iaccho Crater*, the mystic-poetic name for Bacchus. The Soma Cup in India, or Mixing Bowl of Ishtar, the Holy Grail. Akkadian *Mummu-Tiamut*, chaos of the sea, child of Tiamut, the mother of living things. Gives eminence and renown.

Cor Caroli or **Asterion 24♍51**/+38.03 (*alpha 2 Canes Venatici*, Mag 2.9 double, ☿♂) Halley named in honor of the return of Charles II to London on May 29, 1660, when the star was culminating and very bright. Marks collar or heart of Asterion, the starry one, the larger greyhound of Boötes. Ptolemy lists as part of Ursa Major. Loyalty, love of hunting, seeking, running with the pack. Social, friendly, but fierce to interlopers. MM: Restless, strives for action, face challenges and make changes.

Copula 25♍38/+46.20 (*NGC5194* or *M51 Canes Venatici*, Mag 9.6, ☿♂) Gatherings, assemblies of people or information. Good memory. MM: Enhances drive to follow through with intentions and achieve goals.

Alkaid 27♍13/+49.04 (*eta Ursa Major*, Mag 1.9, ♂) aka **Benatnasch** from *Ka'id Banat al Na'ash*, Governor of the Daughters, the chief mourner. Brilliant white star at tip of the tail. In personal charts with good planets - artistic, creative and literary talents; otherwise troublesome. Mundane events - assoc with catastrophic fires and mass calamities. MM: High standards for performance, decision-making, intense concentration.

Zavijava 27♍27/+1.29 (*beta Virgo*, Mag 3.6, ☿♂) or **Zarijan** from *Al Zawiah* or *Alaraph*, the Angle or Corner. Euphratean *Ninsar*, the Lady of Heaven, Persian *Mashaha*. The Correct Weighing. Strong character, assertive, clever and forceful, gain benefits from efforts. Fortunate, very good for career success. MM: Versatility, seeks diverse alternatives for making improvements.

Labrum 28♍50/-23.06 (*beta Crater*, Mag 3.8, ♀☿) A star in the Grail or Chalice. Talents, quests, idealistic. MM: Points out what doesn't work in spite of anger it might arouse.

Markeb 29♍10/-55.14 (*kappa Vela*, Mag 2.5, ♄♃) Star in Argo's sails. Broadminded, education and travel, transforms evil to good. MM: Seek adventure, variety, new experiences.

Galactic North Pole 29♍30/+27. North Pole of the Milky Way Galaxy.

Libra

Intersection of the Ecliptic and Earth's Equator 0♎00. Sun at 0° N/S. Autumn Equinox, Libra Ingress.

Super Galactic Center 1♎08/+13. Located between epsilon Virgo and Coma Berenices.

Ascellus Secundus 1♎23/+51.08 (*iota Boötes*, Mag 4.7, ♂♃) Star in right hand of Boötes. Force, power, determination. Fateful events. MM: Adjust and correct problematic issues.

Ascellus Primus 2♎59/+51.37 (*theta Boötes*, Mag 4, ♂♃) Never sets in northern hemisphere. Star in fist of Boötes beneath thumb. In ancient lore, the hand that turns the plow (Ursa Major). Force, power, determination. Fateful events. MM: Produces commentary, seeks explanations, unique perspective.

Higher Minister 3♎41/+65.39 (*zeta Draco*, Mag 3.1, ♄♂) Star in dragon, fiercely protective, a judge of souls, potential for danger and disease. Acquisitive. Preference for solitude. MM: Coping skills, develop maturity, comprehends unfolding events and needed changes.

Black Eye Nebula 3♎56/+22 (*M64 Coma Berenices*, spiral galaxy)

Beta Coma Berenices 4♎39/+27.37 (*beta Coma Berenices*, Mag 4.2, ♄☿) Losses, sacrifices. Endurance, tenacity, equanimity through distressing situations. Love of traditions and vivid symbolic imagination. Talents in arts, literature, and comedy; a clever, inventive viewpoint. Haste leads to errors of judgment.

Zaniah 5♎07/-0.57 (*eta Virgo*, Mag 3.9, ☿♀) from Arabic *Al Zawiah*, the angle or corner. South Wing of Virgo. Congenial, cultured, scholarly, social and popular. Love affairs. MM: Scrutinize unworkable conditions and seek methods to adjust and improve them.

Eldsich 5♎14/+58.47 (*iota Draco*, Mag 3.3, ♄♂) Acquisitive, danger of disease and or toxic substances. MM: Identify and develop one's true inner nature, gain a personal style.

Diadem 9♎14/+17.16 (*alpha 1 Coma Berenices*, Mag 5.2, ♄ ☿) The Jewel in the Crown. An ivy wreath or Mercury's caduceus. Linked to golden amber. Personal charm, theatrical abilities, idleness or dissipation, baldness. Sacrifice for family, carry burdens of others. The seven stars of Coma Berenices are linked to the Pleiades and Ursa Major. Includes the Pinwheel Nebula-M99, marking the north celestial pole of the Milky Way. MM: Fidelity, faithful to an idea or cause.

Vindemiatrix 10♎13/+10.51 (*epsilon Virgo*, Mag 2.8, ♄ ☿) from Latin for female grape gatherer, right wing of Virgo. Arabic *Al Muridin*, those who set forth. A mischievous star nicknamed The Widow-maker. Great mental concentration; architecture and business acumen. May be hypercritical. With difficult planets - distrustful, suspicious, falsity, irritability, worry, unpopularity. Losses through impulsive actions, writings, legal problems, bad business deals, or love affairs. MM: Compelled to deal with situations that run counter to one's reality, beliefs or expectations.

North Pole of Local System 10♍/+29. Nearest star is xi Ursa Major.

Caphir 10♎25/-1.44 (*gamma 1 Virgo*, Mag 3.6, ☿ ♀) aka Prosa/Porrima, sister goddesses of prophecy, assistants of Carmentis. Arabic *Zawiat al 'Awwa*, the turning (of the line of stars). Left arm of Virgo, called "An Atonement Offering" or "the Submissive One." A courteous, refined, lovable personality. May have prophetic abilities or strong foresight. Hardships in childhood. Being blamed for other's evil deeds brings potential for losses or disputes. MM: Ability to see and discern patterns, shapes, components, complex systems.

Gienah 11♎01/-17.50 (*gamma Corvus*, Mag 2.5, ♂♄) Crafty, patient and ingenious, vengeful, lying, greedy and materialistic, agitators. Prevaricates and procrastinates. Corvus has a negative association with Apollo and his prophetic function (the bird was turned black for bringing bad news), and Hindu sun god Savitar. MM: Ability to interpret life in a unique and personal way.

Alchita or **Al Chiba 12♎31**/-25.01 (*alpha Corvus*, Mag 4.2, ♂♄) Crafty, patient and ingenious, vengeful, lying, greedy and materialistic, agitators, storm crows and bringers of bad news. Prevaricates and procrastinates. MM: Work with others to achieve goals, teambuilding toward objectives.

[The] Green Hill 13♎44/-34.12 (*beta Hydra*, Mag 4.2, ♄ ♀) Wisdom and deep insights, unconventional, mystic. Emotional outbursts. Dangers from poisons and water, bites, suffocation. Poisonous hatred, toxic emotions. Manifestation greatly dependent on nature of planet and its chart connections. MM: Challenges misrepresentations, distortions, falsifications, bias.

Algorab 13♎44/-16.48 (*delta Corvus*, Mag 2.9 binary, ♂♄) from *Al Ghurāb*, the raven. Marks the beak. Delays, restraints. Handle matters badly. Love affairs or marriages that turn sour. Bringer of bad news, destructive, lying, scavenging. Injuries that are difficult to avoid. MM: See reality in a clear, distinct way; able to ignore distractions.

Center of Local System 15♍30/-50. Located near pi Kentaurus.

Merga 15♎44/+46.01 (*38 Boötes*, Mag 5.8, ♂♃) Upthrust left fist of the Driver, never sets in northern hemisphere. Great strength and power to manifest visions. Potent destiny if rising with planets in 1st or 12th house. Punch through social/cultural obstacles to achieve goals, pave the way for others who follow. MM: Make corrections and adjustments, address problematic issues.

Al Tais 17♎26/+67.45 (*delta Draco*, Mag 3.07, ♄♂) Acquisitive, inclined toward mysticism, research, and solitude. Possibility of poisons, toxic substances or emotions, disease and dangers. MM: Effects social changes, introduce new pathways in society.

Kraz or **Tso Hea 17♎39**/-23.41 (*beta Corvus*, Mag 2.6, ♂♄) Delays, excuses, procrastination.

Seginus 17♎57/+38.05 (*gamma Boötes*, Mag 3.0, ☿♄) Right shoulder of the Driver. Carry the weight of a family role or responsibility over time, long career, manage public acclaim or relationship, adjust to trends and social changes. MM: Introduce cultural changes, able to improvise.

Mufrid 19♎37/+18.09 (*eta Boötes*, Mag 2.6, ☿♄) Also Muphrid or **Saak**. Star in right leg or knee of the Driver. Determination, force, athletic skills, pushing into new areas, spreading trends, forging a path for others. MM: Develop mastery of talents, educational opportunities, valuable encounters.

Foramen 22♎26/-59.57 (*eta Carina*, Mag .08 variable) Argo's keel, unstable blue supergiant in the Keyhole or Homunculus Nebula of the southern Milky Way; massive, energetic star.

Spica 24♎07/-11.26 (*alpha Virgo*, Mag 0.98 binary, ♀♂) from Latin *spicum*, ear of wheat in Virgo's hand. Greek *Stachys*, Egyptian *Siru* or *Shiru*; Arabic *Sunbala* from *Al Sunbulah*, ear of corn; also *Al Simak al A'zal*, the Defenseless or Unarmed (no nearby star), corrupted to *Azimech*, *Hazimet Alazel*, the alchemical *Alhaseth*; Hebrew *Shibboleth*, ear of wheat. Star of Juno-Hera. Brilliant talents in arts and sciences, aviation. Wealth and fame achieved because of advancement through others (the wheat doesn't pick itself), patronage and protection; fertility. With malefics, rise followed by fall, loss of previous gains, poverty. MM: Impact on others through actions, ideas and options, a skillful communicator.

Arcturus 24♎31/+18.55 (*alpha Boötes*, Mag 0.04, ♀☿ or ♃♂) Marks the phallus of the Driver, or Ŝupa (Enlil), the god who steers the Plow/Ursa Major. Justice through power. Wealth and renown, prosperity through traveling, good luck. Trendy, fair weather friends, daring or belligerent, forge new paths. Causes own problems by taking bad advice from friends or through litigation. Storms, diseases assoc with bilious temperament. Intense infrared source. MM: Face social injustice, barriers, discrimination, legal problems; seeks equity.

Nekkar 24♎32/+42.18 (*beta Boötes*, Mag 3.6, ☿♄) The head of the Driver. Noisy, wants to be heard, giving warnings or sounding alarms, clamoring for attention. Object 3C299, a strong radio source, is near his left ear.

Izar 28♎23/+26.52 (*epsilon 2 Boötes*, Mag 2.7, ☿♄) Right elbow of the Driver. Power to manifest visions. MM: Inner drive to make an impression; able to craft influential messages.

Southern Intersection of the Local System and Galactic Equators 28♎30/-60

Scorpio

Miaplacidus 2♏15/-69.56 (*beta Carina/Argo*, Mag 1.6) from Arabic *Miyah*, root word Mā - water. Wanderlust, travels for learning, gain knowledge and wisdom. MM: Understands human complexity, motivations, the role of the unconscious.

Menkent 2♏36/-49.14 (*gamma Kentaurus*, Mag 2,1, ♀♃) Cultured, knowledgeable, prone to trouble in relationships. MM: Increases self-confidence, self-development and self-promotion.

Heaven's Kitchen 2♏42/+70.24 (*epsilon Draco*, Mag 3.8, ♄♂) Acquisitive, inclined toward mysticism, research, and solitude. Possible poisons, toxic substances/emotions, disease and dangers. MM: Self-analysis, inner review, can assess implications and effects of events.

Princeps 3♏26/+33.14 (*delta Boötes*, Mag 3.4, ☿ ♄) Staff star near Alkalurops. Keen, studious, profound mind, ability for research. Linguistic skills, can convey emotions and ideas to others. Authority on special topics. MM: Cultivate social popularity, fosters cooperation with others.

Alkalurops 3♏28/+37.18 (*mu 1 &2 Boötes*, Mag 4.5, ☿ ♄) Staff stars, drawn to power, drama, able to manifest visions, good abilities, magical potential.

Ceginus 5♏23/+40.17 (*phi Boötes*, Mag 5.4, ☿ ♄) Top of staff. Drawn to power, drama, able to manifest visions, good abilities, magical potential.

Gacrux 7♏01/-57.24 (*gamma 1 Crux*, Mag 1.6, ♃) Virtuous, spiritual, manifest visions. MM: Desire to understand the motives of others, strong intuition.

Khambalia 7♏ 14/-13.36 (*lambda Virgo*, Mag 4.6, ☿ ♂) From the Coptic word for "crooked clawed." Left foot. Nicknamed Merlin's Star. Impetuous, skillful, and dexterous, eloquent, intuitive, mind over matter, interest in occult or magic.

Nusukan 9♏24/+28.56 (*beta Corona Borealis*, Mag 3.6, ♀ ☿) Highly cultured, gifted in arts and sciences, success in commerce. Fruitfulness, abundance, joyful union, blessings. Poetic (erotic/mystic blend) and intellectual, prone to sex scandals. Green thumb, growing flowers. MM: Motivated to leave a legacy, some deed or product associated with the self.

Mimosa 11♏55/-59.58 (*beta Crux*, Mag 1.25, ♃) Virtuous, spiritual, manifest visions.

Acrux 12♏09/-63.23 (*alpha 1 Crux*, Mag 1.5 triple, ♃) Lucida of the Southern Cross. Vespucci called it the Mandorla (almond). Close to the equinoctial colure. Associated with the cardinal virtues Justice, Prudence, Fortitude and Temperance. Intuition, understand human nature, spirituality, occult interests, rituals and ceremonies. Practical expression of ideas, make visions real. Investigate hidden things. Benefits through spirituality. MM: Curious, inquisitive, questions and assesses conditions.

Alphecca 12♏35/+26.33 (*alpha Corona Borealis*, Mag 2.2, ♀ ☿) aka **Gemma**, the pearl or knot of the northern crown or wedding garland. Latin *Pupilla*, Greek *Kore*, Persephone from Chaldean *Phersephon* [*phe'er*-crown, *serphon*-northern], Amphitrite or Ariadne, Celtic *Caer Arianrod* (house of Arianrod). Long association with underworld goddesses. Highly cultured, gifted in arts and sciences, success in commerce. Fruitfulness, abundance, joyful union, blessings. Poetic (erotic/mystic blend) and intellectual, prone to love scandals. Green thumb, growing flowers. MM: Wants the answer to mysteries, persistent detective who follows leads.

Haratan 12♏35/-36.37 (*theta Kentaurus*, Mag 2, ♀ ♃) Cultured, educated, knowledgeable, prone to trouble in relationships. MM: Able to manage chaotic situations, find the root cause of disorder and repair it.

Zuben Elgenubi 15♏22/-16.15 (*alpha 2 Libra*, Mag 2.75, ♃ ♂) from *Zuben el Genubi*, the Southern Claw. (Formerly the Chelae, claws of Scorpio) "Insufficient Price." Less benefic than the northern claw. Lose status, family problems, situations end badly. Selfish, may be unconcerned about the opinions of others, unconventional maverick, question traditions and taboos. Health problems. Tragic fate. MM: Addresses the differences between people, issues or events at a personal level.

Zuben Elschemali 19 ♏39/-9.34 (*beta Libra*, Mag 2.6, ♃ ☿) from *Zuben el Chamali*, the Northern Claw. "The Full Price." Associated with goddess Bilat or Beltis, the Lady, wife of Bel. Honors and distinction. Studious, sharp mind, literary or speaking skills. Good fortune, lasting results, contributions to society, strong social conscience, able to change bad circumstances to good for self and others. MM: Multi-leveled efforts to address needs, agendas, coordinate activities and people.

Zuben Hakrabi 20♏58/-25.29 (*sigma Libra*, Mag 3.3, ♃ ☿) Studious, sharp mind, literary or speaking skills. Known for achievements, generosity. MM: Improves organization, implements thorough overhauls, learns how to achieve results.

Unukalhai 22♏21/+6.21 (*alpha Serpentis*, Mag 2.6, ♄♂) from *Unk al Hayyah*, neck of the snake. Also called Cor Serpentis. The serpent in hand of Ophiuchus. Intrigue, poisons, drugs, secret crimes, misfortunes, various dangers. A death in the family that has a big impact on the life, leaves a mark. Chronic diseases difficult to diagnose, surgeries. Difficult professional life. MM: Clarifies solutions to problems, devises improvements and puts them into practice.

Agena 24♏04/-60.37 (*beta Kentauri*, Mag 0.6, ♀ ♃) aka **Hadar** (ground) or Baten Kentaurus, the centaur's belly, although the star marks the right foreleg of Southern Centaur. Happiness and success. High status, friends, health, honors, but legal problems or multiple marriages. Strong libido. With malefics, gossip and scandals. Tough learning curves that impose delays and frustrating circumstances. MM: Highly competent and multi-talented in diverse fields.

Arrakis 25♏03/+54.24 (*mu Draco*, Mag 5.1 binary, ♄♂) from *Al Rakis*, the dancer or trotting camel. Marks nose or tongue of the dragon. Mysticism, prefer solitude, gather wisdom and information. Possible toxins, poisons, alchemy, dangers.

Zuben Elakrab 25♏25/-14.58 (*gamma Libra*, Mag 3.9, ♃ ☿) Studious, sharp mind, literary or speaking skills. Known for achievements, generosity. MM: Desires clarity and understanding, develops a sophisticated perspective on life.

Marsik 26♏00/+16.59 (*kappa Hercules*, Mag 5.3, ☿) Also **Marfik**, from *Al Marfik*, the right arm of the Kneeler. A double star of pale yellow and pale garnet. Devotion to goals, strive for perfection in efforts.

Southern Intersection of Galactic and Super Galactic Equators 29♏28/-59 Toliman [alpha Kentauri] is the closest star.

Toliman 29♏48/-60 (*alpha 1 Kentauri*, Mag 0.03 binary, ♀ ♃) Means *shoot of the vine*; probably a misnomer. Also Bungula, Rigel Kentauri, Proxima Centauri. Third brightest star. With beta star Agena, the Sumerian *Nergub-Gudelim*, left foot of the Centaur. Marked the autumn equinox from 3800-2575 BCE. Egyptians associated with Serket. Chinese *Nan Mun*, the South Gate. Arabic *Wasn*, The Weight. Star closest to our solar system at 4.5 light years distance. Refinement, gain social status, selfish, lost inheritances, disputes. Learning, advanced education, spiritual growth through life. Happy relationships spoiled by exceptional circumstances. MM: Needs outlets to express passion, emotions, and creativity.

Sagittarius

Kornephoros 1♐22/+21.23 (*beta Hercules*, Mag 2.7, ☿) Pale yellow star that marks the Kneeler's shoulder. Gain knowledge to improve status or conditions, talent, dedication, may be prolific. MM: Must learn impulse control and to think before taking action.

Kajam 1♐51/+13.59 (*omega Hercules*, Mag 4.5, ☿) or **Cujam**. Star in the club of the Kneeler; given as a separate constellation in Pliny. Force and power to manifest visions.

Dschubba 2♐51/-22.46 (*delta Scorpio*, Mag 2.3, ♄ ☿) from *Al Jabhad*, the front or forehead. Euphratean *Gis-gan-gu-sur*, Light of the Hero. With beta and pi stars, the Tree of the Garden of Light, placed in the midst of the abyss as a reminder of the Tree of Life in Paradise. Meanings similar to Acrab. MM: Must learn how choices affect life and explore different sides of self.

Acrab 3♐24/-19.57 (*beta 1 Scorpio*, Mag 2.6, ♂♄ or ♄☿) aka **Graffias**. Right claw. Research things of hidden or secret nature. Delicate health. Falsehood, treason, bad for finances. Impediments or losses; assaults, falls, toxic family secrets, scandalous behaviors. Mundane events – catastrophes, earthquakes, hurricanes. MM: Heightens the senses and subtle perceptions, ability to interpret meanings and potential influences from input.

Han 9♐30/-10.40 (*zeta Ophiuchus*, Mag 2.5, ♄♀) see Rasalhague. MM: Keen comprehension of the interplay amongst various ongoing factors.

Antares 10♐02/-26.33 (*alpha Scorpio*, Mag .96 binary, ♂♃) Latin - rival of Ares/Mars. Cor Scorpii, Heart of Scorpion. Royal Watcher star *Satevis*. Mesopotamian *Bilu-sha-ziri*, lord of the seed, or *Kak-shia*, creator of prosperity. Egyptian Selket/Serqet. Tough, belligerent, pugnacious. Military and athletic abilities, alertness, strategic skill and courage. Liberal, broad-minded, obstinate. Glory and power. Fleeting wealth and honors. Poison, powerful passions/obsessions. Death from fire, machinery, weapons or war. Linked to optical problems and hard-to-diagnose incurable illness with difficult planets. An intense infrared source.
MM: Becomes involved with clashes of opinion, feuds, disagreements, and treachery.

Rastaban or **Alwaid 12♐15**/+52.16 (*beta Draco*, Mag 3 binary yellow, ♄♀ [or ♄♂]) from *Ras al Thuban*, the Dragon's head, or from *Al'Awaid* - the mother camels. Marks top of head. Cunning, clever, acquisitive but prone to losses and accidents. Criminal inclinations, accidents. MM: Ability to take diverse factors into account and see the overall intention or thrust of situations.

Sarin 15♐03/+24.48 (*delta Hercules*, Mag 3.2, ☿) Marks the right shoulder of the Kneeler. Dedicated, studious, responsible. Linked to toxic spills in mundane charts.

Ras Algethi 16♐26/+14.20 (*alpha Hercules*, Mag-variable double 3.1 to 7, ☿ or ♂♀) from *Al Ras al Jathiyy*, the Kneeler's Head. Double stars of orange and teal. Associated with solar deities Herekhal/Hercules, Ixion, Orpheus, Prometheus, and the Euphratean Izhdubar/Gilgamesh, whose side-kick was the first centaur Ea-bani. Strength of character, fixity of purpose, ardent nature and dangerous passions. Strives to attain the summit of heaven (the celestial north pole). Extreme devotion to goals, strive for immortality, seeker, fanatic, problems in relationships; may live through dark night of the soul and emerge much-changed, more mature and wise. MM: Ability to improvise and adjust to circumstances as they unfold.

Sabik 18♐15/-15.44 (*eta Ophiuchus*, Mag 2.4, ♄☿) Unconventional, amoral, cynical; sorcery and poisons. MM: Create alternatives to reality, portray illusions; spiritual interests.

Graffias 17♐31/-42.23 (*zeta 2 Scorpio*, Mag 3.8, ♂♄) Derived from Greek *graphatos* (crab), or Latin for The Scribbler. Head of the Scorpion. Arabic manzil *Iklil al Jabheh*, the Crown of the Forehead, fortunate; nakshatra Anurhadha – propitious or successful. Contagion, crime, social fringe, dangers. Wealth and success after difficulties.

Maasym 20♐11/+26.04 (*lambda Hercules*, Mag 4.4, ☿) aka **Mi'sam**. A deep yellow star that marks the right arm of the Kneeler. Strive for perfection, struggle to gain knowledge and wisdom.

Ras Alhague 22♐44/+12.31 (*alpha Ophiuchus*, Mag 2, ♄♀) from *Ras al Hawwa*, the Head of the Snake Charmer, aka Azalange. Eccentric, scholarly; doctors and healers of individuals or society. May be secretive, skeptical, suspicious, or a sexual adventurer. Drugs, alcohol, herbs, potions, possible addictions, overindulgence. Humanitarian and imaginative. Prone to bites, rabies, toxic contamination, and risk of infections and epidemics; a sickly spouse. Eventually able to gain wealth, accumulation of goods. MM: Maneuvers to attract and retain the attention of others.

Lesath 24♐18/-37.20 (*upsilon Scorpio*, Mag 2.6, ☿♂) From Greek *lesos* - sting. A stinger star. Desperation, poisons and acids. Victim of clever attacks, sneaky but aggressive adversaries. Spying or subterfuge. Accidents, emergency surgeries like appendectomies. MM: Skill at interpreting and assessing the consequences of life situations.

Shaula 24♐52/-37.09 (*lambda Scorpio*, Mag 1.7, ☿♂) from *Al Shaula*, the Sting, or *Mushalah* – in raised position, ready to strike. Unlucky. In nakshatra Mula, the Root, the recycling bin of the galaxy. MM: Seeks the limelight, self-promotion. May color facts if necessary.

Choo 25♐13/-49.55 (*alpha Ara*, Mag 2.9) MM: Dedication to duty, fulfills commitments.

Cheleb 25♐37/+4.33 (*beta Ophiuchus*, Mag 2.7, ♄♀) Unconventional, amoral, cynical; sorcery and poisons. MM: Ability to plan, test, anticipate, interpret complex possibilities.

Sargas 25♐53/-43.02 (*theta Scorpio*, Mag 1.8, ☿♂) MM: Powerful insights, intuition or clairvoyance, able to perceive subtle input from outside sources.

Aculeus 26♐01/-32.15 (*NGC6405 or M6 Scorpio*, Mag 4.2 variable/nebula, ♂☽) In stinger. Bad for eyesight with Sun or Moon. Stings & attacks, verbal or physical, overt confrontations or covertly undermined. Endure attacks and achieve success. MM: Able to increase the impact of messages, portrayals, or actions.

Galactic Center 27♐07/-28.58 (*Sag A SGR, ii Sagittarius,* Mag 14) The center of our spiral galaxy, the Milky Way. Occupies Bode's Window, a dark area of clouds of stellar dust that makes it invisible to the naked eye. Major components of the Galactic nucleus include sources of high intensity X-ray (subconscious) and infrared (superconscious) emissions: Sag A (26♐10/-29, infrared source), Scorpio X-1 (26♐26/-29, largest X-ray source), Scorpio XR-6, Sag 5 GX5-1, Sag XR-3 and Sag 3-GX9+1. The GC is allegedly associated with truth-telling, a connection with divine inspiration, and deep insights into human nature. MM: Power, influence, ground-breaking efforts, ambition, notoriety.

Eltanin or **Etamin 28♐15/+51.29** (*gamma Draco*, Mag 2.2, ♄♂ or ♃♂) aka **Ettanin**, Arabic *Al Ras Al Tinnin*, the dragon's head. Head or eye of the Dragon. Egyptians associated with Isis-Hathor, Bast, and Sekhet. Prefer solitude, emotional distance from others. Psychic or esoteric skills, deep insights into human nature. Ponder the mysteries. Like all stars of Draco, associated with dangers and poisons. MM: Must seriously consider plans of action or progress of development in work and life.

Acumen 29♐00/-34.50 (*NGC6475 or M7 Scorpio*, Mag 3.2 nebula, ♂☽) sibling star to Aculeus. Difficult outcomes from unanticipated events or attacks. Over time the ability to respond and recover may deteriorate as vigor/enthusiasm is crushed. MM: Ability to probe, explore, inquire and analyze, critique, raise concerns.

Capricorn

Celestial South Pole 0♑00/-90. Sun at greatest separation from ecliptic at 23°26' South. Winter Solstice. Near Spiculum, aka Sagittarius T1, T2, and T3 [stellar T-associations of young stars].

Sinistra 0♑02/-9.47 (*nu Ophiuchus*, Mag 3, ♄♀) Unconventional, amoral, cynical; sorcery and poisons. MM: Seeks balance, reconciliation, develops means for resolving differences.

Trifid Nebula 0♑48/-23.02 (*NGC6531* or *M20 Sagittarius*, Mag 6.3) MM: Desire to clarify objective and purpose. May proceed in spite of objections.

Spiculum 1♑21/-22.30 (*NGC6531* or *M8, M20, M21 Sagittarius*, Mag 5.9 variable nebular clusters, ♂☽) Cluster at tip of arrow. Problems with eyesight. Focus on goal, achievements. Force things to manifest, or an open conduit for manifestation. Linked to the Titan Crius, guardian of the Winter Solstice and his Moon-goddess wife. MM: Realistic; able to face, adjust and adapt to changing conditions.

Al Nasr or Alnasl 1♑32/-30.26 (*gamma 2 Sagittarius*, Mag 2.9, ♃♂) from *Al Nasl*, the point or arrowhead. Also *Al Wazl*, the junction of the arrow, bow and hand. Point of intersection, potent catalyst, actions with consequences. MM: Quick, analytical mind, can deduce solutions and alternatives.

Polis 3♑30/-21.03 (*mu Sagittarius*, Mag 3.8 triple star, ♃♂) Star in the bow. Ambition, keen senses, aggressive, sense of justice. Idealistic and humanitarian. MM: Must learn how to apply discipline to work and proceed in spite of frustration or delays.

Kaus Australis 5♑21/-34.22 (*epsilon Sagittarius*, Mag 1.85, ♃♂) MM: Adaptable, flexible, conceives alternate approaches to resolving difficulties.

Kaus Borealis 6♑36/-25.24 (*lambda Sagittarius*, Mag 2.8, ♃♂) MM: Able to visualize and effectively describe conditions so others understand what's needed and necessary.

Facies 8♑36/-23.52 (*NGC6656* or *M22 Sagittarius*, Mag 5, ☉♂) Star cluster in front of the Archer's face. Problems with eyesight, accidents and illness. Ponders human nature, view things from different, unusual perspective. In mundane charts it's an unlucky star signifying accidents and pile-ups with fatalities. MM: Desire for fulfillment and success. Gains recognition for contributions.

Nunki 12♑40/-26.14 (*sigma Sagittarius*, Mag 2, ♃☿) aka **Pelagus**. Fletching of arrow. Honest, pious, clever, a writer or bureaucrat. Blessed with good friends. Successes may be delayed. MM: Ability to analyze and deduce the core meaning of actions and events. Insightful.

Ascella 13♑55/-20.49 (*zeta Sagittarius*, Mag 2.6, ♃☿) MM: Leadership and management skills, accomplishments, attracts friends and supporters.

Alfecca Meridiana 14♑08/-37.50 (*alpha Corona Australis*, Mag 4.1, ♄☿) Crown beneath front hooves of Sagittarius. Rota Ixiona, the [Solar] Wheel of Ixion. A crown made by Dionysus in honor of Semele, his mother. The Crown of Eternal Life. Lifetime achievements and posthumous fame. The Mesopotamian Cargo Boat taking souls to the afterlife. Military victories and conquests. Cleverness, swift strategic thinking. Possible thievery, destructive, deceit, disgrace, sexual excess or prostitution. Fame or notoriety. Nasty rumors or slanders. Arabic *Al Kubbah*, the Tortoise; Chinese Pi, the Primal Tortoise. Interest in history, symbols, myths and lore, prophetic and divinatory arts. Create body of work, enduring legacy. Success at someone else's expense or a high personal price. MM: Explore one's role in life, seeks to comprehend purpose.

Manubrium 15♑16/-21.40 (*omicron Sagittarius*, Mag 3.7) MM: Serious, dedicated to work and the development of personal ideas and methods.

Vega 15♑36/+38.50 (*alpha Lyra*, Mag 0.3, ♀☿) from Arabic *Waki*, the Harp star. Apollo or Orpheus's lyre, aka Talyn Arthur. Assyrian *Dayan-same*, Judge of Heaven, assoc with Egyptian Ma'at. Refined, changeable, success in business, influential. Magic, charismatic, beauty, artistry, oratorical skills; fashion and fabrics, allure and appeal, sometimes pretentious, fond of luxury. Abilities can be used for good or evil. North star in 10,000 BC; will be North Star in 10,000 AD, linked to a Golden Age. MM: Able to settle differences and disputes and bring reconciliation after distress.

Super Galactic North Pole 16♑20/+15. Nearest stars are zeta and epsilon Aquila, the eagle's wing tip.

Rukbat or **Alrami 16♑55**/-40.32 (*alpha Sagittarius*, Mag 3.9, ♃ ☿) from *Rukbat al Rami*, the Archer's knee. Steady, great inner strength and/or physical strength, education and learning. MM: Able to detect critical factors; concentration, the ability to eliminate mental clutter and distractions.

Sheliak 19♑10/+33.25 (*beta Lyra*, Mag 3.5 variable binary, ♀ ☿) from *Al Shilyak*, the lyre. Refined talents, success and influence. MM: Builds reputation, inspired, highly productive.

Dheneb 20♑04/+13.56 (*zeta Aquila*, Mag 2.9, ♂♃) Green star in Eagle's tail. Leadership skills, generous, success in war. Pirates, robbers and thieves, government or businesspeople that engage in predatory practices. MM: Sets the tone for the group, rules for oversight, ensures quality output.

Sulaphat 22♑12/+32.42 (*gamma Lyra*, Mag 3.3, ♀ ☿) Arabic for tortoise (Hermes made the lyre with a tortoise shell). Refined talents, success and influence. Near the Ring Nebula.

Deneb Okab 23♑55/+3.09 (*delta Aquila*, Mag 3.4, ♂♃) aka **Dheneb**, the Eagle's tail. Ability to command, liberality, success in war, intuitive insights, penetrating intellect, benefits and gains.

Pavo 24♑06/-56.354 (*alpha Pavo*, Mag 1.9) The Peacock star. Symbol of immortality associated with Juno. Self renewal and regeneration. Vain and showy, pride goes before a fall. MM: Charisma, pride in accomplishment, pageantry.

Terebellum 26♑51/-26.10 (*omega Sagittarius*, Mag 4.7, ♀ ♄) Tail of Centaur. Mercenary, cunning, prone to scandals. Good fortune followed by regrets. Sometimes luck arrives during bad times. MM: Restlessness, constantly in motion, urge to move ahead.

Aquarius

Tarazed 1♒13/+10.39 (*gamma Aquila*, Mag 2.8, ♂♃) Penetrating intellect, benefits and gains.

Albireo 1♒32/+28.04 (*beta Cygnus*, Mag 3 yellow-blue binary, ♀ ☿) from *ab ireo*, the iris and sword lily's sweet scent. Head or beak of Swan, aka "Song of the Dying Swan." Beauty and charm. Generosity. Aid is given when in despair, luck in bad times. MM: Desire to study and understand human behavior and how people function.

Altair 2♒03/+8.6 (*alpha Aquila*, Mag 0.7, ♂♃) Neck of eagle. Endurance, courage, generosity. Bold to foolhardy, confident, liberal, sudden wealth, daring, idealistic. Courage to pursue dreams, rise in life. Seize the moment, act quickly. With difficult planets - aggressive action, act without concern or compassion for others, piracy, theft, or predatory behavior. Or could be a victim of theft or sudden attacks. Children taken or adopted from natural parents. MM: Tendency to hold on to ideas/beliefs, cling to decisions.

Al Shain 2♒42/+6.32 (*beta Aquila*, Mag 3.7, ♂♃) Imaginative, passionate, indomitable will, dominating character able to influence others. Clairvoyance, keen penetrating mind, skilled in research. MM: Determination; stick to goals and intentions. Ignore naysayers and detractors.

Giedi Prima and Secunda 4♒03/-12.21 (*alpha Capricorn*, Mag 4.2, ♀♂) Two stars marking the Goat's south horn. Strong desires. Generosity, sacrifices. Peculiar gains and losses, good luck. Love affairs, potential infidelity or carelessness in relationships. MM: Analytical mind able to comprehend and analyze bad decisions, failures, and restrictions.

Dabih 4♒20/-14.38 (*beta Capricorn*, Mag 3, ♀♂) Face of the Goat. Strong desires, lusts, curious and acquisitive. MM: Needs to be first, a pioneer, undertake new efforts, explore new techniques and theories.

Al Shat 4♒42/-12.41 (*nu Capricorn*, Mag 4.8, ♀♂) Face of the Goat. Strong desires, lusts, curious and acquisitive.

Oculus 5♒00/-18.03 (*pi Capricorn*, Mag 5.2, ♀♂) Eye of the Goat. Strong desires, lusts, curious and acquisitive. Sees what it wants and tries to obtain it. MM: Willing to use unproven methods and take risks to achieve goals.

Bos 5♒27/-17.39 (*rho Capricorn*, Mag 4.7, ♀♂) Star in the face of the Goat. Strong desires, lusts, curious and acquisitive. MM: Able to work with others to develop easier modes to achieve goals.

Al Bali 12♒00/-9.19 (*epsilon Aquarius*, Mag 3.8, ♄☿) from *Al Sa'd al Bula*, the Good Fortune of the Swallower. Fortunate, good friends, social success, profitable. MM: Desire to influence or shape culture through criticism or commentary.

Armus 13♒01/-19.40 (*eta Capricorn*, Mag 4.8, ♄☿) Star in body of Goat. Studious, technical or scientific skills. MM: A reformer, one who institutes change and offers fresh ideas in a field of study, the arts, or in large social-political venues.

Dorsum 14♒07/-17.02 (*theta Capricorn*, Mag 4, ♄☿) Star in body of Goat. Studious, technical or scientific skills. MM: Communicates ideas in an emotional, forceful way.

Rotanev 16♒37/+14.39 (*beta Delphinus*, Mag 3.7) from Syriac-Chaldean *rotaneb* or *rotanew*, swiftly running. Meaning similar to alpha star Sualocin. MM: Builds the foundation for and introduces cultural shifts and new ideas.

Sualocin 17♒40/+16.05 (*alpha Delphinus*, Mag 3.7, ☿♀) from Arabic *scalooin*, swift. Also call *Al Ukud*, the Pearl or Precious Stone. Ptolemy wrote that it is one of the stars cognizant of human births, with influence on character. Philanthropy and devotion to children. Shy, naïve, and overconfident. Comedy, laughter, outrageous sense of humor, teasing, mockery, satire and parody. MM: Consistent in thought and action, firmly adheres to position on issues.

Castra 20♒29/-19.15 (*epsilon Capricorn*, Mag 4.6, ♄♃) body or tail of the Goat. Drawn to the seas, assess risk versus profits, travel for career. MM: Communication skills, able to craft impactful messages that influence others.

Nashira 22♒04/-16.27 (*gamma Capricorn*, Mag 3.6, ♄♃) Tail of the Goat. Drawn to the seas, assess risk versus profits, travel for career. MM: Able to develop a unique personality with colorful style; gains public attention.

Sadalsuud 23♒40/-5.21 (*beta Aquarius*, Mag 2.9, ♄☿) from *Al Sa'd al Su'd*, Luckiest of the Lucky. Left shoulder, top of urn. Akkadian *Kakkab Nammach*, the Star of Mighty Destiny. Peculiar lifestyle, luck through speculation. Gushing effect, associated with great wealth; great quantities, multiplies opportunities. MM: Able to develop deep understanding and acute perceptions for social interactions.

Deneb Algedi 23♒49/-15.54 (*delta Capricorn*, Mag 2,8, ♄♃) Double tan and aqua stars. Tail of the goat. Extremes of luck and destruction, wealth, fame, help from old clergyman.

Inventor, physicist, radical thinkers; lawyer, councilor, positions of trust. High integrity with good stars. Possible losses. Impervious to poison and venom. Sobriety. Star has useful protective qualities for astrological talismans. MM: Must learn to handle responsibility, power, and life's gifts in positive ways.

Sador 25♒07/+40.25 (*gamma Cygnus*, Mag 2.2, ♀☿) or **Sadr**. Central star of the Swan or Northern Cross. Great talent, skill at blending different methods, multi-disciplinary. Significant influence on others. Wide-spread distribution. MM: Experiences life lessons about the limits of own abilities, and to know when enough is enough.

Gienah 28♒01/+34.09 (*epsilon Cygnus*, Mag 2.4, ♀☿) Star in tail of Swan. Interest in myths and story-telling. MM: Focus on personal interests/agenda or on getting public attention.

Pisces

Helix Nebula 1♓40/+20.33 (*NGC 7293 Aquarius*, Mag 7.3) MM: Must learn how to retain objectives while dealing with the implications and fallout of deteriorating circumstances.

Enif 2♓10/+10.06 (epsilon Pegasus, Mag 2.3, ♂☿) Nose of the horse. Ambition, intuition, enthusiasm, capricious, sometimes bad at risk assessment. MM: Must learn to take a stand on issues and address them effectively.

Sadalmelek 3♓38/-0.05 (*alpha Aquarius*, Mag 2,9, ♄☿) from *Al Sa'd al Malik*, the Lucky One of the King. Right shoulder. Wealth, occult interests, sciences, lucky for gains and prosperity. MM: Develop skill at personal decision-making, reconciling with events, find peace.

Fomalhaut 4♓08/-29.22 (*alpha Pisces Australis*, Mag 1.6, ♀☿) from *Fum al Hut*, Mouth of South Fish. Persian Royal Watcher star *Hastorang*, marked winter solstice in 3000 BCE. Amplifies tendencies of good or difficult planets. Mystic, magic, charismatic, may assume archetypal roles. Fame, lasting name, fortune, power. Tricky secrets, occult/spiritual interests, narrow escapes. Potential fall from grace. MM: Inconsistent, flighty, blows hot and cold, contradictions.

Deneb Adige 5♓36/+45.27 (*alpha Cygnus*, Mag 1.2, ♀☿) aka **Arided**, a corruption of Scaliger's name *Al Ridhadh*. Tail of Swan, aka the Northern Cross. From *Al Dhanab al Dajajah*, the Hen's Tail. Caesius called it *Os rosea* or the German *Rosemund*, linking it to the fragrant rose. Leda, mother of Castor and Pollux. Ingenious, clever, quick to act, fiercely territorial. Powerful, determined, strong will and sharp temper. Artistic, literary or scientific skill and gains from these; possible sales records, vast distribution. May have wide-spread influence over others through work. MM: Powerful creativity and ingenuity that may influence culture and change history.

Sadalachbia 6♓59/-1.17 (*gamma Aquarius*, Mag 4, ♄☿) from *Al Sa'd al Ahbiyah*, the Lucky Star of Hidden Things or hiding places. In the head of Water Bearer. Personal charm, ingenuity. May have mathematical, technical, mechanical, or scientific skill.

Biham 7♓07/+6.17 (*theta Pegasus*, Mag 3.7, ♂☿) aka **Baham**. Marks the horse's head. Curious and impulsive, drawn to high-risk activities. MM: Talented, inspired, creative, but must learn to channel these gifts effectively.

Skat 9♓09/-15.34 (*delta Aquarius*, Mag 3.7, ♄♃) from *Al Shi'at*, A Wish, or *Al Sak*, the shin bone. Right leg of Water Bearer. Good fortune, lasting happiness, able to attract and keep loyal friends, get aid from friends and give generously to them in return. Spiritual and occult studies. Many blessings.

South Pole of Local System 10♓/-29. Nearest major star is Fomalhaut, alpha Pisces Austrinus.

Achernar 15♓36/-56.59 (*alpha Eridanus*, Mag 0.46, ♃) from *Al Anir Al Nahr*, the end of the river. Success, benefits, spiritual wisdom, strong faith. Sometimes a risk-taker, prone to crisis and difficulties, risk of rapid endings. Signifies fires and floods in mundane charts. MM: Need for acceptance, appreciation, and understanding from others.

Ankaa 15♓45/-42.03 (*alpha Phoenix*, Mag 2.3) aka **Cymbae**, Arabic *Na'ir al Zaurak*, bright one in the boat. A griffin or eagle, the Egyptian Bennu bird, or Chinese Fire Bird. Linked to immortality. MM: Drawn into conflicts, controversies, arguments, divergent opinions.

Homan 16♓25/+10.55 (*zeta Pegasus*, Mag 3.6, ♃♀) alternate spelling **Homam**, from *Sa'd al Humam*, the lucky star of the hero, or *Al Hammam*, the Whisperer. Neck of horse. Capricious, daring, curious, loves travel but at risk for accidents.

Markab 23♓46/+15.28 (*alpha Pegasus*, Mag 2.4, ♂☿) from *Matn al Faras*, the horse's withers, shoulder. A saddle, vehicle, anything ridden upon. Skilled speaker or writer, energetic, intellectually alert, math skills, potential for wealth and fame. Arrogance or impulsive actions can bring dangers and disappointments; cuts, stabs, fire, freak fatalities. MM: Gains depth of insight and more sophisticated ideas with age.

Sadalbari 24♓39/+24.42 (*mu Pegasus*, Mag 3.7, ♂☿) from *Sa'd al Bari*, the good luck of the excelling one. Shoulder of horse. The Arabic *Sa'd* is the good luck associated with life-giving spring rains. Attracts and creates nourishment and abundance.

Matar 25♓59/+30.39 (*eta Pegasus*, Mag 2.9, ♂☿) Knee joint of horse's foreleg. Fortunate, prosperous. MM: Fights for acceptance, convince others to adopt one's outlook, interpretations and viewpoints.

Azelfafage 28♓32/+51.16 (*pi Cygnus*, Mag, ♀☿) from *Al 'Azal al Dajajah*, the Tail of the Hen. The tip of the Swan's tail gives a flair for story-telling and unusual journeys.

Galactic South Pole 29♓30/-27. Celestial south pole of Milky Way Galaxy.

References (see page 42 for complete citations)

Vivian E. Robson, *The Fixed Stars and Constellations in Astrology*.

Richard Allen, *Star-Names and their Meanings*.

Diana K. Rosenberg, *Secrets of the Ancient Skies, Vol I and II*.

Elspeth Ebertin, Reinhold Ebertin and Georg Hoffmann, *Fixed Stars and their interpretation*.

Bernadette Brady, *Brady's Book of Fixed Stars*.

Part II

Working
with Fixed
Stars

Origins

Star Names

The ancient traditional star names are usually from Arabic, Greek or Latin sources. Ex: Algol (*beta Perseus*) is the Arabic *Al Ghul*, the ghoul or ghost star, head of Medusa. Pleiades (*eta Taurus*) is the Greek name for the seven daughters of Atlas. Bellatrix (*gamma Orion*) is Latin for Female Warrior.

Johann Bayer added Greek letters to clarify star designations in **Uranometria**, 1603. This became the standard practice. The alpha star is the lucida (brightest) followed by the beta star. Ex: Capella is alpha Auriga. Schedir is alpha Cassiopeia. Nebulae are usually referred to by their Messier classification. Aculeus is M7 Scorpio, a Mag 3 nebula at 28 Sagittarius.

Arabic star names were frequently mangled, corrupted or compressed by medieval translators. Example: Rastaban (*beta Draco*) is from the Arabic *Al Ras al Thuban*, the dragon's head. The same star is also called Alwaid, the mother camels, from an alternate Arabic constellation. Both names are used. Important secondary names and monikers are given in the star list.

Important stars have accumulated many names from different cultures. The name Regulus (*alpha Leo*) the diminutive of Rex, was given by Copernicus. Other names for this star include: Sharru (Akkadian, the king); Magha (Hindu, the mighty); Miyan (Persian, the center) and Taran-Masa (the hero); Malikiyy (Arabic, kingly); Regia (from Pliny); Basiliscus (Tycho Brahe); Al Kalb al Asad (Arabic for the lion's heart); and Gus-ba-ra (Euphratean, the red fire of the house of the east). Richard Allen's book **Star Names** (1899) provides a comprehensive background and history.

Star Lore

Star meanings incorporate a polyglot of astrological traditions, lore inherited from multicultural stories and myths, and from traits conferred by lunar mansions. The stars that outline human figures gain motivation, purpose and behavioral traits. Stars that outline animals and objects relate to their mythic roles, utility, and the reason for their placement in the sky. The deity that constellated the animal, person or object may impact the interpretive contents. Contemporary authors sometimes insert a modern gloss into star stories, either to make star meanings more comprehensible or less nasty. Tread cautiously in this area. Modernist revisions are rejected by traditional astrologers as presumptuous and unnecessary. Readers should examine these sources and make independent assessments of whether updated meanings are useful or not by putting them to the test in chart interpretations.

Constellations are placed in groups that relate to shared legends. For example, the contiguous constellations of Hydra, Crater and Corvus belong to a legend about the Crow's delay in bringing bad news to Apollo. Hercules is near Sagittarius, relating to the Euphratean tale of Gilgamesh and his centaur side-kick, Eu-bani. Aquila, Cygnus, and Lyra were, at one time, the three Stymphalian birds. Lyra is also near Hercules, a constellation linked to Orpheus, the musician who traveled to the Underworld to save his girlfriend Euridice. The stars of Hercules are near the Capricorn Gate, the entrance to the afterlife, which is guarded by Centaurs. The death and deification of Hercules is a significant finale to this hero's story.

Star stories are not static and not uniform! Some constellations, like Hercules, participate in many different stories. Other constellations belong to tales that passed from one culture to another, like that of Perseus and Andromeda. Shared myths evolved through many centuries with assorted variations. Acquiring knowledge of constellation groupings greatly enhances the context for understanding star meanings.

As can be seen in the star list, star names reflect the diversity of cultural input. They also show extensive corruption from translation and transcription errors. Problems developed through centuries of illustrations, as particular stars may be shown to occupy different parts of a constellation's figure in different drawings and descriptions. Albrecht Dürer's illustrations of constellations in La Lande's **Bibliographie Astronomique** (1515) became the definitive constellational figures, along with his 48 drawings for Ptolemy's catalog (1537).

Old constellation and star lore lingers with stubborn intractability. Some stars once belonged to different cultural constellations or to constellations that were discarded in antiquity. Meanings may be contradictory and awkward. For instance, Antares is regarded as a very difficult star in western lore but has lucky and protective features in China. Caput Algol, by way of constrast, is regarded as absolutely evil by absolutely everyone. Yet it has the potential to perform very well in individual natal charts when connected with benefic planets. It's also a very useful star for protective talismans in astrological magic.

Careful study of star-related myths for tiny but significant details bears fine fruits for interpretive clues. As each person's natal chart is a unique life signature, the impact of fixed stars on natal planets is similarly personalized. Fixed stars are many-faceted jewels! Natal planet-star contacts highlight selected facets of these celestial gems. A prime example is a client with Jupiter conjunct Algol. He is by trade a welder and the guitarist for a death-metal band. Another client with a Sun-Algol conjunction works in the mining industry. The story of the Gorgon Medusa includes the detail that her scales were made of metal. It is unknown if the cyclic "winking" of Algol due to its variability as an eclipsing binary star has an impact on natal interpretations. It is possible that a bright Algol yields better influences, while a dim Algol confers the darker ones.

Western culture does not have a monopoly on star lore! There's plenty of great information to be gained from reviewing the Hindu nakshatras, as these are based on star asterisms (groupings) and their imagery. More rich sources of star lore can be found in the Arabic lunar mansions (manzils), star stories from the South Pacific Islands, the Chinese, the Mayans, the ancient Egyptians, African Yoruba and Lucumi lore, and Native American myths.

Suggestions for Interpretation

Working with fixed stars requires some basic astronomical terminology.

Magnitude: brightness of star in comparison to Sirius, the brightest star at Mag −1.4. Mag 1 stars are brightest, most powerful and have given names. Mag 5 may not be visible if night isn't exceptionally clear with no light pollution. Mag 1 stars include Antares, Arcturus, Aldebaran, etc. A star's magnitude may change over time, growing brighter or dimmer.

Binary, Trinary or Variable stars. Binary and trinary stars may appear to be a single star to the naked eye. Ex: Antares – red and green binary star. Many Mag 1 stars are double or triple stars. Variable stars have a range of brightness. Ex: Algol is a eclipsing binary star that appears to wink when the smaller, darker star is in front of the larger, brighter star.

Young and Old Stars: Stars are not the same age. Example: most stars in Orion are fairly young blue-white giants except for Betelgeuse, a very old red-orange giant star in an entirely different star system. Constellations can include stars from different galaxies!

Messier Objects and NGCs: Astronomical classifications for nebulae and cluster galaxies. French astronomer Charles Messier catalogued celestial objects and published his list of 103 objects in 1781. Messier numbers are still used. *The New General Catalogue of Nebulae and Clusters of Stars* (abbreviated as NGC) was compiled by John Louis Emil Dreyer in 1888 to expand on the work of William and Caroline Herschel's general catalog. Nebulae are usually associated with eyesight and blindness. Ptolemy assigned the Mars-Moon attribution to nebulae and clusters. They were used as an ancient vision test for archers and night watchmen. Example: Praesepe (the Manger), aka the Beehive Cluster or M44, is a feature in the constellation of Cancer. Its new designation is NGC2632. Some nebulae are named, and these names can be whimsical or funny. Apparently astronomers have a sense of humor.

Lucida: The brightest star in a constellation, and usually the alpha star. Some alpha stars have decreased in magnitude over the centuries. Stars may increase in magnitude, too.

Occultation: An occultation occurs when a planet passes in front of a fixed star, in both longitude (zodiacal degree) and declination (north or south). Stars must be in the range of planetary orbits for this phenomenon to occur. Unless a planet exceeds 27° north or south out-of-bounds, stars above or below 27° N/S will never be occulted. The Moon makes the most frequent occultations of stars and planets.

Planet Attributions: named stars may be associated with one or two planets. The earliest star list is in Ptolemy's *Almagest*. Associations have been added over the years. Ex: Hamal (alpha Aries) is a Mars-Saturn star. Planet attributions give clues to the star's nature and energies, as well as the features and meanings that particular natal planets that will emphasize.

Orbs

Use orbs of one degree or less for conjunctions, especially for stars less than magnitude 1. Conjunctions are the aspect considered as **stars cast no light** (i.e., do not make aspects). Over the years exceptions to that rule have become more accepted. There are significant fixed star oppositions and star squares which, when highlighted by natal planets or axis points, can have a powerful influence in a natal chart.

Declination

There's debate about whether stars to the extreme north or south have a reduced influence on planets. The path of the planets is confined within 23°33' north or south, although occasionally planets may stray out-of-bounds. A planet that's conjunct a star by both degree and declination (i.e., an occultation) has a profound connection that yields a notable manifestation of the star's influences.

A good example of a planet-star occultation occurs in J. R. R. Tolkien's chart. His natal Uranus occults Khambalia, aka The Merlin Star. Tolkien's books highlight the role of wizards in the events of Middle Earth. The great achievement of Gandalf was stage-managing the transition from the age of the Elves to the age of Humans, a notably Uranian occupation.

Precession

Fixed stars don't move much, but they *do* move. The rule of thumb is about 1 degree in seventy years, although different stars move at different rates of speed. Keep this in mind when examining birth charts from previous centuries. For example, when Leonardo da Vinci was born in 1452, his natal Venus was conjunct the Pleiades at 24 Taurus and his North Node was conjunct Vega was at 6 Capricorn. Remember to take the subtle movement of stars into account when viewing older charts.

Cosmic Structure

This list includes twenty points of celestial orientation. Intersections of the ecliptic, galactic equator, super-galactic equator, and local galactic system are crossroads between greater and lesser cosmic structures. Our cosmos features a hierarchy of celestial associations much like that of city, state, nation and globe. Crossroads are symbols of orientation, decision, cyclic beginnings and endings. The individual with contacts to these may have keener awareness of connections on different levels of existence, and perhaps a greater sense of the ripple effect that actions have on the world around them.

Other celestial points include the centers of the local system, the galaxy, and the supergalaxy. The center of our galaxy, the Milky Way, pulses with burgeoning life. It's a star nursery for millions of baby stars and a massive emitter of X-rays, gamma rays, ultraviolet and infrared light. The emissions may operate on a subconscious or subliminal level that's difficult for short-lived humans to process. Nevertheless, these cosmic centers are the beating hearts of space and exert the forces and ordering principles of the space-time continuum. More research needs to be done on their astrological impact, especially on charts with planets contacting these galactic points.

How Stars Work

A planet that is conjunct or parallel a star (a parallel conjunction, aka occultation, is the most powerful connection) acts as a conduit, pattern buffer and filter for the star's energies. The nature of the planet, its dignities and chart relationships determine the facets of a star's meaning that manifest through personality, life events, relationships, career path, etc.

A star's planet attributions offer additional clues about how a natal planet-star association will manifest. If Mars or Saturn is conjunct Hamal (*alpha Aries, 7♉40*), a Mars-Saturn star, the effects will tend to be more aggressive, violent and destructive.

The whole natal picture must be considered. In 1973 Triple Crown winner Secretariat's chart, Mars and Saturn-Hamal are in mutual reception with the Moon in Capricorn, while Venus in Aries is in mutual reception with Mars in Taurus. The horse became an immortal champion. Saturn and Mars are in the fifth house of progeny. Secretariat sired over 600 foals. Offshoots from his bloodline continue to appear in the winner's circle. The most desir-

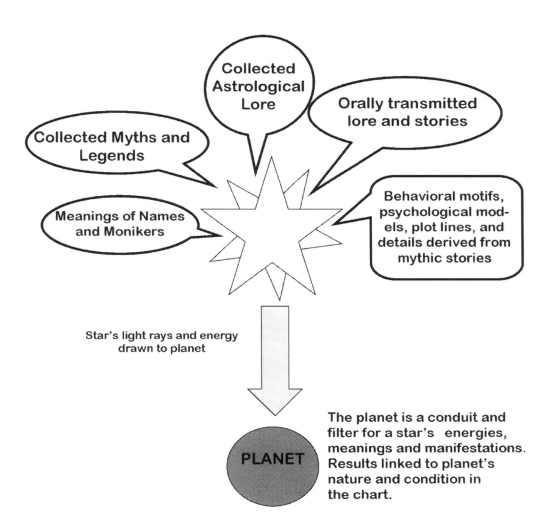

able effect of a natal Saturn conjunction to a fixed star includes a notable legacy, a body of work, or a dynasty. The benefic planets Venus and Jupiter modify and soften stars associated with Mars and Saturn. The malefic planets Mars and Saturn bring out the darker and more unfortunate meanings of Venus, Jupiter, and Moon-associated stars. More details about working with these are in Chapter 3.

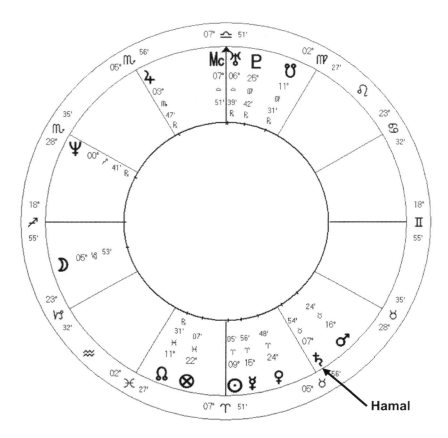

Hamal

Secretariat
March 30, 1970
12:10 am EST
Doswell, VA
Tropical-Placidus
True Node

Data from "Secretariat's
Meadow" biography

THE ROYAL WATCHER STARS

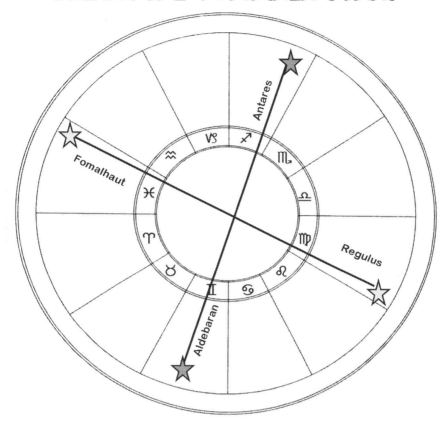

The Adversaries—both red stars
Aldebaran 10♊04/♂ opposite Antares 10♐02/♂♃
The King and Queen—both blue stars
Regulus 0♍06/♂♃ opposite Fomalhaut 4♓08/♀☿

All four are Magnitude 1 stars. Aldebaran (Taurus), Regulus (Leo) and Antares (Scorpio) belong to zodiacal constellations. Fomalhaut marks the mouth of Pisces Austrinus, the Southern Fish.

Brady states that Royal Watcher Stars are "*amplifiers*" that magnify the qualities of the planet or chart point. If these stars are connected to important planets or chart points, the individual may be wildly ambitious and have a strong drive to achieve. The person may become identified with his/her field of achievement as an icon, leader, or an archetypal figure.

The Aldebaran-Antares axis can give exceptional talents that require huge dedication and personal sacrifices. The native must learn self-control of appetites and drives. This axis heightens competition and the potential for career scandals and rivalries. The person must fight and struggle to keep what's been gained, but must also preserve his/her integrity and high ethical-moral standards in the process. A nemesis may arise if power is abused, if the ego becomes overinflated with success, or if the person becomes a law unto themselves. Then the rise to fame is followed by a fall, or an ignominious loss to a rival that's publicly visible. Antares is linked to chronic illnesses and terminal diseases that are sometimes difficult to diagnose or remain hidden for many years.

The Regulus-Fomalhaut axis has similar issues. The meanings and implications of Regulus are close to those of Aldebaran-Antares: the drive to attain power and wealth; the potential for ugly scandals; and the penalties for power abuse or loss of personal integrity with a rise followed by a big fall. Fomalhaut is a less power-hungry star. It gives great talent, luck and beauty along with good fortune, charisma and mystical or magical qualities. The allure of the artistry or creative outlet the individual becomes involved with may have a tricky and/or insidious influence on the imagination; the person becomes wrapped in its tentacles and their perspective on life and relationships can veer in a bad/self-destructive direction. The person's connection with reality may erode or the perceptions/senses can become warped. (More danger of this if the contacting planet has hard aspects or is in bad dignity or a bad house). The good fortunes and favoritism of Fomalhaut can also trigger jealousy in others. There is a potential fall from grace or narrow escapes with this star. Royal star natives include Maria Callas (ASC-Sun-Antares), Jeanne Dixon and MacGregor Mathers (both ASC-Aldebaran).

Interpretive factors

Natal planets conjunct a fixed star, along with dignity factors and aspects, influence how a star's energies are translated and manifest over time. Interpretative factors include the star's meanings and the constellational myth.

A preponderance of natal fixed star conjunctions (more than three or four) implies a greater degree of fatedness and an impulse to enact aspects of the mythic models associated with those stars. It may indicate that the individual is more likely to be at the right place in the right job at the right time to acquire notoriety and fame, and more likely to be remembered for achievements. The individual has more "star power."

While an abundance of natal star contacts may seem desirable, it depends greatly on the stars and planets involved. It may not always work out in a good way. Stars confer a distinctive agenda that must manifest in some way. A chart may contain star contacts at cross-purposes or contain an excess of difficult star contacts. A minimum of very close natal planet-star conjunctions (less than three) confers a greater degree of personal choice and free will. Exceptionally good natal planet placements are just as effective at generating fame and fortune without all of the star agenda-driven baggage!

A Sun-star contact heightens the impact of the constellational myth, including the character(s) and behavioral models featured in the legend. Examine the chart to determine the **heliacal rising star**, i.e. the star that rose with the Sun. A major Mag 1 star may perform that function over five to seven days. This is a highly significant contact that impacts personality and life-direction. The Sun, of course, remains conjunct that star before and after sunrise, so the connection is valid for birth times around the clock. Profound effects accrue if the Sun and the heliacal rising star are both conjunct the Midheaven. Stars conjunct the Ascendant and/or Midheaven are also highly significant.

Working with Stars and Planets

Star-Planet Attributions

Planet attributions underscore the star's meaning and how natal planets will translate it. A star's planet assignments are provided in Part I if available. The earliest source is Ptolemy's *Almagest*. The planets relate to a star's meaning. There is not universal agreement on these assignments.

When a single planet is affiliated with the star, the full spectrum of planetary significations become attached to the star. The star will function most characteristically when in contact with its affiliated planet.

If there are two attributed planets, the order is highly significant. The first planet indicates the initial conditions or situations and the second planet indicates the outcomes. To give a general idea of how these operate: a **Jupiter-Saturn star** augurs benefits or rising status followed by losses or refinement over many years, whereas a **Saturn-Jupiter** assignment gives difficulties and losses followed by benefits. A **Mercury-Mars** combo brings clever but impulsive actions followed by contention, whereas **Mars-Mercury** gives contention followed by ingenuity and silver-tongued excuses to escape troubles. Necessity is the mother of invention here.

Mars-Moon is assigned to nebulae and star clusters and is always associated with eye problems. In practice this combination implies family and/or emotional disruptions and estrangement. The individual may be challenged to confront dysfunctional family patterns. **Venus-Mercury** and **Mercury-Venus** affiliations give talents and skills, popularity, and sometimes fertility, but can indicate fickleness, vanity, or an excessive focus on sexuality or luxuries. **Mars-Venus** and **Venus-Mars** combinations increase powers of attraction and fertility, but also increase the likelihood of infidelity, multiple love affairs and marriages, perhaps with scandals. **Sun-Mars** relates to the use of will power and physical vitality. **Jupiter-Mars** suggests gains in wealth and status followed by struggles to retain these gains or a fall or overthrow, with losses from lawsuits. **Mars-Jupiter** indicates military triumphs, personal battles to gain justice, followed by rising status and wealth.

Star-planet attributions help to ascertain the relative amity or adversity between a star and a natal planet. Benefic planets (Moon, Venus, Jupiter) improve star meanings and minimize negative star meanings. Malefic planets (Mars, Saturn, Pluto) bring out more difficult and contentious meanings and increase the likelihood of dangers with stars of a violent nature.

Uranus, Neptune and Pluto highlight odd side-effects and unusual qualities of fixed stars. There may be a greater connection to the collective, like being swept up in massive cultural movements and trends, participating in technological developments that impact society, or being affected by far-reaching social upheavals like economic crashes, wars or epidemics. Uranus and Neptune trigger scientific, technological and occult qualities. With difficult stars, these planets can trigger bizarre injuries, rare diseases, poisonings or side-effects from drugs. Pluto increases an obsessive emphasis on the star's qualities or uncontrollable, eruptive manifestations of it.

Natal Contacts

The impact of a fixed star depends on the natal planet that's conjunct the star.

Sun – influences personality, physical body type, facial features, hair, personality and temperament, life story, the predominant theme of life. Consider the myth connected with the entire constellation for greater insights

Moon – influences family and personal connections, type of thinking, daily or cyclic exchanges and flow, connections with the public, collective/historic events

Mercury – influences skills, wits, intellect, ingenuity, scholarship, ability to assess personal crossroads and life choices, transactions, salesmanship, communications, and modes/frequency of travels

Venus – influences love, sexual norms and preferences, fertility and children, creativity, artistry, the sector of society to which one is attracted, desire for peace and harmony

Mars – energy, ambition, motivation, physical dynamism, aggression, military, physique or outstanding physical characteristics, potential for injuries and wounds, use of tools and engines, heat sources

Jupiter – expands and dramatizes the star's meanings, education, religion/philosophy, potential for wealth and leadership, foreign connections, broadmindedness, status within community, good reputation. With some stars (like Castor) can lean toward excesses.

Saturn – structural or developmental difficulties, behaviors or traits that are a liability until controlled, inherited problems, or liabilities that may ease with maturity. Hardships and limitations, burdens, unhappy or unwonted results, dealings with dishonest people, or long-term experiences that lead to mastery in one's field. Lifetime works, substantial cumulative opus, great refinement of character, high integrity and impeccable reputation.

The Moon's Nodes and Stars

The Nodes move in the same apparent direction as the stars, so nodal contacts are indicative of specific and destined manifestations and destinations whether or not the person has any interest or proclivities in that direction. The Nodes have magnetic properties that funnel a star's influences. The brightest stars have the most powerful effects. A North Node contact may impel the individual to perform a familial or social role or function, with or without conscious acknowledgment. If a star-node contact fits the rest of the chart and coincides with the person's interests and talents, it gives a sense of being in harmony with one's destiny. If at odds with the rest of the chart, however, the contact can pull the person away from the desired course or career. The concomitant disruptions may evoke struggles, insecurity, and self-doubts. A South Node contact is more unpredictable because the dragon's tail thrashes around. The manifestation of the star contact may be sporadic or unplanned, creating once-in-a-lifetime opportunities or disasters, depending on the nature of the star. Venus and Mercury are node-friendly and will tend to attract good things, while Mars and Saturn bring out the more negative effects of the South Node.

Star-to-Star Relationships

Star Pairs

In some constellations there are pairs of stars that work together or evoke different facets of a concept. Examples include Castor and Pollux (alpha and beta Gemini at 20 and 23 Cancer)

and Zuben Elgenubi and Zuben Elschemali (alpha and beta Libra at 15 and 19 Scorpio).

Star Conjunctions
Sometimes two stars occupy the same degree of longitude (zodiacal degree). Their influences may be mingled but usually the more powerful star is brighter and/or closer to the ecliptic. Examples include Polaris-Betelgeuze (28-29 Gemini); Sirius-Canopus (14-15 Cancer); Vega-Rukbat (15-16 Capricorn); and Arcturus-Spica (24 Libra). Bernadette Brady offers more details about star pairs and conjunctions in her fixed star books.

Star Oppositions
Aldebaran—Antares; Rigel—RasAlgethi/Graffias; Sirius—Vega; Scorpion's Stinger stars (Aculeus/Lesath) and the Galactic Center—El Nath/Betelgeuze/Polaris and the Anti-Galactic Center; Capulus/Algol—Agena/Toliman; Acrux—Almach.

Star Squares
Pollux-Spica; Rigel-Achernar; Agena-Sadalsuud/Deneb Algedi; Algenubi—Zuben Eschamali. Regulus-Toliman (0 Virgo/29 Scorpio).

Stellar oppositions and squares are only relevant if natal planets conjunct *both* stars. This is not an exhaustive list! Star oppositions that straddle the ASC-DSC axis impact self-knowledge and relationships. Star oppositions that straddle the MC-IC axis impact the overall life path, family, and career. The specific effects depend on the meanings of the stars.

I call Hyades-Regulus "The Armada Square." Saturn was conjunct the Hyades and Jupiter conjunct Regulus on July 28, 1588 OS, when the tiny British Navy drove off the huge Spanish Armada with the aid of a great storm, a David vs Goliath type of event. The Hyades are linked to storms, too. Rigel-Achernar is "The Wild Ride Square" and appears in the natal charts of Arthur Rimbaud (French poet) and Syd Barrett (Pink Floyd co-founder). It connects individuals to the whirlpool of mass cultural movements and emerging social trends. The individual may become iconic, but may be hurt or destroyed in the process.

Brits send the Fire Ships into the Spanish Armada
July 28, 1588 OS *
12:01 am LMT, Calais, France
Tropical-Placidus-True Node

The sea battle occurred over several weeks. The British fire ships were the turning point. Strong winds pushed the fire ships into the Armada. Several ships burned and the Spanish crescent formation was broken.

*Alison Weir, *The Life of Elizabeth I*, Ballantine Books, 1998, pg. 391.

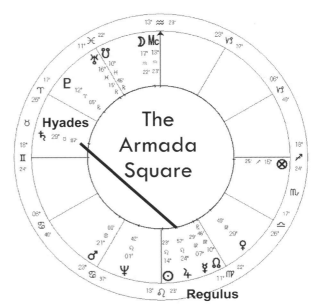

Bird Stars

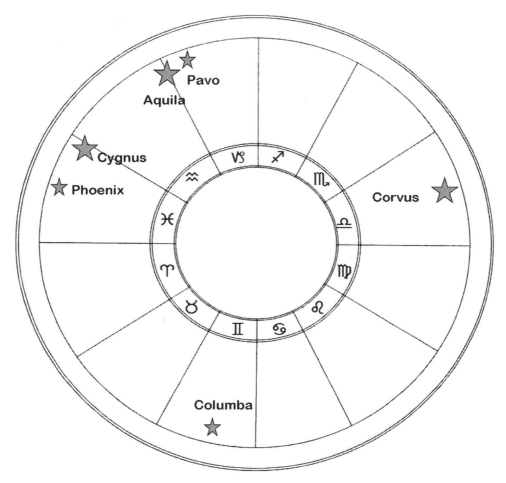

Aquila the Eagle is near the ecliptic. Cygnus the Swan (the Northern Cross) is a large northern constellation that stretches across Aquarius and Pisces. Corvus the Crow and Columba the Dove are beneath the ecliptic. Pavo the Peacock is in the extreme south.

Hearts and Eyes

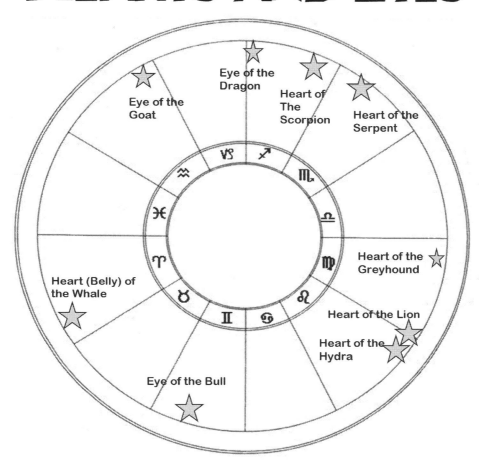

Baiten Kaitos (Heart of the Whale) 21 Aries
Aldebaran (Eye of the Bull) 10 Gemini
Alphard (Heart of the Hydra) 27 Leo
Regulus (Heart of the Lion) 0 Virgo
Cor Caroli (Heart of the Greyhound) 24 Virgo
Unukalhai (Heart of the Serpent) 22 Scorpio
Antares (Heart of the Scorpion) 10 Sagittarius
Etamin (Eye of the Dragon) 28 Sagittarius
Oculus (Eye of the Goat) 5 Aquarius

DANGER ZONES!

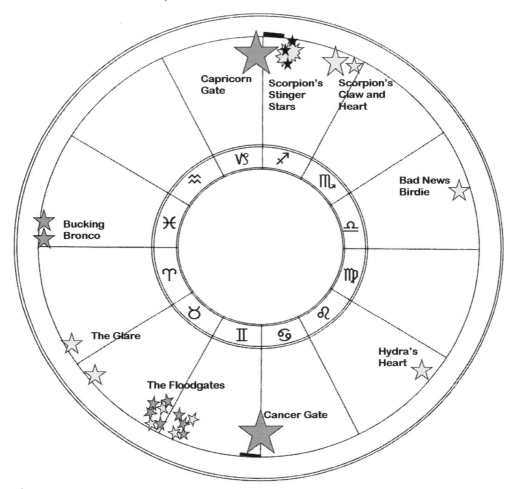

Be wary of these places in the zodiac, especially in mundane charts: The Bucking Bronco is Pegasus. Cetus the Whale of Sea Monster lurks just beneath the ecliptic and is a threat to passing planets. The Floodgates are the Pleiades and Hyades, both connected to rain and floods. The Cancer Gate (last five degrees of Gemini) is populated with difficult stars. The Hydra's Heart, Alphard, is linked to poisons. The Bad News Birdie is Corvus the Crow. The Scorpion's Heart (Antares) and claw star (Acrab) are unlucky and linked to disease. The Scorpion's Stinger stars Sargas, Lesath, Aculeus and Acumen signify attacks. The Stinger stars curl around the Galactic Center like a poisonous barbed wire fence, posing dangers for souls passing through the Capricorn Gate.

Stellar Danger Zones

Red flag these fixed star zones for potential trouble.

The Glare – Bernadette Brady conferred this name on the stars of Cetus that lie just below the ecliptic and glare upward at the planets on the Via Solis. This zone goes from Baten Kaitos at 21 Aries to Menkar at 14 Taurus. It's associated with attacks, ambushes, cultural upheavals and natural disasters that pull the individual off course. The individual may be exiled for a period of time, in the belly of the whale. Example: the mass flight of civilians from Syria in 2016 while Uranus was conjunct Baten Kaitos.

The Flood Gates – the Pleiades and the Hyades, from 0 to 6 Gemini. These star clusters are associated with the rainy season, floods and storms, but also with tears, separations, and family estrangements.

The Cancer Gate occupies the late degrees of Gemini at the solstitial border; it includes Al Hecka, Polaris, and Betelgeuze. Although the person may be able to navigate for others, s/he may experience great difficulties in life and be unable to navigate a satisfactory personal path.

The Serpent's Heart is Alphard at 27 Leo. It can signify poisoning, contamination, and drug overdoses, especially when affiliated in some way with the eighth house or the ruler of it.

The Bad News Birdie is Corvus, from 10 to 17 Libra. This zone can signify someone who is badgered by friends and relatives who are disaster magnets, who is blamed for problems s/he didn't create, or whose life is trashed by an overweening solar-ego type person.

The Scorpion's Claw and Heart – Acrab and Antares at 3 and 10 Sagittarius are dangerous stars associated with assaults, toxic family secrets, and crash-and-burn situations.

The Capricorn Gate is from 24 to 29 Sagittarius along the solstitial border. It includes the Scorpion's stinger stars, the Galactic Center, Etamin, and Sinistra. It is the term of Mars and face of Saturn. The nakshatra Mula, the root, ruled by Nirritti, the Calamity Jane of the Hindu pantheon, overlaps the Capricorn Gate from late degree tropical Sag into Capricorn. This is a place of exceptional danger for natal planets. A good motto for this zone is "curiosity killed the cat." In the pursuit of deep, ancient, or occult knowledge, the individual may tumble into dangerous situations that are beyond control. It is the cosmic recycling bin. Dumpster divers beware!

Ancient Greek pottery features illustrations of fierce Centaurs guarding the Capricorn Gate. The Mesopotamians and Egyptians placed a many-breasted Scorpion goddess at this portal, named Ishara-tam-tim or Selket/Serket, respectively. It is the gate to Paradise, but one encounters dangerous creatures before gaining entrance.

References and Resources for Fixed Stars

In addition to personal experience with fixed stars over many years and Michael Munkasey's original commentaries, these texts have provided useful summaries of star meanings and other data:

Richard Allen, **Star-Names and their Meanings.** G. E. Stechert, 1899 [available as a free download in multiple formats at *archive.org*]

Bernadette Brady, **Brady's Book of Fixed Stars**. Red Wheel/Weiser, 1999
Planet-Star Combinations. The Wessex Astrologer, 2008

Reinhold Ebertin and Georg Hoffman, **Fixed Stars and Their Interpretation**. Translated by Irmgard Banks, AFA 1971.

Vivian E. Robson, B. Sc., **The Fixed Stars and Constellations in Astrology**. Weiser, 1923, 1979.

Diana K. Rosenberg, **Secrets of the Ancient Skies**, Volume I and II. Ancient Skies Press, 2012.

Resources for Constellational Myths

Ovid, **The Metamorphosis**
Robert Graves, **Greek Myths**
Aratus, **Phainomena**

Star myth stories are provided at *www.constellationsofwords.com*

A comprehensive Greek mythology site with primary resources is at: *www.theoi.com*

Please note that fixed star sources sometimes give conflicting details. Every effort has been made to provide the most correct and up-to-date data. Any errors in star classifications, names, or positions or other details are my own.

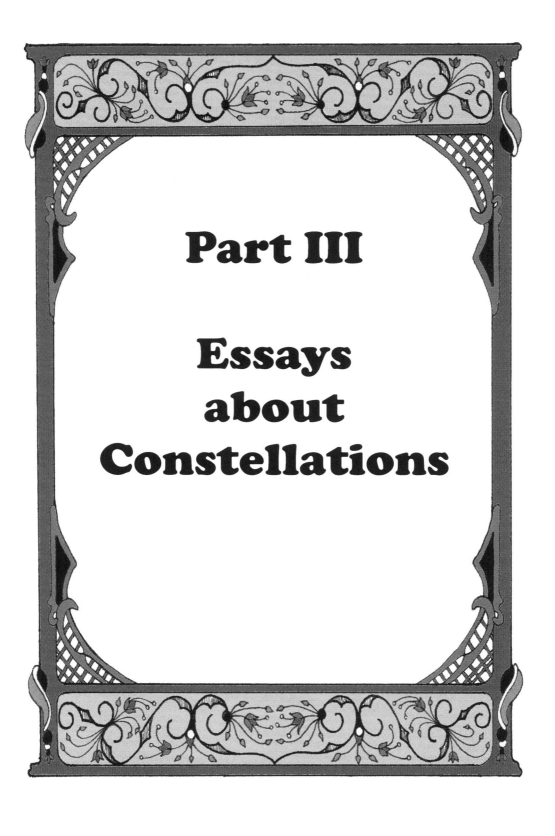

Part III

Essays about Constellations

Introduction to Part III

Modern astronomers recognize eighty-eight constellations. The series of short essays in Chapter 4 on non-zodiacal constellations were published in NCGR's *E-News* from 2017 to 2019. I wrote them because they're much less familiar to astrologers. The effort helped satisfy my own insatiable curiosity and provided greater understanding about how these stars operate in charts and why particular meanings have accumulated over time. Constellation maps, birth charts and illustrations accompany these essays for the first time. Hopefully readers will find these to be useful supplements to the written material.

I chose to examine Boötes and Auriga because they are mysterious and misunderstood. The Celestial Crowns are small but mighty. Examining them was an opportunity to answer some questions: how are they different? how are they similar?

The essays in Chapter 5 about Orion, Eridanus, and Hercules were written at different times. I have attempted to excise redundancies; please pardon those that remain. Orion is one of the largest and most visible constellations in the sky. It's helpful to understand his lore and stars, as well as his celestial adversary Hercules. Both are exceptionally ancient constellations and their celestial opposition signifies struggles toward human evolution.

This section concludes with two full-length articles about Gemini and Capricorn. These zodiac signs are of special interest because of their unique star-planet attributions make them unlike other zodiacal constellations. These articles appear here for the first time. I find star-planet attributions enormously useful for delineating planetary contacts. My interest in them stems from my work with tarot attributions and the occult Law of Correspondences. It's possible that star attributions are more relevant when working with star longitudes and less useful with star parans. You, the reader, are quite free to review the information and accept or reject it, as you please. As Terry Pratchett said, it would be a funny old world if we were all alike.

References and end notes are at the end of each essay and article.

Non-Zodiacal Constellations

Aquila the Eagle – The Cosmic Velociraptor

It's a bird! It's a plane! It's Superma....no, wait, it's a bird. The Eagle soars along the edge of the Milky Way during the nights of summer and rises with the Sun in mid-to-late January. Aquila is exciting, noble, fierce and beautiful, sometimes in a cruel and dangerous way. The Eagle's most familiar story is about Zeus's infatuation with a beautiful boy. He sent the Eagle to snatch Ganymede and bring him to Olympus to serve as a cup-bearer. Hera was annoyed because this was her daughter Hebe's job, so Zeus transformed the boy into Aquarius the Water Bearer. This myth caused all kinds of problems by legitimizing relationships between older men and younger boys (tips for conducting these relationships are forever immortalized in Plato's naughty **Phaedra**). The social and legal rights of women in Greece deteriorated as this myth gained popularity.

The Eagle carried and retrieved Zeus's thunderbolts. The great raptor was the Roman standard and associated with emperors. Appearances of eagles that were connected to a Roman emperor's ascent to the throne or death were taken very seriously. Emperor, the Latin *imperator*, originally meant "field marshal" rather a having dictatorial connotation. The constellation is associated with conquerors, generals, armies, and weapons of war. Native Americans called it the Thunderbird, a personification of the angry sky sending storms, high winds, roiling clouds, and fast-changing weather fronts.

Eagles fly higher than any other bird. Their eyesight is keen and their vast wings make them exceptionally swift. Natal contacts to Aquila's stars may inspire intellectual and spiritual flight, skill at seeing or spotting things long before others are aware of it, and a propensity for speed and swiftness. The Ptolemaic Mars-Jupiter attribution to Aquila's stars connects it to militaristic pursuits and opportunistic grabs. Contacts may bring quick wealth, possibly through looting or the karmic violation of "borrowing with intent to keep." The Mesopotamians referred to the star group as The Living Eye of God, a divine eye that saw everything on earth. This manifests as hyper-curiosity that leads to the acquisition of information. Like the Living Eye, Aquila natives accumulate knowledge, becoming walking encyclopedias and know-it-alls that are always ready for juicy intel-grabs. Aquila's spiritual visions can inspire religious movements, music or literature. The Ganymede legend connects the constellation to kidnapping and swift assaults. In contemporary usage, this can extend to children taken from parents for one reason or another, infant adoptions, or child snatchings.

The figure of Antinoüs was added beneath the Eagle's claws by the Roman Emperor Hadrian in 132 CE upon the death of his young male companion. An oracle predicted the death of the emperor unless the one he loved most died. Young Antinoüs drowned himself in the Nile and courtiers pointed to the stars of Aquila overhead carrying his soul into the heavens. The figure was discontinued by astronomers in 1933.

The constellation currently occupies tropical degrees from 18 Capricorn to 4 Aquarius. Aquila hovers over the Centaur's rump and Lyra, and is beneath Albireo, the Swan's head. Bright stars Altair, Albireo, and Vega form "the Summer Triangle," a figure that's easy to spot in the northern skies at that time of year. The Eagle's head and neck stars are above the Goat's horn and eye stars in the early degrees of Aquarius. This doubly emphasizes keen perceptions, visionary abilities, and the proclivity for self-serving acquisitiveness. Aquila is just above the ecliptic so planet-star occultations are possible.

The main stars of the Eagle include **Altair** (alpha, 2≈07/+8.54, Mag 0.9), **Alshain** (beta, 2≈ 42/+6.27. Mag 3.9), and **Tarazed** (gamma, 1≈12/+10.39, Mag 2.8) in the head and neck.

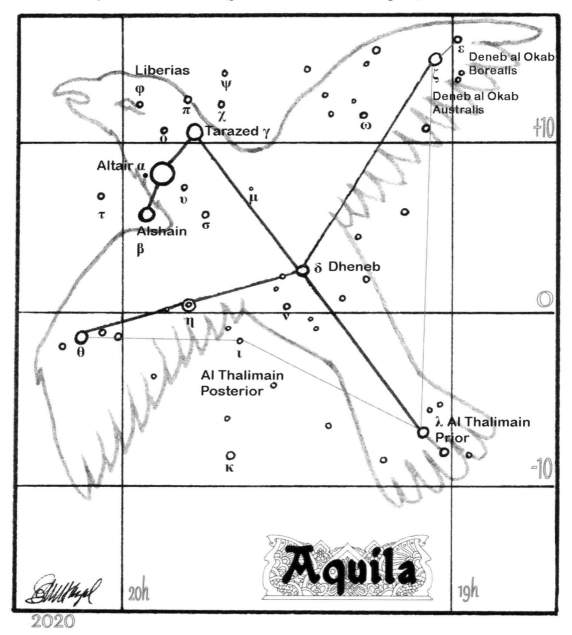

The main tail stars are **Dheneb** (zeta, 20♑04/+13.53, Mag 3) and **Deneb Okab** (delta, 23♑ 56/+3.09, Mag 3.4).

Famous criminals who exemplify the Eagle's ruthless attacks and loot-grabbing include early 1930s automobile bandit Clyde Barrow, who had two natal Aquila contacts (♂-Dheneb and ♅-Deneb Okab), and Mafia syndicate gangster Lucky Luciano (☊-Tarazed).

Military and political figures include: George Washington (MC-Altair, ☽-Dheneb); Niccolo Machiavelli (ASC-Dheneb); Clara Barton (☽-Dheneb; she followed the Army of the North during the Civil War as a nurse); Benjamin Franklin (☉-Tarazed/Albireo, known for his pithy remarks and some sexual opportunism as the French ambassador), Napoleon Bonaparte (☽-Altair, a classic mark for a conqueror), and German PM Konrad Adenaur (☿-Deneb Okab).

Literary examples are: Robert Anton Wilson (♂-Altair); Jules Verne (♅-Altair); Paracelsus (♂-Deneb Okab); Clare Booth Luce (⚷-Deneb Okab in the third house sextile Sun in the fifth; she was an author and playwright, had hit-and-run sexual affairs, was elected to Congress, and served as US ambassador to France); William Powell, author of **Anarchist Cookbook** (♃-Altair, ♀-Tarazed, spent months in NYC library snatching intel from army manuals on guns and bombs for his book); Mark Twain (♆-Alshain); William Blake (♀-⚷-Deneb Okab, had numerous visions); early sci-fi author Shirley Jackson (☊-Dheneb), and Bertold Brecht (♀-☊-Tarazed).

Musicians and actors include: Beethoven (♀-Tarazed and ♇-Dheneb; his productive years coincided with the Napoleonic era and he originally dedicated his Fifth Symphony to Napoleon); The Doors guitarist Robbie Krieger (☉-Dheneb); Edith Piaf (♀-Deneb Okab, snatched from drunken mother as a child by her father, who gave her to his mother to raise. Her songs inspired French Resistance members during WWII); Canadian pianist Glenn Gould (♄-Tarazed in Grand Trine with Chiron/Taurus and Mercury MC/Virgo, high speed soaring on piano); Bruce Willis (☽-Altair, like Napoleon – frequently in action film roles handling weapons and fighting); and Ben Stiller (♀-Deneb Okab; he portrays characters pitched into bizarre situations [*The Zero Effect*, *Night at the Museum*] that sometimes include romance [*Zoolander*]).

Religious examples are: Church of the Latter Day Saints (Mormon) founder Joseph Smith (♂-⚷-Deneb Okab, multiple convictions and jail time for fraud); St. Bernadette Soubirous (☉-Dheneb and ♄-Tarazed); and Pope John Paul I (♅-Tarazed).

Auriga the Rein-holder

Auriga has identity issues! The Charioteer doesn't have a chariot, and why is there a goat on his shoulder? Auriga's accumulated legends and stories provide diverse layers of meaning. Furthermore, the stars of Auriga, a northern constellation, occupy nearly the same zodiacal degrees as Orion, so the impact of Auriga's stars might be overlooked when the brighter stars of Orion are close to natal planets.

These stars have served in different groupings. The oldest image, circa 5000 BCE, is of a shepherd holding a goat. The alpha star Capella marked Spring Equinox in 3853 BCE. The Shepherd and Goat were eventually displaced by Taurus, then by Aries—all domesticated animal images. Chariots were invented during the third millennium BCE. The stars were reconfigured into a king holding a staff and reins in a chariot. Though that figure didn't last long, the idea of a chariot stuck. The Babylonians split the stars into 2 constellations, Rukubi (The Chariot) and Mul-Gam (The Crook). Shepherd's crooks represent husbandry and royal authority. Eventually the crook became a whip.

Ptolemy attributed Auriga's stars to Mars and Mercury. Isadorus called the constellation "Mavora," a poetic term for Mars, father of Romulus, patron of shepherds. Hermes-Mercury was also a patron of shepherds associated with fecundity. The Greek legend of Erichthonius sustains the figure of a Charioteer. Hephaestus attempted to rape Athena. She wiped his sperm off her leg and dropped it on the ground. Mother Earth gave birth to an infant with snakes for legs. Erichthonius inherited Hephaestus's lameness and craftsmanship. He was raised by Athena and became the king of Athens. He invented the chariot so he could be mobile. Auriga is associated with damaged legs and wheelchairs.

The alpha star Capella, the Little She-Goat, is a red giant with two smaller companions. It is the sixth brightest star and the most northerly bright star. It's been called the Horn of Plenty, the Food-Bearer, Brahma Ridaya (the heart of Brahma), Ptah the Opener, The Messenger of Light, and the Star of the Gate. In China it was the Celestial Treasury. The star is connected to abundance and riches. Manilius said that Capella gives a fearful, timid, cringing nature along with curiosity and the urge the seek the unknown. **Capella** (22Ⅱ08) and the stars that mark her two kid-goats, the **Haedi** (Sadaltoni at 18Ⅱ38 and Hoedus II at 19Ⅱ27) are associated with storms and high winds. The twin he-goats signify frivolousness, lustful urges and promiscuity, criminal behavior, and indulging in bad habits unto death.

El Nath (22Ⅱ34) does double duty as gamma Auriga and beta Taurus. It marks the tip of the north horn of the Bull and the foot of the Shepherd-Charioteer. El Nath is the star closest to the Galactic Anti-Center (27Ⅱ05). The tip of the horn augurs prodding, pushing, and forcefulness. This star can give fortune and status, with interests in science or spirituality, but also problematic relationships, wounds, accidents and leg or foot injuries that limit mobility.

Hindu lore associates Auriga with the **Bhagavad Gita**. Krishna directs Arjuna's chariot while lecturing on right action and karmic law. In Plato's **Phaedrus**, a metaphoric chariot is the vehicle of the soul. The rational intellect—the Rein-holder—must control the horses, who symbolize primitive urges and passionate impulses. The theme is self-control, discipline, and shouldering responsibilities.

Auriga is bisected by the Galactic Equator. In Mesopotamian terms, this meant the Rein-holder stood between the realms of Enlil and of Anu, i.e., between human realities and the realm of divine immortality. Many ancient star myths boil down to one big question: *what does it take for a person to become immortal and/or ascend into the heavens?* Auriga's legs are deformed, and he holds two misbehaving, ungrateful goat kids, symbolizing obstacles in the upward path to Capella—the Star Gate to Enlil's celestial realm, the heart of Brahma, or the Horn of Plenty. Isn't it curious that physical disabilities and troubled parent-child relationships are the final hurdles to the passage to immortality?

The constellation contains an unusually high number of special celestial objects: multiple eclipsing binary stars, seven open clusters that include M36, M37, and M38; two O-Associations, two bright diffuse nebulae, and one T-Association. Auriga's stars are slowly precessing toward the intersection of the Galactic Equator and the ecliptic, the summer solstice point. Menkalinan at 00♋11 has crossed the doorstep of the solstice point at 0° Cancer and the other stars will follow like sheep or goats.

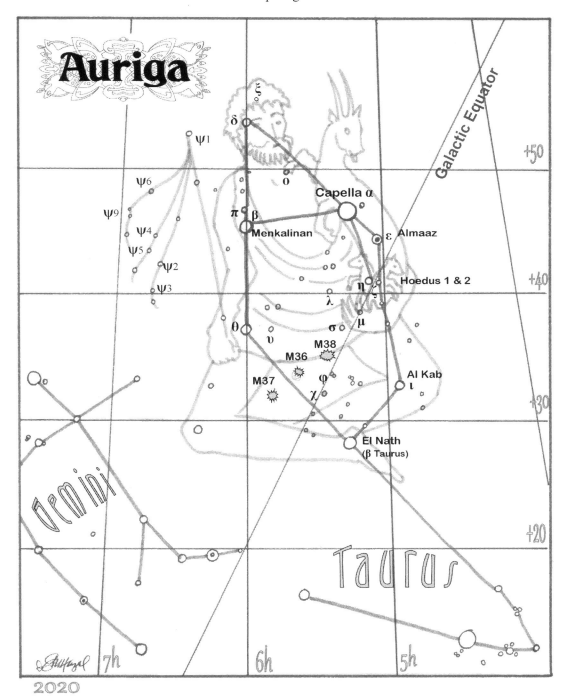

I ruminated on this constellation for several days and concluded that Auriga's major theme of right action and karmic law arches over three sub-stories and a nasty little codetta.

The first story is about mothers—the Nanny Goat and her twin kids. Horace called the Haedi "*hirrida et insana sidera*" and "*insana caprae*" - the horrid insane stars or the crazy goats. Amalthea's foster son Zeus supposedly broke off her horn in play, thus creating the Horn of Plenty. The Goat rests on the Shepherd's left shoulder, the feminine-yin side. The Nanny Goat is a generous, all-giving mother who is disappointed or wounded by her children, perhaps afraid of them. She may be a mother projecting hopes and dreams onto her children and feels betrayed when they choose different paths as adults.

Joan Crawford's natal chart has Pluto sandwiched between Sadaltoni and Hoedus II with Mercury in an applying square from Pisces. Joan adopted five children. The oldest son and daughter were intensely difficult children. Joan died in 1977. Christina Crawford wrote *Mommie Dearest* (Nov 1978), a memoir alleging that Joan beat and tormented her children. Joan's younger children and some friends denied the allegations, while other acquaintances

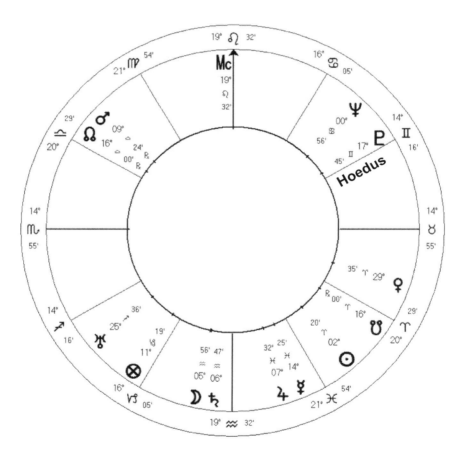

Joan Crawford
March 23, 1903, 10:00 pm
San Antonio, Texas
Geocentric-Tropical-True Node-RR: A

affirmed instances of abusive behavior. Even Bette Davis, Joan's arch-enemy, pitied Joan for her two awful older children. In 1999, the American Film Institute rated Crawford as tenth on its list of the greatest female stars of Classic Hollywood cinema. She won an Academy Award for playing the title role of *Mildred Pierce* (1945), a mother coping with a duplicitous daughter. Her posthumous fame was tainted by her alleged behavior as a cruel parent.

The second story is about fathers. **Menkalinan** (*beta Auriga*, 00♋11) marks Auriga's right/ yang shoulder. It's minutes away from another right shoulder star, **Betelgeuse** (*alpha Orion*, 29♊02). The star combination emphasizes shouldering burdens and responsibilities on a paternal and professional level. These stars give a powerful drive to achieve, but also deep distress, sorrows, and disappointments that are met when striving for the highest levels of accomplishment. Menkalinan signifies the potential to inherit parental strengths and weaknesses. Menkalinan and Betelgeuse's current positions at the threshold of the Cancer Gate highlights humanity's collective responsibilities for the planet.

The third story centers on **El Nath** (*gamma Auriga*, 22♊51) and **Al Kab** or **Hasseleh** (*iota Auriga*, 16♊54), the stars that mark the Shepherd's right knee and foot. They emphasize mobility or the lack of it. El Nath prods, gores, and causes injuries, accidents, or paralysis. Necessity or injury demand new modes of locomotion, innovation and creativity, whether in a literal or figurative sense.

The nasty codetta is from the ten little Mag 5 psi stars [ψ^1 to ψ^{10}] that form the whip. They're called the Goads, or the Latin *Dolones* or *Stimulus*. The Whip stars, now at 8–10 Cancer, can signify a mean streak, ruthlessness, cruelty, or even demagogues who whip up the masses into a frenzy.

Auriga's star stories highlight the best and worst sides of human nature, life's inevitable burdens and the struggle to move through life in a responsible, ethical way. Most will never attain fame but what each person does, and what humanity does, matters greatly.

Boötes Bears Watching

Boötes and Auriga share identity problems because of conflicting cultural legends. Too many make-overs have caused confusion about their form and purpose. Both constellations feature a famous northern lucida but are otherwise formed from fainter stars. They lost importance as precession shifted them away from the equinoxes over the centuries.

Boötes is known as the Bear-Watcher or Bear-Hunter because of his close proximity to the Great Bear, Ursa Major. In some depictions he holds a staff in one hand and the leashes of his two dogs, Asterion and Chara, in the other. Boötes' identity problem stems from Ursa, which has been depicted as a bear, a wagon, and a plow. Sole reliance on Greek myths is a liability because it confounds the celestial jobs and star meanings. The Mesopotamians saw a celestial avatar guiding the plow in a circle around the celestial North Pole, while the Greeks superimposed their regional myth of Kallisto and Arcus, the mythic founder of Arcadia, being harried by a hunter chasing the big angry mama bear.

Historic evidence yields a protective deity in charge of ordering the cosmos and destiny rather than a hunter-killer. The god-king Šupa (Shu.Pa) or the Egyptian hippo (Isis as Rennenutet) are earlier sky figures who held "the mooring post" of heaven and earth. Šupa is the celestial moniker for the great god Enlil. Šupa's position in the sky underscores Enlil's role in determining the destiny of the land and royal dynasties. It also highlights the impact of the plow on agricultural development. Enlil was, like Zeus, the king of the divine pantheon and patron god of farmers. The Arabic title *Al Haris al Sama*, The Protector of Heaven, and the Chaldean name for Arcturus—*Papsukal*—the Guardian Messenger, convey the idea of a powerful divine royal figure with crucial celestial responsibilities.

Arcturus occupies the phallic zone of the god-king. A consistent feature of god-kings, like Enlil and Zeus, is their semi-divine offspring who link them to humanity and earth. Arcturus -Papsukal is a symbol of divine seeds descending from a highly elevated position of the sky. Semi-divine offspring do great deeds, make an impact on the people around them, and have a shot at immortality. Arcturus and Spica share the implication of engendering special "seeds" that land on earth. While Spica implies the greatest offspring of human origin, Arcturus implies semi-divine status or god seeds. There are many human figures in the sky; none but Boötes has a major magnitude star marking the organ of generation.

Coma Berenices, the crown of love and sacrifice, is near Šupa's left knee. Corona Borealis, the crown of triumph and rewards, is near the hand holding the staff. The crowns underscore Šupa-Enlil's royal status along with his responsibility for ensuring the celestial movement around the axis at the northern celestial pole and North Star, the mythic residence of goddesses of fate and destiny. Šupa-Enlil is the distributor who channels well-earned rewards or imposes sacrifices, and who calls warnings before dangers arrive. This is a highly potent and heroic figure upon whom the orderly movement of the cosmos depends.

Where Cygnus the Swan evokes sweet floral scents, Boötes is linked to sounds. Object 3C299 (13♎), a strong radio source, is near his left ear. One of his nicknames is The Shouter: *Vociferator* and *Clamator*. The clamor used to be a warning of stormy weather, that farmers should finish their tasks and sailors should stay home. This constellation may signify individuals who clamor for attention and demand to be heard.

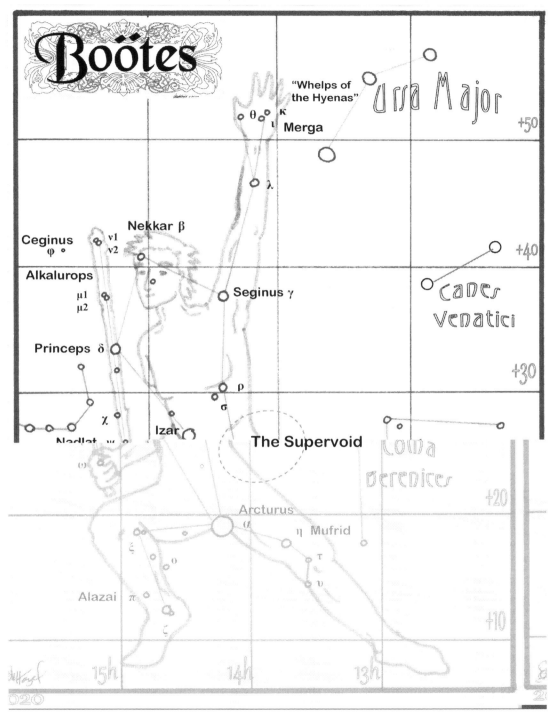

The named stars of Bootes include: **Merga** (38h/iota Bootes, 15♎44/+46.02, Mag 5.8) the elbow of the left hand; **Mufrid** (eta, 19♎37/+18.09, double, Mag 2.8) in the left leg; **Seginus** (gamma, 17♎59/+38.05, Mag 3.0), his left shoulder; **Arcturus** (alpha, 24♎31/+18.55, Mag .20) a red giant, the 4th brightest star, in the phallic region between his legs; **Nekkar** (beta, 24♎32/+42.18, Mag 3.6) the head; **Izar** (epsilon, double, 28♎23/+26.52, Mag 2.7)

the right elbow; **Princeps** (delta, 3♏26/+33.08, Mag 3.5), **Alkalurops** (mu, 3♏28/+37.18, Mag 4.5), and **Ceginus** (phi, 5♏23/+40.17, Mag 5.4) near the top of the staff. Arcturus is attributed to Jupiter-Mars, the rest of the stars to Mercury-Saturn.

The constellation has eccentricities linked to its appearance. It sets slowly over eight hours in a perpendicular position during the spring and summer. Merga and the stars of the extended left fist never sets in the northern hemisphere. The Chinese called this group "the whelps of the hyenas." Aratos wrote that Boötes rises "all at once" like a jack-in-the-box during the autumn when the Sun is in Libra and Scorpio.

Boötes' rising or setting in a chart makes a difference. Boötes rising seems to indicate one-shot wonders or people known for a single achievement or event. Look for this in charts with Libra or the early degrees of Scorpio on the Ascendant. Harper Lee has Boötes rising with her Ascendant. She wrote **To Kill A Mockingbird**, her only novel, to great acclaim. Controversial photographer Robert Mapplethorpe gained notoriety when an exhibition of his work was censored and removed from a Cincinnati gallery. Sculptor Niki de St. Phalle is famous for a garden of tarot trump figures that took decades to build.

Frank Herbert, author of the **Dune** series, has Ascendant-Izar, Mercury-Seginus and Sun-Merga. His books are imbued with the heroic qualities inherent in Boötes-Supa. The lead character Paul Atreides is the son of a nobleman who gains semi-divine status through the course of the series.

People with Boötes setting in the seventh or eighth houses have longer-lasting careers and more achievements over time. These include Michael Jackson, who was born just after sunset with North Node-Arcturus and Jupiter-Izar. The Divine Miss M, Bette Midler, also has Jupiter-Mufrid and Chiron-Seginus sinking toward the Descendant.

Fist star Merga gives force and intensity. David Carradine has Mars-Merga and Moon-Mufrid, the elbow and knee stars. He conveyed Bruce Lee's work into the mainstream in the **Kung Fu** TV series and remained an icon in the world of woo-shu until his tragic death. Jim Henson has Mercury Rx-Merga and Venus-Arcturus, quite appropriate for the most famous puppeteer of the 20th century. His voice (*Clamator*) was more well known than his face! Astronomer Johannes Kepler had Mars-Merga, and French PM Emmanuel Macron has Pluto-Merga.

Arcturus and Spica are only 36' minutes apart. Their gifts include fortune, fame, and wealth. Spica, the wheat sheaf, doesn't pick itself but does attract patrons and highly-place supporters. The downside of Arcturus is the tendency cause one's own problems through the consequences of public visibility, sycophants and fair-weather friends. Natives include Marie Antoinette (Moon) and Jane Austen (Saturn, with Moon-Seginus). Lenny Bruce (Mercury-Arcturus) certainly clamored for attention with this comedic social critiques and like Boötes had a great rise and fall. After his death he became known as the patron saint of modern comedy. Bernie Sanders has Venus-Arcturus, and has affiliated himself with strong female politicians.

Angela Lansbury has Sun-Spica-Arcturus and Mercury-Izar rising in her third house. A film-industry friend plucked her out of a retail job and boosted her into a decades-long film career. Lansbury starred as Eglantine Price in ***Bedknobs and Broomsticks*** (1971) holding a staff, declaiming spells, and shepherding two refugee children. Later in life she gain more mainstream recognition in the TV series ***Murder She Wrote*** in her role as Jessica Fletcher the writer (3rd house).

The staff is an ancient symbol of power and nobility that was eventually transformed into a scepter. The tradition of using a "speaking stick" in group discussions was revived as Pluto transited those stars in the mid-1980s. The staff stars Alkalurops and Princeps are quite close and work together. People with these stars are attracted to power, drama, and the power of language. Natives of the staff stars include Sarah Bernhardt (Sun, with Mercury-Seginus); Hillary Clinton (Sun); Terry Gilliam (Mars, with Venus-Arcturus); and Ed Sullivan (Mercury).

Eusebius wrote "a mystic goad the mountain herdsman bears." There does seem to be some magic connected with Boötes. The Ganesha Milk Miracle on September 21, 1995 (4:30 am IST, New Dehli, India) features Ascendant and Sun ruler Mercury Rx conjunct Mufrid and North Node-Izar rising in the second house.

The Celestial Crowns

Corona Borealis, Corona Australis, and Coma Berenices have strange and peculiar characteristics. The two Coronas symbolize crowns or wreaths, while Coma Berenices is hair sacrificed to a goddess and stolen from the temple, then placed in the sky. These beautiful constellations play host to unusual celestial objects, galactic clusters and nebulae.

Corona Borealis, the Northern Crown

Corona Borealis the **Northern Crown** extends from 5 to 25 Scorpio. It is in close proximity to Hercules and above the head of Serpentis, the snake held by Ophiuchus. Ptolemy attributed Northern Crown stars to Venus and Mercury. It's depicted as a gem-encrusted crown made by Hephaestus, or as a wreath of flowers created by Dionysus to use during his wedding to Ariadne. Greek Orthodox weddings still feature floral crowns on the heads of both bride and groom. The crown was placed in the sky by Venus. The constellation is also linked to Arianrhod and Persephone, whose name is derived from the Chaldaean *Persephon* (phe'er [crown]-serphon [northern]).

There are two named stars: **Alphecca** (α, 12♏35/+33) and **Nukasan** (β, 9♏24/+28, Mag 3.7). The Blaze Star, a recurrent nova, is at 20♏08. The epsilon star (19♏10) was known in China as **Koon-So**, the Money String. It is associated with great wealth. A cluster galaxy at 8♏21 is part of the crown. Some of the stars of the constellation form a circle that represents the crown. Others represent ribbons that extend outward from the circle. Alphecca is the large gem or pearl at the front of the crown.

Ariadne is the Cretan princess who gave Theseus string to find his way out of the maze after slaying the Minotaur. Theseus took Ariadne with him when he escaped. Her dreams of a happily-ever-after were crushed when he ditched her on Naxos. Dionysus, a composite solar-vegetation god associated with wine and death/rebirth cycles, subsequently claimed her as his bride. Theories about the origin and purpose of labyrinths and mazes suggest these struc-

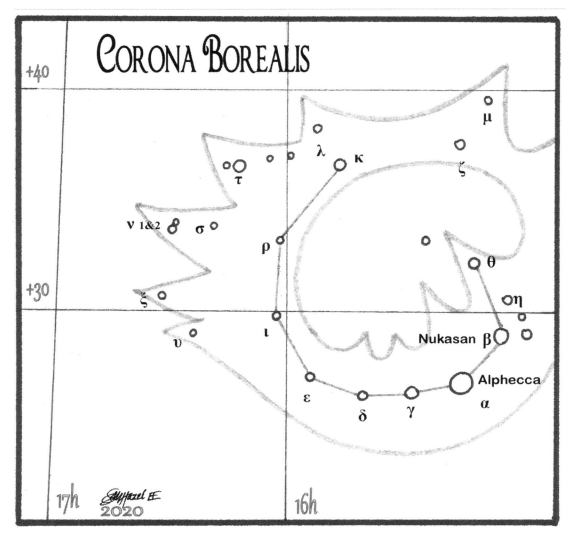

tures are a physical representation of ancient seasonal dances depicting or celebrating the Sun's seasonal turnings and/or the path of transmigrating souls. The Solstices, or Sun's turnings, are associated with reincarnation. Ariadne and Dionysus share mythic ties to the underworld. Ariadne's father King Minos became a judge of souls in the underworld because of his great wisdom. Ariadne may have been a Moon goddess. Her union with Dionysus links the Sun and Moon with vegetative cycles of death and rebirth.

Manilius wrote that this constellation fosters an interest in gentle pursuits like gardening and perfumery. It's associated with accumulating collections and the creation of a body of work (songs, poems, jewelry, paintings, etc). This author links it to "foppishness" in the charts of men; to the arts of adornment, debauchery and momentary pleasures.

A crown usually elevates the wearer and confers status. It implies honors and high attainments, but it is also a circle symbolizing time and duration. Fame and recognition may be conferred after death. Flowers are transitory and regenerative, so natives may have periodic seasons of blooming and retreat. The influence of Alphecca and Nukusan merge with the depth and intensity of Scorpio. Natives of these stars probe deeply into their fields of interest. An alternate name for the constellation is the Crown of the Serpent, giving its stars an association with profound occult or spiritual delving and transformations.

Nukusan natives include Oliver Stone (Venus), Ezra Pound (Sun) and John Lennon (Mercury). Nicholas Culpeper is a perfect example of Sun-Alphecca with his fascination with herbs, plants, and the combinations of these that are effective for medicinal purposes. Other Alphecca natives include Joni Mitchell (Mercury); and Frank Herbert (Venus). H. G. Wells and Gore Vidal share Saturn-Alphecca. Vidal wrote biographies of historic individuals. The French painters Séraphine de Senlis and Henri Toulouse-Lautrec, both born in 1864, share North Node-Alphecca.

Séraphine is a particularly good example of the creative and distillation processes associated with Alphecca. [1] Her North Node-Alphecca opposes South Node-Pluto-Menkar, the mouth of Cetus. These natal placements straddle her MC-IC axis. She taught herself to paint after seeing a vision of the Virgin Mary. Lacking any resources for supplies, she concocted secret recipes for her paints using locally available herbal and organic materials that have stood the test of time. She painted in obscurity for years, generating a massive collection of paintings in her small flat. Séraphine's work was discovered by a German art dealer in the 1920s. She had a brief blooming period of prominence and wealth that ended abruptly when the effects of the 1929 stock crash were felt in Europe. She was institutionalized with paranoid schizophrenia and died of breast cancer in the late 1930s. Her work was forgotten and swallowed (Menkar) by the tumult of the second World War. Interest in her strange life story and surviving works revived at the dawn of the 21st century as Neptune in Aquarius squared her MC-IC and Nodal axes.

References: Richard Allen, **Star-Names and their Meanings** (1899)
Diana Rosenberg, **Secrets of the Ancient Skies** (2015)
[1] E. Hazel "Séraphine de Senlis: The Lots of Angels." *Geocosmic Journal*, Spring 2016, pp 25-32.

Corona Australis, the Southern Crown

The **Southern Crown**, **Corona Australis** or **Stephanos Notios** is a celestial figure that lies beneath Sagittarius the Archer. This rough, oblong circle is south of the bracing arm holding the bow and arrow and loops between the two front hooves. Aratus (3rd c BCE) knew it as an unnamed circlet. It was first distinguished as a separate figure by Hipparchus (2nd c BCE). It occupies the early degrees of tropical Capricorn and includes no notable bright stars. The Southern Crown currently occupies the early-to-mid degrees of tropical Capricorn, beginning with Globular Cluster NCG 6541 at 1♑35. The lucida or alpha star is called **Alfecca Meridiana** (14♑08/-37.50) and is a faint magnitude 4.

Corona Australis has less traditional mythic lore than Corona Borealis. Centaurs were sometimes shown wearing crowns or wreaths in Greek art, a convention that may have been influenced by the halos of the Gandharvas, the celestial horses of India. Late myths credit the crown to Dionysus who placed it in the sky in honor of his mother Semele. An earlier legend regards the star group as a bundle of radiating arrows known as the Rota Ixionia or the Wheel of Ixion. The centaurs or Kentauroi were descended from Ixion (the sun) and

Nephele (clouds). They were a Bronze Age mountain tribe who hunted bulls on horse-back with spears (*ken*—spear or prod, *tauroi*—bull). The Mesopotamians placed the Archer Pabilsag in the zodiac to guard the Capricorn Gate, the exit portal into the afterlife. From this lore comes the alternate name, the Crown of Eternal Life. The Northern and Southern Crowns share implications about lifetime achievements and posthumous fame.

The Mesopotamian Centaur was linked to Nergal, a god similar to Mars. In this culture and in Egypt, the crown was The Cargo Boat bearing souls into the afterlife. The Crown's meanings include military victories and conquests. Ptolemy gave the brightest stars of this constellation (α, β, γ, δ) an attribution to Saturn and Mercury. Star-planet assignments are from a much-earlier work by Hipparchus that is no longer extant. The Saturn-Mercury attribution implies cleverness, strategic and tactical thinking, being fast on one's feet, and a degree of cunning. In negative manifestations this can amount to thievery, destructive tendencies, deceitfulness, disgraceful behaviors and sexual excesses. Fame can shift to notoriety when these traits are at the forefront.

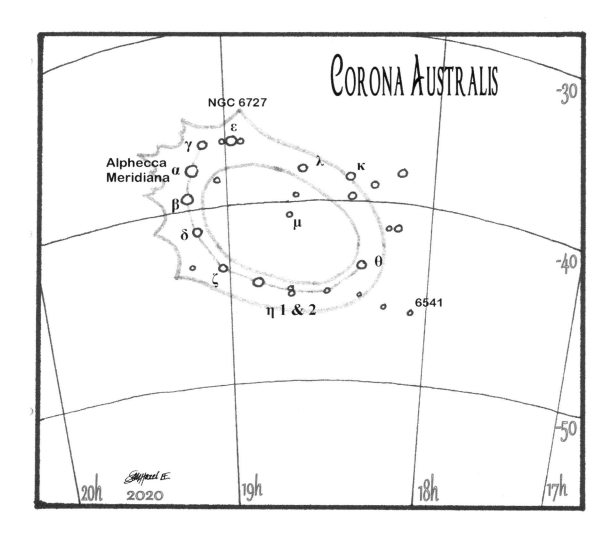

The Chinese used the fainter stars of the figure in an asterism called the Winnowing Tray, the Manure Basket, the Mouth of the Winds or the Big Mouth in China. A basket was a symbol of a big mouth that spreads nasty rumors and slanders, and was further associated with adultery and prostitution. Winnowing and the removal of manure echo the overlapping Mula nakshatra, a cosmic recycling bin associated with intense destruction and regeneration. The Mouth of the Winds moniker also implies fires, terrible storms, destructive natural phenomena, and military depredations.

Another Chinese asterism now in the early degrees of Capricorn was called The Celestial Market. This zone signified community wealth and personal fortunes, but also the potential for social and economic destruction and plagues. The Arabic manzil *Al Na'a'im*, The Ostriches, has meanings that include the destruction of community wealth. On September 11, 2001, Mars was at 1 Capricorn with the South Node at 3 Capricorn. The Solar Eclipse at 4 Capricorn on December 25-26, 2019 heralded a global pandemic. This is a dangerous area of the zodiac!

The bright stars (α, β, γ, δ) formed an asterism called *Al Kubbah*, the Tortoise, by the Arabs. The Chinese called it *Pi*, the Primal Tortoise. Pi the Tortoise existed before the earth and sky. These stars give an intense interest in history, cultural roots, symbols, myths, and folklore. Fu Ti invented the I-Ching when inspired by the markings on the tortoise's shell, so the Tortoise stars in the region of 13°-14° Capricorn lend themselves to the prophetic and divinatory arts. The Chinese associated this asterism with seasonal inundations and storms.

Gamma Corona Australis at 8♑53 is in close longitudinal proximity to Facies (M22 Sagittarius, 8♑36) although somewhat below it in declination. The influences of these stars are merged. Rosenberg specifies that Facies is a cluster *in front of* the Archer's face that creates a unique lens of perception and imagination. It confers visionary tendencies, a sense of personal destiny and great willpower, but also the potential for poverty, ostracism, and chronic health problems. The native must have patience in order to overcome monumental challenges. Facies is from the Latin *facere* – to make or do something. The *Liber Hermetis* associates these degrees with prophecy and foresight, and the desire to look into the future. That said, Facies frequently turns up in mundane disaster charts.

As with the Northern Crown, the Corona Australis is associated with gems and flowers, gathering, growing, or creating a body of work that may become an enduring legacy. The downside is that the constellation and the Arabic and Chinese asterisms indicate greater risk factors as the works of men and cultures can be destroyed by war and violent manifestations of Nature. Triumphs associated with the Southern Crown may come at someone else's expense or at a high personal price. Natives with natal planets in the Southern Crown include Adolf Hitler (Moon-Jupiter), Larry Czonka (Mars), Heidi Fleiss (Sun), Florence Griffith-Joyner (Saturn), Nancy Kerrigan (Mars), Vivien Leigh (Jupiter), Frank Sinatra (Venus), and Clara Barton (Sun, Uranus, Neptune).

References
Richard Allen, **Star-Names and their Meanings** (1899)
Diana Rosenberg, **Secrets of the Ancient Skies** (2015)

Coma Berenices

The shape and meanings of **Coma Berenices** are similar to the Northern and Southern Crowns, so it is included as the third crown in the series. It's depicted as a circular hank of hair, although this star grouping has taken many forms. The name *Berenice* is the Greek word for amber, both the stone and the hair color. Hair has magical properties. For men, hair relates to physical strength and virility (Sampson). Female hair is a "crowning glory" that enhances powers of sexual attraction and a woman's intuitive powers.

Coma Berenices became a distinct constellation in 234 BCE during the reign of the third Macedonian Greek pharaoh of the Ptolemaic dynasty, Ptolemy Euergetes. His sister-wife Berenice donated her hair to the temple of Arsinoe-Aphrodite. The hair was stolen and the pharaoh created this constellation to commemorate it. Aphrodite-Venus is credited with placing the constellation in the sky.

Crowns, long golden hair, organic wreaths, and halos symbolize of the beaming rays of the rising sun (Ascendant/East). The rising sun alludes to people who embody the highest and

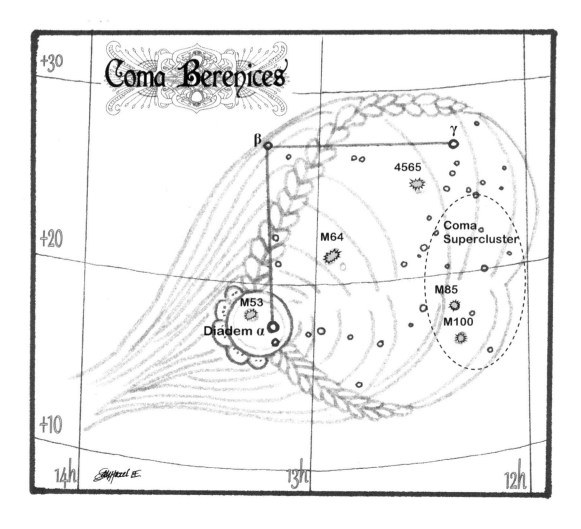

best traits of humanity. Crowns confer the power of royal status and command. Halos are earned through holiness and martyrdom, wreaths are awarded to champions or give special status to a bride and groom. Hair is the only one of these that can be cut away. Berenice's amber hair was a willing sacrifice to the goddess of love, so Coma Berenices is a Crown of Giving.

Earlier associations with other constellations and figures have left residual meanings. The Arabic *Al Halbah* or *Al Dafirah*, the Coarse Hair or Tuft, placed this star group at the tip of Leo's twitching tail, giving fidgety mannerisms, facial ticks, epilepsy or convulsions. Coma Berenices co-rises with Boötes' hand and were depicted as a dove by the Assyrians. The alpha, beta and gamma stars are an Arabic asterism called *Kissin*, possibly a species of ivy, morning glory or a climbing dog rose. On the Dresden Globe it's shown as an ivy wreath, elsewhere as a floral wreath. The link to ivy gives tenacious clinginess. As a part of the Virgo constellation it was the Caduceus or alternately a distaff, thread and woof and called *Fusus vel Clous, Fila et Stamina*. Weaving goddesses are associated with wisdom, talent, and the threads of fate. Coma Berenices retains links to talents and destiny along with a heightened sense of karmic ties and obligations to others.

Coma Berenices occupies tropical zodiac degrees from 1 to 11 Libra. The Autumn Equinox occurs at the intersection of the ecliptic and Galactic North Pole at 0♎00. The Coma Supercluster NGC 4889 at 1♎30 (+27.59) leads at the front edge of the constellation. Natal planets at the celestial crossroads kick open William Blake's doors of perception through visionary experiences and unique insights.

The bright stars and objects include M64, the Black Eye Nebula spiral galaxy at 3♎56; the beta star at 4♎39 (+27), and alpha star **Diadem** at 9♎14 (+17). The Ptolemaic attribution Saturn-Mercury was assigned to the stars of both Coma Berenices and Corona Australis. The attribution precisely describes the events that named the constellation: one person makes a sacrifice or endures a loss (Saturn) and another person runs away with it (Mercury). This can be a recurring life pattern for natives, although they seem to endure these episodes with exceptional tenacity and equanimity.

Other traits include a love of ancient traditions and a vivid symbolic imagination. These stars confer exceptional talents in the arts, literature, and comedy, which requires a clever and inventive viewpoint. Natives put incredible effort into achieving goals. Sacrifices taken to extremes can lead to martyrdom. Feverish pursuits can erode critical thinking skills and judgment. Actions and choices influenced by Coma Berenice can be mind-boggling. Common sense may leave the building.

Ground-breaking French poet Arthur Rimbaud's Moon rose with Diadem and Venus in the 12th house in advance of his first house Libra Sun. Although he only wrote poetry for five years, Rimbaud's work changed poetry forever. His poems were published posthumously and the impact rippled through the following century of writing. Lenny Bruce's tenth house Mars-Diadem accompanied his Sun and Mercury in Libra. His career in comedy was controversial and fraught with legal problems caused by obscenity and drug charges. Lenny's scathing yet hilarious social commentary on bigoted politicians and money-hungry religions mocked institutions operating far short of social ideals. Like Rimbaud, Lenny changed the course of American comedy and is considered a patron saint of free speech to contemporary comedians. Coma Berenices can give posthumous elevation to sainthood, but it should be noted that Coma's saints may be glorified rebels.

The chart of Dr. Edward Bach has Uranus-Diadem and the Sun-Supercluster NCG 4889 trine Pluto in Gemini. He was dedicated to healing British soldiers wounded during WWI. The available medicines failed to address PTSD and psychosomatic illnesses. He spent several years developing flower remedies. His extreme dedication included testing all of the remedies on himself to ascertain precise profiles on the symptoms each flower would relieve. Dr. Bach's quasi-homeopathic simples rely upon wild flowers (the floral wreath) and native tree buds. His invaluable gift to humanity is a collection of nearly three dozen flower remedies that includes Rescue Remedy, the indispensable five-flower blend.

People born around September 30, October 1 or 2 with Sun-Diadem may have a pattern of soap-opera entanglements in family dramas. Three clients with Sun-Diadem share similar patterns. As young adults they were highly attractive, talented individuals with numerous romantic choices. Marital commitments led to decades of care-taking burdens. These clients clung tenaciously to spouses and family members in spite of financial or emotional sacrifices. Their extremely high level of commitment persists although they are fully aware of deleterious effects on their own lives.

References
Richard Allen, **Star-Names and their Meanings** (1899)
Diana Rosenberg, **Secrets of the Ancient Skies** (2015)

The Northern Cross: Cygnus the Swan

Cygnus the Swan soars across the Milky Way in the far north circling around the edge of the circumpolar constellations. The enormous Swan extends from the early tropical degrees of Aquarius to the late degrees of Pisces. Although the Romans standardized the constellation as a swan, it as been *Volucris* (a bird), *Avis Veneris* or *Myrtilus* (bird of Venus), and *Phoebi Assessor* (Sun's bird). The Euphratean name was *Urakhga*, the Roc. The Arabic figure *Al Dajajah*, the Hen, was eventually corrupted into *Adige*. It has been a pigeon and a partridge, too.

Cygnus is also known as the Northern Cross. The α, γ, η, and β stars parallel the Milky Way, while the ζ, ε, γ, and δ wing-stars form the perpendicular line. Gamma star Sador is the point where the lines intersect. This area of the sky is dominated by red and orange stars and known as the Red Region.

The Greek myth tells of Zeus transforming into a swan to seduce the beautiful Leda. Leda laid two eggs, each bearing two children: Helen and Polydeuces (Pollux) who were immortal, and two mortal children Castor and Clytemnestra by her husband Tyndareus, King of Sparta. While the Twins rise with the Sun in May and June, their Swan-parent is fully visible throughout the night. The Chinese have a story of thwarted romance between the stars of the Ox Boy (Altair and Albireo) and the Weaving Girl (Vega) separated by a river (the Milky Way). The monogamous swan mates for life. Cygnus stars may confer the traits of romantic devotion, thwarted or unrequited love.

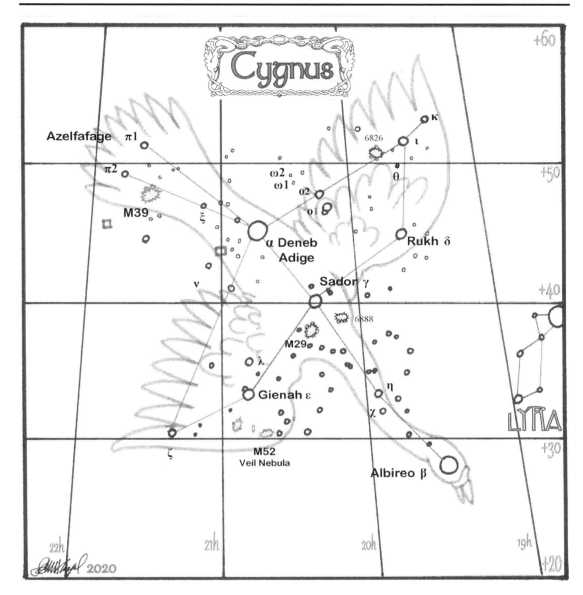

The Swan's Venus/Mercury attribution confers charm, beauty, social popularity and talents. The head of the Swan is **Albireo** (1≈32/+28, *beta Cygnus*, Mag 3.2, a golden-azure binary). The Arabs called it *Al Minhar al Dajajah*, the Hen's Beak. The modern name is a mangled translation of *ab ireo*, the sweet-smelling root of the iris. Orris root's scent is sweeter and stronger than the flower, useful in perfumery for unifying blends and making the scent last longer. Albireo natives are capable of bringing disparate elements together into something stronger, sweeter, and more durable than the sum of its parts. Iris, aka sword lily or flags, require full sun to thrive. Likewise, Albireo is especially notable with Sun conjunctions. Natives may have a beaky nose and speak or sing with sporadic honks or barks like a goose.

The gamma star is **Sador** (25≈07/+40.25), from *Al Sadr al Dajajah*, the Hen's Breast. Sador natives also merge disparate elements and their works may have an extended influence on others. The epsilon star is **Gienah** (27≈45/+34.09) from the Arabic *Al Janah*, the Wing. It gives talent and sharp minds eccentricities and quirks. **Azelfafge** is from *Al 'Azal al Daja-jah*, the Tail of the Hen (*pi Cygnus*, 28✶32/+51.16). It gives story-telling flair and unusual journeys.

The Swan's lucida is **Deneb Adige** (5✶36/+45, *alpha Cygnus*, Mag 1.3), from *Al Dhanab al Dajajah*, the Hen's Tail. This star emphasizes a swan-like tendency toward fierce territoriality, a strong will and sharp temper. It's also called *Arided*, a corruption of Scaliger's name *Al Ridhadh*. Caesius called it *Os rosea* or the German *Rosemund*, linking it to the fragrant rose. Deneb Adige produces creative people whose ideas and products gain phenomenal success and mass distribution, although all Cygnus stars share this quality to some extent. The trait also applies to products released when the Swan's stars are activated. Cygnus contacts generate catnip-like attraction, so natives with well-placed planet contacts sometimes exceed all expectations.

Natives with planets conjunct more than one Swan star gain more benefits! Those looking for natal Cygnus contacts should keep in mind that the positions listed above are for 2020. Stars precess about 1 degree every 70 years.

People with natal contacts to **Deneb Adige** include: Evangeline Adams [☉], Honore de Balzac [♇], Alice Cooper [☿], and Sybil Leek [☉♂]. Macabre cartoonist Edward Gorey is a triple native [☉/Deneb Adige, ☽/Gienah, ☿/Sador].

Natal contacts to intersection star **Sador** are in the charts of: Charles Darwin [☉], Louisa May Alcott [☽], Tallulah Bankhead [♂], Judi Dench [♄], and Claude Monet [☊]. Double natives include the mother of the modern tarot deck Pamela Colman Smith [☉/Gienah, ☊/

Janis Joplin
January 19, 1943
9:45 am CWT
Port Arthur, TX
Tropical-Placidus
True Node
RR: AA

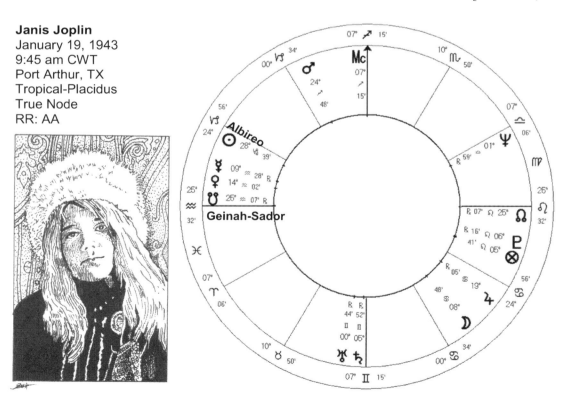

Sador], Jules Verne [☿/Sador, ♅/Albireo], and Judy Blume [☉/Sador, ♀/Gienah]. Bobbi Kristina Brown's ♄/Sador and MC/Deneb Adige echoes the sad Ox Boy-Weaving Girl story.

Wing star **Gienah** natives include: Havelock Ellis [ASC], Margaret Mead [☽], JD Salinger and Jacqueline Susann [♅]. Double natives are baseball hero Jackie Robinson [♀♅/Gienah, ♂/Deneb Adige] and Lauren "Baby" Bacall [♂/Gienah, ☋/Sador].

Head star **Albireo** natives include flashy, recognizable personalities: Dolly Parton [☉], Federico Fellini [☉], Jane Fonda [♃ rising]. Double natives include hot-tempered Janis Joplin [☉/Albireo, ASC-☋ / Gienah-Sador] who often wore feathers on her head; Jackson Pollack [♅/Albireo, ⚷/Deneb Adige]. Charts with both head and tail star contacts include George Balanchine [☉/Albireo, ♂/Deneb Adige] who choreographed Swan Lake, and Benjamin Franklin [☉/Albireo, ☽/Deneb Adige].

The children of tail star **Azelfafage** include the Mother Goose of Wicca Doreen Valiente [☽], Hans Christian Anderson [♀], John Milton [♂], and humorist Erma Bombeck [♅].

The Good Earth by Pearl S. Buck was released on March 2, 1931 with ☿/Gienah. It was on best seller list for 2 years, won the Pulitzer Prize, Howells Medal, and Nobel Prize in 1938. YouTube, launched February 14, 2005, is a triple native with ☿-☉/Gienah, ♅/Deneb Adige, and ⚷/Albireo. Anyone hoping to have a successful book release should seek an election chart with a strong contact to one of the Swan stars. Hoping to benefit from the benevolent Swan stars, *Little Book of Fixed Stars: Expanded 2nd edition* was released with Mars/Deneb Adige and Saturn/Albireo!

The Kneeling One

Hercules is 1,225 square degrees, the fifth largest constellation in the sky. It's stars aren't very bright, yet it's a highly significant and extremely ancient sky figure. The Summer Triangle formed by the alpha stars of Cygnus, Aquila, and Lyra to his right. To his left are the Corona Borealis and Boötes. Ophiuchus and Serpens are beneath him, and the Big Dipper is above. Hercules rotates around the edge of the circumpolar zone in a bizarre position, with head down and his knees along the circumpolar circle. Hercules stars range from tropical degrees 25 Scorpio to 20 Sagittarius, wider than Orion. All of its stars are attributed to Mercury. This is an oddity as the constellation's lengthy history offers numerous associations with solar deities.

The constellation's most ancient title is simply The Kneeler. The etymology is strange. Eudoxos called it Ἐνγούνασι (Engounasi); Hipparchos *Engonasi* or *d'en gonasi kathemenos*, that is – Bending on his Knees. Ptolemy used *en gonasin*. Aratos added *Oklazon*, the Kneeling One, and *Eidolon*, the Phantom, and wrote "...of it can no one clearly speak, nor to what toil he is attached...labouring on his knees, like one who sinks he seems..." [1]

Eratosthenes suggested the figure was standing on Draco. The Euphratean myth of Izhdubar (Gilgamesh) includes the defeat of the dragon Tiamat. This is probably the source of the Greek myth of Hercules and the Lernaean Hydra. A cylinder seal from 3500-3000 BCE shows these figures in this exact position, so Eratosthenes had it right. The labors of Gilgamesh and Hercules echo the Sun's journey through the twelve zodiac signs; both are Sun-related mythic characters. Hercules shares a winter solstice birth date with other solar gods. [2]

In Phoenicia, the constellation represented the sea god Melkarth. The Romans called it *Genuflexus* (Kneeler) and used other names relating to his legendary skills: *Saltator*, the

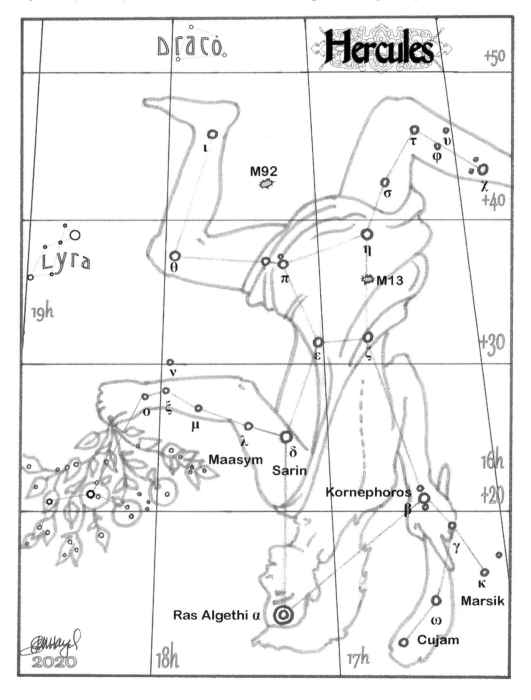

Leaper; Χάρωψ (Charops) the Keen-eyed One; and *Clavator*, the Club-bearer. *Sanous* is a Sabine-Umbrian-Roman name for a geographic location involved in a story. Varro estimated that there were forty-four regional versions of the Hercules myth, attesting to the enormous popularity of this hero's stories. [3]

Hercules is usually illustrated as a strong man wearing a lion's skin. He holds a club in one hand and apple branch on the edge of the Milky Way in his other hand. The apple branch symbolizes the golden apples of the Hesperides featured in one of the Herculean labors. Ladon, the dragon that guarded the tree, is the nearby constellation Draco. The Arabs called it *Al Rakis*, the Dancer, as well as *Al Jathiyy a'la Rukbataihi*, the One who Kneels on Both Knees. This degenerated into Algethi, the name of the star that marks the figure's head.

For such a famous and elderly constellation, only a few of its stars bear names: **Ras Algethi** (alpha 16♐26), variable double stars of orange and teal that marks his head. **Kornephoros** (beta 1♐22, pale yellow) is his left shoulder star; **Marsik** (kappa 26♏00, double stars of pale yellow and pale garnet) is near his right hand or club, depending on how the figure is drawn. **Maasym** or Mi'sam (lambda 20♐11, deep yellow) is near his right elbow near **Sarin** (delta 15♐02) the right shoulder star. **Cujam** (omega 1♐51) is in the club, which is given as a separate constellation in Pliny.[4] **M13** is a nebula near his hip. The **Apple Branch Cluster** is formed by stars 93, 95, 96, 98, 101, 102, 106, and 109 Hercules.

The Kneeler's predominant associations with solar deities makes the Mercury attribution a head-scratcher. Very few stars have the Sun as an attributed planet. The Mercury affiliation could trace back to legends and lore that predate written myths, or with Egyptian lore that hasn't yet been deciphered, or was deciphered erroneously. The shape of the constellation has similarities to certain Egyptian hieroglyphs.

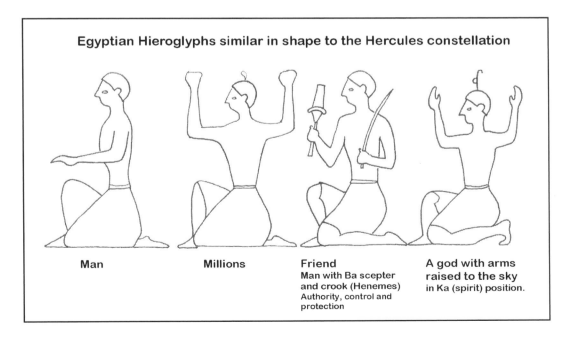

Egyptian Hieroglyphs similar in shape to the Hercules constellation

Man

Millions

Friend
Man with Ba scepter and crook (Henemes) Authority, control and protection

A god with arms raised to the sky in Ka (spirit) position.

The Kneeler has mythic links to Ixion, Prometheus, and Orpheus. Orpheus is a convincing association as Lyra, his harp, is quite close. Mercury's caduceus enables the god to travel back and forth between the underworld and Olympus. A key feature of the Orpheus legend is his journey to the underworld to save his beloved Eurydice. The journey to the under-world or afterlife is important for all of the stars in the *helice*. The Orphic cult was a wide-spread prominent mystery religion in the ancient world. Orphic doctrine was absorbed into the later Neo-Platonic Hermetic cult with the focal deity Hermes Trismegistus. The golden apples of the Hesperides confer immortality. They belonged to Hera-Juno, a goddess that placed several constellations in the sky. The Kneeler has strong religious and devotional meanings that are evident with the name of *Genuflexus,* as people genuflect in religious ritu-als. Ancient mystery religions—Orphic, Eleusinian, Hermetic Neo-Platonism—were pri-marily concerned with preparing the soul in life for its journey in the afterlife. Hermes is the psychopompos, the guide of transmigrating souls.

Hermes as shepherd
from small bronze
circa 520-500 BCE

The meanings of The Kneeler's stars offer clues, too. These include the word "devotion." The most ancient role of Hermes (Mercury) was as a patron deity of shepherds and flock herders. Other meanings include "dedication" and "seeker of knowledge," traits that imply watchfulness and ardent curiosity. One word given for Kornephoros is "prolific," cer-tainly a chief concern of shepherds. Mercury was more closely associated with fertility in ancient times than in modern astrology. Leo is not a fertile sign, and the Sun has minimal associations with fertility. Perhaps early star watchers saw the Kneeler as a herder of souls that were exiting or en-tering incarnations through the *helice*. This would be the obvious link to the most ancient aspects of Hermes-Mercury.

Egyptian lore is worth exploring, particularly because their myths are so much older. The Egyptians were very concerned with the *helice* and the stars in this area. The circumpolar zone was the special province of Isis-Renenutet, the hippo form of the goddess. Joanne Con-man posits that Set is the planet Mercury.[5] Images of Ra (the Sun) riding in the solar boat show Set at the front, guiding the ship and protecting the Sun from Apophis, a snake-like monster that wants to "eat the Sun," or destroy Time itself. The Sun was said to turn the cos-mos with his "strong arm" aided by the magic of Isis, a metaphysical rather than mechanical notion of the heavenly rota-tions. The legendary conflict between Set, Osiris, and Horus is quite different from the rela-tionship between Ra (Sun) and Set (Mercury). Egyptian myths changed a lot over 3,000 years! Set guards the borders and boundaries to keep foreigners from entering Egypt, protects the Sun from destruction, and guides the Sun's boat through the Duat, the Lake of Night.

A theory called "the Apex of the Sun's Way" proposes that the Sun, the pilot of our solar system, is moving toward the stars of Hercules. Allen credits this idea to Johann Tobias Mayer in the 1760s. Herschel proposed in 1806 that our Sun was heading toward Maasym (lambda Hercules). Contemporary astronomers have recalculated and estimate the Sun is moving toward the vicinity of Lyra or Cygnus. Although the Apex of the Sun's Way is credited to 18th and 19th century astronomers, the idea for it came from an ancient source. The Kneeling One (Set-Mercury) is guiding the Sun on its course, shepherding it along in the right direction, just as Set guides the Solar Boat in Egyptian iconography. This link, perhaps more than any other, points directly toward an Alexandrian-Egyptian source for the star-planet attributions.

The excavations at Nabta Playa (Egypt) and Gobekli Tepi (Turkey) suggest star tracking activities as early as 10,000 to 11,000 BCE. How old *are* the constellations? The Kneeling One's lengthy history and multiplicity of names suggest that it's incredibly old. The evidence for a detailed body of star lore handed down from the Paleolithic herding tribes of southwest Egypt to the Egyptian Nile culture is increasingly compelling and is supported by ongoing archeological discoveries.

References

[1] Allen, **Star-Names and their Meanings**, p 239. Allen quotes Aratos, *Phainomena*
[2] Robert Graves, **Greek Myths**, pp 451. Some Hercules legends are clearly variants of the Gilgamesh legend.
[3] Graves, pp 450
[4] Allen, pp 244-246
[4] Joanne Conman, **Ancient Egyptian Sky Lore**. Decan Wisdom Books, 2013, p 162-63.

Eridanus: River of Golden Tears

Eridanus is a meandering trail of stars rising from the bottom of the southern hemisphere to the ecliptic. Most are magnitude 3 or less. The path of the river extends across a full zodiacal quadrant from Pisces to Gemini. In ancient times the River terminated at the theta star Acamar at 40° south declination. After the Age of Exploration, astronomers added more stars so the river's source is now the star Achernar at -60°.

Eridanus has been conflated with Homer's Ocean Stream flowing around the earth, and with numerous Terran rivers that flow into the ocean from northwestern Europe. Ancient poets linked it to precious amber, a stream of golden tears shed by the Heliades at the death of their brother Phaëthon after his failed attempt to drive the chariot of Apollo. In that legend, Eridanus was placed in the sky to console Apollo for the loss of his son.

Eratosthenes and scholiasts on Germanicus and Hyginus equated it with the Nile, a river that flows from south to north, a somewhat unusual characteristic that mimics the direction of Eridanus. Egyptians along the north-flowing Nile were obsessed with the path through the stars leading to the afterlife. Names that follow this train of thought include Mulda and Melo, from the Greek Μέλας, or Black. The name of Egypt, Khem, has the same meaning, as it describes the color of the dark soil left after the river's inundation. Allen also mentions a Euphratean passage about a stellar stream called the River of Night from the Akkadian *Aria-dan*, the Strong River. It may also be the Euphratean *Erib-me-gali*. [1] Old illuminated star maps of this constellation feature a river deity with an urn and aquatic plants lying on the surface of the stream of stars.

Named stars in Eridanus include **Cursa** (beta, 15♊33), the northernmost river star three degrees northwest of Rigel and easily seen. Other river stars are **Zaurak** (gamma, 24♉09), **Azha** (eta, 9♉01), and **Acamar** (theta 1, 23♈33, the former terminal star), and **Beid** (omicron 1, 29♉42). **Angetenar** (tau, 2♉54) marks a bend in the river). A group of faint stars called **Beemim and Theemim** (upsilon 1, 2, 3, and 4, 0♊09/-30.31) are rarely used in for interpretive purposes.

The Argonauts sail down Eridanus in their quest for the Golden Fleece in Virgil's **Aeneid**. They travel to the underworld so Aeneas can obtain advice from the shade of his father. Virgil describes the journey: "*On they went dimly, beneath the lonely night amid the gloom,/ Through the empty halls of Dis and his unsubstantial realm,/Even as under the grudging light of an inconstant moon lies a path in the forest.*" Dis is an alternate name for Pluto, and the forest is a forest of stars. Aeneas's father Anchises relates fascinating information relating to soul transmigration and what happens to a soul after death.

One of the greatest conundrums of transmigrational cosmology is that the path to the afterlife is as likely to go *up* toward the Celestial North Pole as *down* to the Celestial South Pole. The most commonly-cited soul portals are the solstitial points at 0° Cancer and 0° Capricorn (although there are others mentioned in ancient literature on this topic). The stars of Eridanus aren't anywhere near those points! Inconsistencies are the norm in journeys to afterlife. What's consistent is the link to stars. The Underworld is not beneath the Earth's surface but in the sky, and the paths to the afterlife always involve traveling into the cosmos.

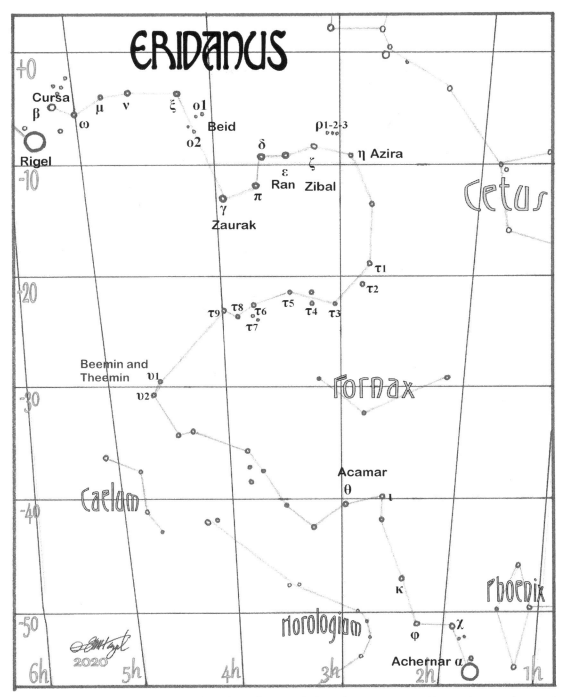

After the great battle between the Olympians and the Titans, Kronos (Saturn) was chopped into pieces and cast into the furthermost reaches of Tartarus, the realm of Hades. In the Platonic Cosmos, the lower end of the Earth's axis, the Southern Celestial Pole, rests upon the Cube of Saturn. The Saturn-attributed stars of Eridanus are a symbolic path of the dead to the underworld linked to Apollo's grief at the death of his son. The Sun god symbolizes life and Saturn symbolizes death.

The stars of Eridanus are associated with accidents, sorrows, and losses. They are linked to maritime professions, a common meaning for Saturn in the ancient world, and voyages of discovery that lead to skills and wisdom gained through experience. The legends suggest travel to other realms through out-of-body experiences and dreams, or through theoretical means like quantum string theory and alternate dimensions. There could be encounters with spirits and ghosts. The passage of time, history, and antiquities are other topics of interest to individuals with chart connections to the stars of Eridanus.

References
[1] Allen, **Star-Names and their Meanings**, p 217

Stars and Earthlings

Neptune and the River

It's no secret that I have the film tastes of a 13-year old boy. I've been fascinated with the Marvel Universe series since the first **Iron Man** film. The heroes and villains are bigger than life. There are huge fight scenes with stunning FX, fantastic chase scenes, lots of things get blown up and people even get pushed out of the air lock (outer space defenestration!). What's not to love? It was difficult to watch **Infinity Wars** and **Endgame**. I enjoy the DC Comics films, too. I never thought Ben Affleck would make a good Batman, but he may be the best one yet. And Jason Momoa as Aquaman, what a knuckle biter!

The M. Night Shymalan film **Unbreakable** was released in 2000. I'll watch anything with Bruce Willis. For a long time there were rumors about a sequel. Many years passed before **Split** with James McAvoy was released in January 2017, followed by **Glass** with Samuel L. Jackson in January 2019.

A strange notion occurred to me during that gob smacker of a Full Moon in Aries on October 13, 2019. Multiple hero-focused film series ended in 2019. Films and comics are what passes for mythology in our culture. They delineate right and wrong, good and evil. Heroes

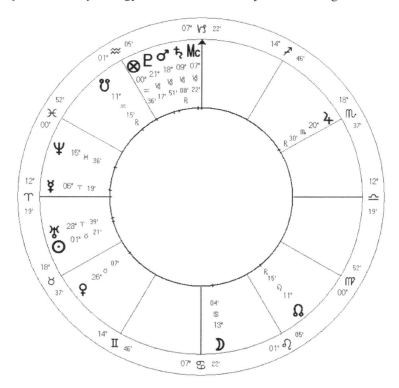

First Neptune-Achernar conjunction

April 21, 2018
5:27 am PDT
Los Angeles, CA
Tropical-Placidus
True Node

struggle to overcome bad guys who want to take over the world. Or the cosmos. But at the end of these film series, some of the heroes got wasted along with the villains in the process.

Neptune crossed over the longitudinal point of Achernar four times in two years: April 2018 (*see chart on previous page*), August 2018, February 2019, and finally in November 2019. Jupiter, ruler of Pisces and Achernar's attributed planet, squared Neptune-Achernar three times in 2019. Some kind of wisdom dangles like a carrot at the end of the stick. It's being shoved into our faces on the silver screen. That's what Jupiter-Neptune does!

The third **Star Wars** trilogy ended in a collision with studio execs. The Marvel Universe film series began with several "origin" films that explained how the members of the Avengers came into existence. The scattered threads of these stories coalesce in **Marvel's The Avengers** and **The Avengers: The Age of Ultron.** The mythic arc became tightly focused on the battle against Thanos, an alien being obsessed with gathering all six Infinity Stones. **The Black Panther** (2018) features an invisible nation hidden in Africa. Various Avengers travel into outer-space on the quest to overcome Thanos but are soundly and tragically defeated in **Infinity Wars**. **Endgame** features a time-travel adventure to collect the Infinity Stones before Thanos gets them and undo the damage he's done. The quest is successful but at least one Avenger dies in the quest.

The Shymalan films aren't as elaborate as the Marvel or DC films when it comes to flashy costumes and special effects. The stories underscore the point of discovering one's powers. Elijah Price (Samuel L. Jackson) prods David Dunn (Willis) into recognizing his superpowers and using them to protect people in **Unbreakable**. Dunn becomes The Overseer. He can sense criminal activities and can't be injured, although water is his Kryptonite. Once Dunn embraces his role as a protector, Elijah can fully embrace his villainous identity as Mr. Glass. In **Split**, Kevin Crumb (James McAvoy) struggles with a multiple-personality complex involving twenty-three personalities. A hidden persona called The Horde emerges under stress and at the end, the Overseer has to stop him. All three characters wind up in a facility for the criminally insane in **Glass** (2019), where Elijah has been incarcerated since the end of the first film. They discover that there's a league of people murdering superhumans, both heroes and villains. The Overseer overcomes The Horde, but all three characters die in the end.

These mythic-comic characters reach the end of their river and disappear, apropos of Neptune. Neptune's super-power is invisibility. Hail Wakanda! Neptune transits can make a person feel invisible. It's an illusion with smoke and mirrors, but that doesn't invalidate those feelings. Another star is close to the same longitudinal degree as Achernar: **Ankaa** (alpha Phoenix at 15 Pisces 45). The Phoenix is a constellation near the South Celestial Pole. One of the portals to the Underworld is through the South Celestial Pole. The Phoenix is a creature of dramatic rebirth. It explodes into flames to die and then is reborn.

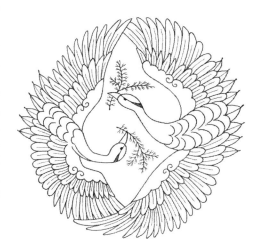

A phoenix is featured at the end of J. K. Rowling's **Fantastic Beasts: The Crimes of Grindewald** (2018). The final film of that trilogy is scheduled for release in 2021. It's also strangely synchronous that Neil Gaiman's masterwork **American Gods** became a TV series during this period. Old gods struggling to adapt to the 21st century are in conflict with powerful new gods.

I don't think it's an accident that all of these films and series are appearing or culminating and ending as this decade winds to a close. *As above, so below.* These fictional cinematic conflicts reflect contemporary human conflicts with good and evil, right and wrong. Power is a golden apple with a banana peel beneath it. Some people simply shouldn't be trusted in powerful positions because they're apt to misuse and abuse it. The Saturn-Pluto conjunction in Capricorn is bringing that truth home to roost.

The heroes and villains of these epic films fade and disappear, just as people strut onto the world stage, cause a lot of sound and fury, and eventually (in some cases hopefully) disappear, too. Maybe we learn from those experiences, maybe we don't. Art reflects life and life reflects art. The past few years have seemed like an especially perilous journey down the river of life. What is there to learn from that? What super-powers can regular people develop to overcome evil? Where is the line in the sand? I don't have all the answers, but simply offer awareness about the dramatic story lines that contemporary film-myths are depicting as Neptune reaches the source of the river. What clues are you picking up as you take your own journey down the river? Think about the 2010s and your personal story lines. Neptune's lengthy transit of Achernar might have made patterns more visible as the 2010s ended.

Orion and the Whirlpool

One of the sky's most potent stars is Rigel, the left foot of Orion. The constellation of Orion depicts an enormous man with one foot in the waters that gush from the mouth of Eridanus, a wandering river of stars that descends to Achernar, a star near the South Pole. Orion is accompanied by his faithful dogs, Sirius and Procyon (Canis Major and Minor) chasing Lepus, the hare.

Orion is a legendary hunter known for his excessive appetites. He importunes goddesses and nymphs, giving offense to the divine feminine. His name is derived from the Greek root "uri," the root of "urine." Given the ancient Greek sense of humor, one might suspect his name could be roughly translated as "the big pisser." Orion boasts that he plans to kill one of every animal. This angers the Moon Goddess Diana who sends the Scorpion to kill him. The Scorpion chases Orion through the sky: as Orion sets, Scorpio rises. As Scorpio rises, Orion sets.

Orion's body is defined by blue-white giant stars: right shoulder star **Bellatrix** (*gamma*, 20Ⅱ57/+6.21, ♂♀); his feet/knee stars **Rigel** (*beta*, 17Ⅱ07/-8.11, ♃♂) and **Saiph** (*kappa*, 26Ⅱ34/-9.40, ♃♂). The red-orange giant **Betelgeuse** (*alpha*, 29Ⅱ02/+7.24, ♂♀) is his left shoulder. Betelgeuse may be on the verge of going super-nova within the next several decades. Astronomers have noticed its magnitude is changing at a faster pace. Orion's famous Belt stars are **Alnilam** (*epsilon*, 23Ⅱ45/-1.11, ♃♄), **Alnitak** (*zeta*, 24Ⅱ58/-1.56, ♃♄), and

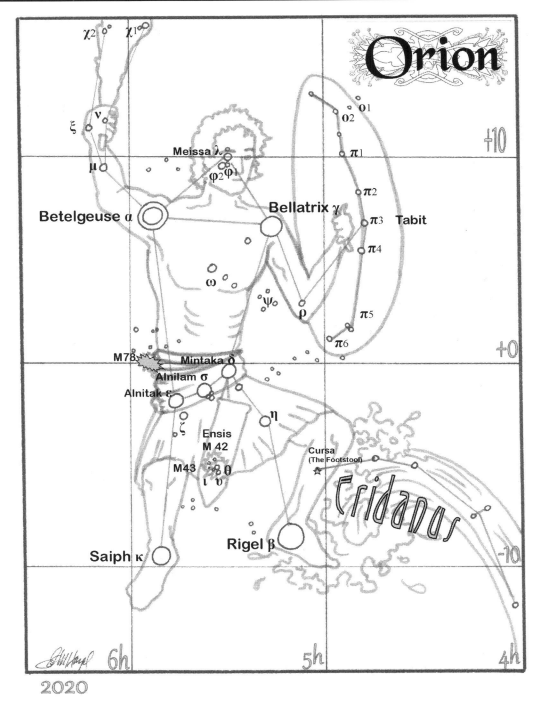

Mintaka (*delta*, 22Ⅱ38/+0.22, ♃♄). The belt marks the ecliptic. Orion's head is **Meissa** (*lambda*, 23Ⅱ56/+9.56, ♃♄), a faint 3.7 magnitude star cluster. His bright body stars are surmounted by a dim head! Orion is bold and strong but stupid and insensitive. He is driven by bodily appetites and impetuous urges.

Orion has the opportunity to evolve. He and his faithful dogs are poised for a long south-ward journey. The stars of Eridanus are generally unfortunate, so he'll have difficult tests and lessons along the way. But if he reaches Achernar, the source of the river, he has the potential to acquire wisdom. Orion is a crucial archetype of humanity. He represents the potential to learn, grow, and develop a global conscience. He could transform into a responsible steward that values and cares for Mother Earth rather than thoughtlessly destroying her land and creatures.

Rigel is the first step on the journey to wisdom. It's close to **Cursa** (*beta*, 15Ⅱ33/-5.02, ♄), the star at mouth of the river. The heliocentric node of Venus is at 16 Gemini, making her retrogrades in this area especially significant. Rigel, Cursa, and Venus's Node are a massive confluence of thought and energy called **The Whirlpool**. People with natal planets in the middle degrees of Gemini thrive in the swirling waters of their ambient culture. They contribute or have access to the zeitgeist or pulse of the times. Whirlpool natives have enormous potential to benefit from the gushing flow of trends and developments in their contemporary culture.

Members of the Great Generation born in the early 1900s have either natal Neptune or Pluto in close proximity to the Whirlpool. This generation fought in WWI, then survived the Depression and WWII. Their lives swirled through major cultural upheavals but they experienced the spread of new technologies that changed how people traveled, communicated and thought about their world. Apropos of these two outer planets, members of the Great Generation were in the vanguard of movements to destroy social barriers to women and minorities. Others led rebellions on a microscopic level by developing medicines that destroyed life-threatening bacteria and viruses.

Whirlpool contacts often appears in the charts of writers, poets, or artists associated with specific movements. Federico Garcia Lorca, a prominent member of the Spanish Generation of '27 movement, has Sun and Pluto conjunct Rigel, his heliacal rising star. Poet T. S. Eliot's Moon, Erza Pound's Chiron, and Anne Frank's Mercury are conjunct Rigel. A number of rock 'n roll pioneers born in 1946 have Uranus in close contact with Rigel, and of course, rock 'n roll was a major music and cultural movement that spread across the world from the US and Britain in the early 1960s. Cher and Syd Barrett (founding member of Pink Floyd) share this placement. Donald Trump has his Sun-Uranus-North Node near the Whirlpool. It manifests through his name-branding, use of social media, slogans and symbols (a red hat), reality TV, and his ability to manipulate the masses in chaotic Uranian ways. Style subordinates truth and facts, but that's how the turbulent Whirlpool operates.

That's the quintessential Whirlpool – more knowledge, more communication, more ways to spread ideas, concepts, and data! People born after 1980 with Whirlpool contacts tend to have access to huge databases or other information-gathering/storing digital technologies. The link between the Whirlpool and cellular-wireless technologies is an important one. The North Node transited through Gemini in 2002. An annular solar eclipse on June 10, 2002 at 19 Gemini had the Sun and Moon conjunct Saturn and Rigel, all in opposition to Pluto Rx at 16 Sagittarius. Wireless technologies swept the globe during the first decade of the 21st century, giving the masses portable calling and internet access. Problems were inevitable with Pluto's link to the dawn of the cellular era. Concerns about privacy, deaths from texting and driving, and serious health risks from 5G have all surfaced since that time.

When contacts to the Whirlpool appear in natal and mundane charts, it presages a connection to the swirling pulse of the times, involvement in hot cultural trends, or the expression of contemporary ideas through the arts, fashion, and architecture. In charts after the 1980s, contacts emphasize access to mass connectivity and/or enormous databases.

The Brute and the Dreamer

The stories of the constellations reflect universal human experiences and concerns. Some contiguous constellational groups embody a full mythic cast like the autumn cluster of King Cepheus, Queen Cassiopeia, the maiden Andromeda, Perseus, and Cetus the sea monster. Star stories also take place across the zodiacal axis. The massive constellation of Orion, whose stars occupy Gemini (16 – 28 degrees) shares mythic ties with two constellations in tropical Sagittarius – Scorpio and Hercules.

Orion was a lust-driven jerk. The image of a man in the sky is extremely ancient, perhaps even 30,000 years old. His body is formed of brilliant blue-white baby giant stars except for the alpha star Betelgeuse, an old red-orange giant star. The Greek name Orion comes from the root word "uri," and means "he who walks on water." To people on the Mediterranean coastal regions, Orion's setting phase made him appear to sink into the sea.

Orion's club and animal skin show his hunting prowess. In myth he threatened to kill one of every animal on earth. The Moon Goddess Artemis, protector of forest creatures, wasn't amused and sent the Scorpio to kill Orion. These two constellations chase each other through the skies.

The star marking his left foot is **Rigel**, a very bright 0.3 magnitude binary star. Rigel is Orion's "foot in the river" of Eridanus. The waters of Eridanus flow in a meandering line from the southern mouth of the river, **Achernar** at -60 declination, to **Cursa** (aka Orion's footstool) at the river's delta. On clear nights, Cursa is visible just a bit to the right of Rigel. The dog Canis Major (with the brightest star **Sirius**) accompanies Orion on his journey from ignorance to wisdom. He is like the Fool card in the tarot, foolish and prone to disaster, but also open to possibility and gaining knowledge along his journey. Orion symbolizes the raw potential of the individual and of humanity at the start of the quest along the river of life. The goal is to attain wisdom, knowledge, perfection or enlightenment by reaching the bright star Achernar at the end of the river.

The constellation Hercules, or The Kneeler, is almost directly above Scorpio on the opposite side of the sky. The head of The Kneeler is **Ras Algethi** (alpha Hercules), a variable star at 16 Sagittarius that opposes Rigel at 17 Gemini. Where Orion is raw potential, Hercules represents great refinement, devotion to a goal, and striving for immortality through achievements. Hercules, Orpheus and Gilgamesh all traveled to the underworld and returned. Small nearby constellations include the Lyre (Lyra) whose music is said to soothe him, and the Northern Crown, Corona Borealis, a symbol of awards and achievements.

Hercules, like Orion, is another enormous constellation. But the stars of Hercules are rather dim, none above magnitude 3. In contrast to Orion, Hercules's brightest star is Ras Algethi, the star that marks his head. This is the brainiac star!

The zodiacal opposition between Rigel (the left foot) and Ras Algethi (the head of the dreamer) implies that while one may travel great distances and have amazing experiences, the mind can travel even further and even reach new worlds and different dimensions. One can be caught up in the whirlpool of humanity in the river, or be "in the world but not of it," floating above the masses and dedicated to pondering the mysteries of life, death, and immortality.

The opposition between Orion and Hercules illustrations a potential alchemical transformation: a soul burdened with karmic debts versus a soul cleansed by moderation, good deeds, and striving for enlightment and wisdom. One figure is carnivorous (Orion holds a dead animal) while the other is vegetarian (Kneeler holds the branch of a fruit tree). The Heracles stars pi and nu are within circle of North Stars. Nearby Vega (*a Lyra*) was the Pole Star linked to the "Golden Age" (circa 7500 BCE). Perhaps that's why this constellation is so ancient and revered.

When Jupiter transits Ras Algethi, people of refined, educated, and well-developed character will have important things to disclose, while others may absorb new truths or arrive at moments of self-discovery. The quest for better education, for spiritual wisdom, and for higher truths could become imperatives for several months.

Venus with Rigel or Ras Algethi contacts emphasizes dedication to the arts, the creation of beauty, and children of the mind. The role of women in steering humanity toward understanding the import of current events and taking greater care of the Earth and her creatures may be evident. These combinations underscore the imperative to understand humanity as a family, not as a group of hostile races or nations battling for power.

**Lunar Eclipse on the
Rigel-Ras Algethi axis**

June 5, 2020
3:12 pm EDT
Washington, DC
Tropical-Placidus
True Node

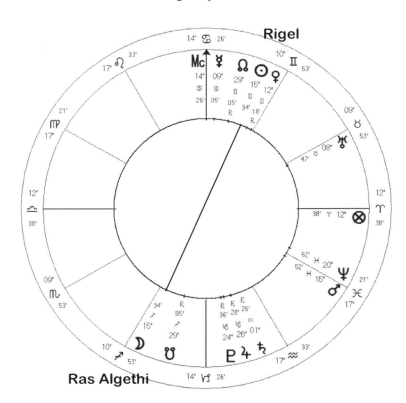

A full moon or eclipse along the Rigel/Ras Algethi axis could take place with a Gemini Sun and Sagittarius Moon, or a Sagittarius Sun and Gemini Moon near the 16 Gemini-Sag star axis. The Sun and Moon can be given a bit of extra orb for star conjunctions. A full moon on this stellar axis occurred on December 12, 2019 followed by a lunar eclipse on June 5, 2020. The whirlpool of humanity swirls with a high-tide of spectacularly momentous events that are flung into the spotlight of public awareness. The difference between the crude and brutish and the evolved and wise may seem greater than ever. Individuals may feel the gap between their public and social selves and the needs of the evolving inner self.

✸ Celestial Portals ✸

The Cancer Gate

The Cancer Gate is a name for the last five degrees of Gemini that precede the Summer Solstice point at 0° Cancer. Cosmic gates imply luminal thresholds where things change and transform. Various commentators of the ancient world posited that the Cancer Gate was a portal for souls returning to incarnate into a physical body. Incarnation is a commitment to a change of status and release from whatever conditions existed in the spiritual realm, whether a term of punishment or of rest. Plato's *Story of Er* in **The Republic**, Book 10, outlines what returning souls may choose and aspects of life determined by lots.

The planets with dominion over the Cancer Gate include **Mercury**, the sign ruler, **Saturn**, ruler of the bound/term, and the **Sun**, the Chaldean face (decan) ruler. The Sun is a significator of life, the spirit or *elan vital*. Saturn is the outermost visible planet, the gate-keeper, and significator of physical form. It's also the Lord of Karma and death, the burdens and gifts that become ingrained upon a soul through multiple lifetimes. Negative karma must be expunged through evolution and enlightenment. An evolved soul may pass through Saturn's boundaries to reunite with the Divine. Mercury the Psychopompos guides souls through the

portals of incarnation. These three planets are permanent zodiacal arbiters and functionaries of the Cancer Gate.

The slow apparent movement of precession causes the stars at the Gates to shift over time. The stars and celestial points that currently occupy the Cancer Gate include:

Al Hecka (25♊04/+21, *zeta Taurus*, Mag 3, ♂ or ☿ ♄)
Wezn (26♊42, *beta Columba*, Mag 3.12, ♄ ☿)
Saiph (26♊34/-9.4, *kappa Orion*, Mag 2.2 triple star, ♃ ♄)
The **Galactic Anti-Center** (27♊05/ +29) in close proximity to **Taurus T-4**, a stellar T-association or star nursery

within a dark nebula
Polaris (28♊51/+89, *alpha Ursa Minor*, Mag 2.1, ♄♀),
Betelgeuse (29♊02/+7, *alpha Orion*, variable magnitude,
♂♀).

<table>
<tr><td colspan="3" align="center">**THE CANCER GATE**</td></tr>
<tr><td colspan="3" align="center">25° ♊ - 0°♋</td></tr>
<tr><td colspan="3" align="center">Sign Ruler ☿</td></tr>
<tr><td colspan="3" align="center">Bound ♄</td></tr>
<tr><td colspan="3" align="center">Face ☉</td></tr>
</table>

These are not user-friendly occupants! If one accepts the notion of the Gates as soul portals, the slowly shifting stars suggest that cosmic road conditions aren't static but change through the aeons, thus presenting wayfaring souls with different traveling conditions. If the Gates are simply considered as specific zones of the zodiac that merit extra attention in birth charts, the celestial conditions planets traverse upon approach to the Solstice points are laden with potential dangers. It's notable that a collection of famous prison escape charts revealed the propensity for planets to occupy sign boundaries, but most particularly the Cancer Gate! [1] It's a place where people and situations have the potential to change on an earthly and spiritual levels.

Al Hecka is the tip of the southern horn of Taurus. Its meanings include intellectual abilities and strategic thinking, but a tendency to have bad habits and scoundrels for friends. It also augurs the potential for ambushes and accidents. It's within the ecliptic so planet-star occultations are possible. This is a gory star (pun intended).

Wezn is the sweet note in a strident cacophony of stellar energies. Columba is the dove released from the ship Argo to find land. The stars of the Dove signify generosity and luck as well as adventures into unknown, uncharted, and unexplored places.

Saiph is not safe! It's Orion's right foot or knee and the name comes from *Saif al Jabbar*, the sword of the giant. It's a triple star that brings trampling and violence. Other people's emotions and needs may be ignored through an inconsiderate and unsympathetic temperament.

The Galactic Anti-Center and **Taurus T-4** occupy a zone filled with interstellar dust and variable stars. Variable magnitudes signify sporadic situations and conditions. The dark nebula is a strong infrared emitter. Infrared influences the subconscious mind where dreams and memories reside, and where primal hunches and gut instincts are generated. This pulsating cluster sends intermittent signals to the primal mind.

Polaris currently holds the job of being the North Star or Lode Star. In India it's *Grahadhara*, the pivot of the planets. The Arabic *Al Kath al Shamaliyy* means the North Axle or spindle. Polaris is a navigational star, so its meaning includes the ability to find the right direction. The star's attributed planets Saturn and Venus imply that the way is hard and many lessons are learned along the way before arriving at a place of comfort and pleasure. Polaris natives are often excellent guides who can lead others toward their destinies but struggle to navigate their own life-paths. As a star of Ursa Minor, the meanings include violence, difficulties, losses, and evil legacies. This is an unfortunate North star, and it will hold sway for another 2,000 years until Altai in Cepheus become the pole star in turn.

The troublesome meanings of Polaris may be offset by **Betelgeuse**. The stars are only eleven minutes apart in longitude, but Betelgeuse is near the ecliptic at +7, while Polaris is soars above the planetary highway at +89. There are various opinions on the relative influence of stars outside of the ecliptic. If a planet occupies 27-28-29° Gemini (taking precession into account over the past 70-80 years), check its declination. A planet-star occultation, both conjunct and parallel, is a remarkably potent connection that allows a planet to act as a conduit for a great range of a star's influence.

Betelgeuse is a red-orange giant star whose name derives from the Arabic *Ibt al Jauzah*, the armpit of the Giant or Central One (Orion). This favorable star signifies good fortune and honors, military prowess, ingenuity, wealth, noble qualities, blessings and success. It's variable and an intense infrared source, so a planet in close proximity may channel the influences of Betelgeuse and Polaris in sporadic intervals. Betelgeuse's attributions to Mars-Venus suggest struggling or fighting to achieve one's Venusian desires, whatever they may be. Great consideration should be given to the particular natal planet that contact Polaris and Betelgeuse. The three planets that hold dominion over this zone—Mercury, Saturn and the Sun—have the potential to gain command over the stellar energies. Natal Mars implies more struggles and battles in life. Natal Venus highlights the specific desires and goals that motivate efforts. Venus makes promises she doesn't always deliver, so her presence in these degrees needs support from positive aspects to gain results.

[1] Hazel, Elizabeth. "The Astrological Art of Escape". *ISAR International Astrologer*. Vol 49. Issue 1. April. 2020. Page 41.

The Capricorn Gate

Macrobius wrote in his **Commentary on the Dream of Scipio** that the Summer Solstice was the "Gate of Men" where souls return to earth to be born into the world. The Winter Solstice point was the "Gate of the Gods" where the souls of the dead "return to rightful abode of immortality to be reckoned among the Gods." In this commentary, the natural home of souls is in the Milky Way. In other traditions the Milky Way is the Path of the Dead, a road leading to the afterlife.

Different cultures had soul portals in different zodiacal locations. The notion of a "stairway (ladder or rope) to heaven" was passed from the Mesopotamians and Egyptians to the Greeks. Egyptian soul travel was entwined with exceptional knowledge about fixed stars. Their word for star (*seba*) shares the root word for soul (*ba*). Separate pathways were used by shades of the dead to return for ancestral festivals in late May and October. The Chinese and Romans honored the dead during these months, too. Cinco de Mayo and Samhain/Halloween occur with the Sun midway between the Equinoxes and Solstices. These "hinge" dates are portals for the visiting spirits.

THE CAPRICORN GATE
25° ♐ - 0° ♑
Sign Ruler ♃
Bound ♂
Face ♄

The Capricorn Gate occupies the last five degrees of Sagittarius. This area is filled with strange and difficult celestial occupants: **Lesath** (*mu Scorpio*, 24♐18), **Shaula** (*lambda Scorpio*, "the sting" 24♐52); **Grumium** (*xi Draco*, 25♐ 01), **Kelb Alrai** (*beta Ophiuchus*, shoulder, 25♐35); **Sargas** (*tau Scorpio*, 25♐53); **Aculeus** (*M6 Scorpio*, 26♐01); **Etamin** (*gamma Draco*, the eye, 28♐ 15); and **Acumen** (*M7 Scorpio*, 29♐01).

The Scorpion's stinger stars are linked to attacks, poisons, and undoings. Sinistra is connected to sorcery and poisons. The Centaur's bow and arrow stars are energetic, focused, and powerful. The nebulae Aculeus, Acumen, and the triple T-associations of Spiculum are bad for eyesight, particularly with the Sun or Moon (which rule the eyes). Sometimes the inner eye is more powerful. J. R. R. Tolkien's natal Mercury Rx is precisely conjunct Spiculum, and he imagined entire worlds and aeons of its history. The eye of the Dragon hovers far above in the circumpolar region, cherishing solitude and pondering occult mysteries.

The **Galactic Center** is located at 27✗07 between the curling line of stars and nebulae that form the Scorpion's stinger and the Centaur's arrow, which points straight at the GC. It occupies a dark zone of the Milky Way called Bode's Window. Cosmic dust obscures this intense light source from the naked eye. There's a star nursery that generates radio waves and infrared with a massive nearby black hole.

The GC was known in ancient times. The Capricorn Gate has fierce guardians while the Cancer Gate's guardians, Orion and Auriga, pose challenges for soul evolution. Centaurs quite appropriately serve this role since they descend from Ixion, a fallen Sun god linked to the solar wheel. The Egyptian Serqet or Selket and the Euphratean Ishara-tam-tim are portal guardian deities depicted with a woman's head and many-breasted torso on top of a scorpion body. She is simultaneously venomous and nurturing. The sidereal nakshatra Mula (the Root), the lunar mansion of destruction and cosmic recycling, currently overlaps the tropical Capricorn Gate. It is ruled by Nirritti, the Calamity Jane of the Hindu pantheon.

These mythic guardians give a clue to what emanates from this cosmic portal. Hybrid creatures imply human-animal duality. Venom and destruction infer that Death is an absolute of the human condition. The multi-breasted Serqet implies that total destruction is followed by regeneration. The cosmos is a place of renewal where transformation is a constant.

The lords of the Capricorn Gate are the three visible planets outside of Earth's orbit: **Jupiter**, ruler of Sagittarius; term/bound ruler **Mars**; and face ruler **Saturn**. For people with planets at the Capricorn Gate, consider the placement and relationships of Jupiter, Saturn and Mars to determine how the Gate's energy may be used or channeled.

Natal Gate planets offer benefits through exploration, discovery, and invention. There are also terrible risks. Pink Floyd co-founder Syd Barrett's Mercury and South Node are in the Gate zone (born January 6, 1946, Cambridge, UK). He wrote lyrics for their first album, *Piper at the Gates of Dawn*. Syd was engrossed with fairy tales, legends, Tolkien's novels, and mystical-spiritual explorations. One weekend he ingested too much LSD and began to exhibit signs of schizophrenia. Within a year he was no longer able to work with the band or function in society. The song "Shine On You Crazy Diamond" is a tribute to Syd. His pattern of hyper-creativity followed by tragedy and loss reflects the dark potential of the Capricorn Gate.

Individuals with natal Sun at the Gate (late degrees of Sag) include John Milton, Brad Pitt, and Frank Zappa. In one way or another these men explore the darker side of human nature and philosophical ideas.

Mercury seems especially sensitive to the Capricorn Gate, underscoring this planet's role as a psychopompous or guide to migrating souls. J. R. R. Tolkien, Spanish dictator Francisco Franco and author C. S. Lewis all have Mercury Rx here. Examining the Gate's planetary lords delineates why Lewis was an author and mathematician and Franco a brutal dictator: Franco's Mercury is unaspected, his Jupiter opposes Saturn, and Mars squares his Sun. Lewis has Sun trine Mars with Jupiter in Scorpio and Saturn in Sagittarius approaching the Gate. His Narnia series begins with **The Lion, the Witch and the Wardrobe** (1950). The wardrobe is a portal or gate to another world.

Research on charts with Capricorn Gate placements suggests that individuals with planets in late Sag *and* the very early Capricorn degrees seem to be insulated from the worst effects of the Gate. Steven Spielberg's Sun at 26° Sag is balanced by Mars at 1° Capricorn. Perhaps the innate conservatism of Capricorn adds a greater propensity for more cautious risk assessment.

References
Richard Allen, **Star-Names and their Meanings** (1899)
Diana Rosenberg, **Secrets of the Ancient Skies** (2015)

The Great Bears

The constellations in the *helice* (a Greek term for the zone surrounding the north celestial pole) have been the focus of elaborate story-telling for aeons. The myths surrounding the Bears are multi-cultural, extensive, and inconsistent. Richard Allen's book **Star Names** devotes 28 pages to Ursa Major and its stars.

The best-known tale is that of Kallisto, one of Zeus's lovers, who transforms into a bear to escape the wrath of Hera. While in that form, her son Arcos attempts to shoot her. Out of pity, Jove took the mother and son and placed them in the sky as a pair of bears guarding the North Celestial Pole. A regional Greek alternative myth suggests that the bears were elevated because Arkas was the progenitor of the Arcadian or bear race. The Greater Bear may be a wandering mother seeking her lost children, that is, stars that are no longer visible. [1]

A variant story gives the two bears as the nymphs Helice and Melissa, nurses of the infant Zeus. Helice is the name of the city of Kallisto's birthplace in Arcadia. Helice is the Greek root of helix, a spiral; while Melissa is a bee-goddess. It's charming to imagine the stars as bees spiraling around the Earth's axis. It alludes to a second mother-child connection to the constellation. Hyginus and Germanicus used the masculine form Ursus and Arctus, so the figures aren't always or exclusively feminine in nature.

A further and perhaps more sensible legend calls Ursa's stars "young and beautiful maidens highly skilled in spinning and weaving." The motion of the constellation creates "rays of light to a weaver's web." The Celestial Pole is sometimes known as The Spindle. The North Celestial Pole is a mythic hotbed of multi-cultural weaving and spinning goddesses, like the Greek Moirae, the three Fates who spin, weave, and snip the threads of human life.

The Wheel of Fortune from **Tarot Pink**
(2015)
Cerridwen means *crooked* or *turning path*.

Her hair is the Milky Way. She holds the spindle, a symbol of the cosmic axis. The North Star is at the top of the axis.

Her Milky Way hair leads to her cauldron, a symbol of rebirth and soul migration. The dove is a soul rising. It grasps a thread of destiny in its beak. The thread is one of many spun on the rotating Wheel of Destiny and Fortune.

Weaving goddesses are always linked to the threads of fate and destiny in human lives and occupy the North Celestial Pole in most mythologies.

This image merges Neo-Platonic-Hermetic cosmic structure with Celtic goddess lore. You don't have to be crazy to work here, but it helps.

The Sanskrit name *Riksha* signifies "bear" and "a star", "bright," or "to shine" (in both genders), which led to the later title of Ursa's stars: the *Rishi* or the Seven Sages. The same name appears as *Seitsen tahtinen* in the Finnish **Kalevala**. [2]

Ancient writers sometimes conflate the bear and wagon, suggesting they were uncertain about which shape the constellation should be associated with. Aratos called it the "Wain-like Bear," alluding to the title Ἅμαξα (Amaxa), from ἄξων (axon) or axle, i.e., the axis of the heavens. Hesychios used the word Ἄγαννα (Aganna) from an archaic word ἄγειν (agein - "to carry"). This is similar to the Akkadian title for the constellation, *Aganna* or *Akkana*, the Lord of Heaven. The Roman moniker *Plaustrum* refers to a two-wheeled ox cart. The three stars protruding from the rectangle are the horses or oxen drawing the wagon. [3]

Ursa Major and Minor are illustrated as bears with peculiarly long tails. The legends attempting to explain the long tails are ridiculous and don't make sense. The need to have large, fierce, protective beasts guarding the Pole does make sense. The North Celestial Pole is a portal for souls and visiting gods. Yet the stars of Ursa Major are attributed to Mars. The Great Bear is usually female, yet is associated with planet that's considered masculine by modern astrologers.

Mars has a powerful protective function in mythology and astrology. This choleric planet's temperament is hot and dry, but it's a triplicity lord of the earth and water signs. More importantly, Mars belongs to the Moon's nocturnal sect along with Venus. These ancient associations give Mars a decidedly more feminine quality.

Mars is associated with heat-related professions like metallurgy, baking, and glass-making. It's consistently credited with military prowess and aggressive tendencies. It's bright red and easily identifiable in the sky. Two of these characteristics are most closely associated with Ursa Major: the protective function, and a violent, fierce, and vengeful nature. The action-oriented qualities of Mars are more consistent with the Northern European and Arabic view of the constellation as a chariot, wagon, or funeral bier. The Norse called it Thor or Odin's Wagon. The Arabs envisioned a funeral bier bearing the body of Al Na'ash, who was murdered by Al Jadi (the current pole star Polaris in Ursa Minor). The rectangular bier is led by his three daughters who seek revenge upon his

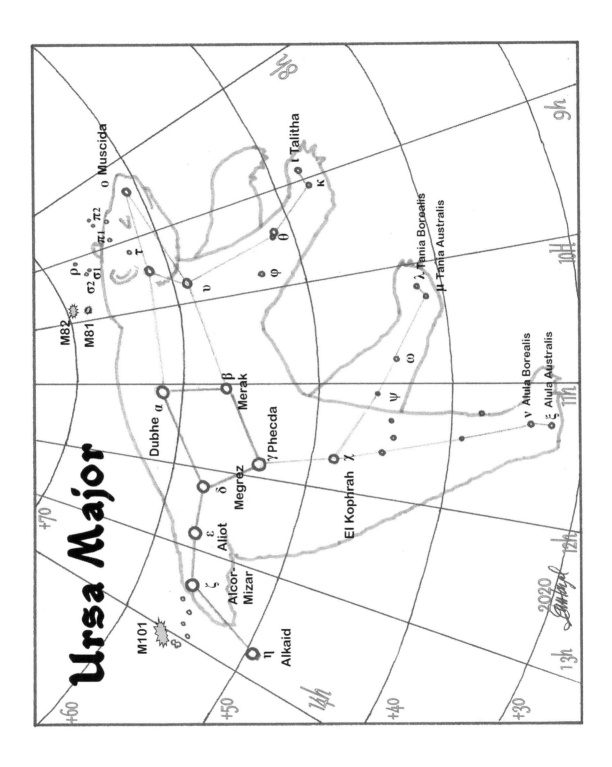

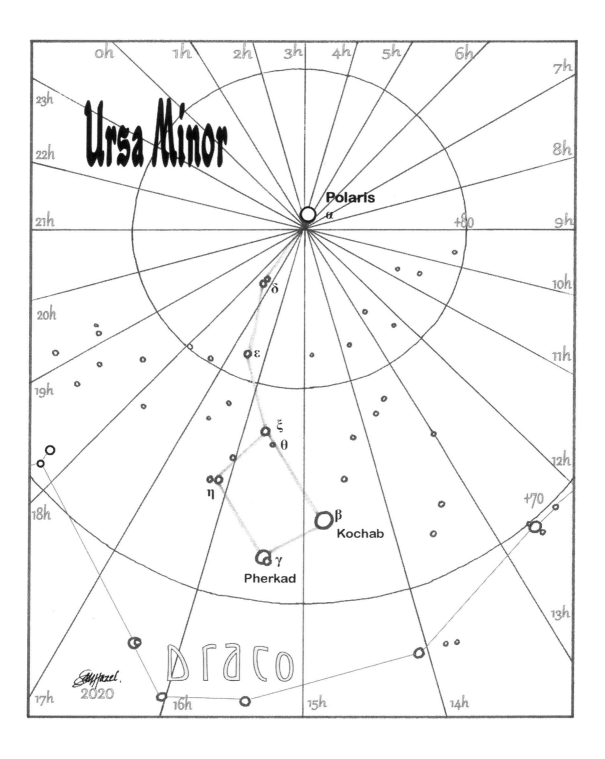

killer. The slow and stately procession of the constellation is why Ursa Major and Minor's star meanings include inactivity and laziness. [4]

The myths of Mars (or the Greek Ares) include challenges, wars, and duels. It didn't take much to arouse the fury of this god. Greeks myths depict him as a hot-head with little control over his lusts and emotions. This trait parallels another Ursa star meaning, which is uncontrollable forces of nature – storms, earthquakes, mudslides, sinkholes, high winds, tornadoes and hurricanes, etc. The Egyptian moniker for the star group is "The Dogs of Apophis (Typhon)." Typhon was known as the "father of fierce winds." Black dogs are sacred to Mars.

The gods can't control Mars's temper any more than humans can control weather patterns or other natural forces. Natural laws like gravity, the speed of sound and light, the spinning of Earth and the cosmos around our planet are other forces outside of human control. Ancient gods are—first and foremost—personifications of natural forces, and Mars was the most violent of all. Ancient peoples were more greatly victimized by natural disasters. The contemporary ability to predict storms and earthquakes is very recent, and even so, not always effective in preventing damage and death.

Another property of Mars is its association with fevers and diseases that are hot and dry. Records of comets traveling through Ursa Major coincide with highly contagious plagues and epidemics. Astrologer Rod Smith's survey of comet appearances through history appears to verify the link to plagues. Pliny outlined the factors that determined the portent of comets and terrible events, writing that "the direction in which a comet begins to move, the star from which it draws its strength, the things it resembles and the places in which it shines, are all important factors." [5] Comets passing through the two Bear constellations are linked to great winds, fierce heat, and Mars-related diseases that provoke the high fevers and skin eruptions. These symptoms mirror the symptoms of historic plagues, smallpox, and measles.

The stars of the Pleiades are linked to the stars of Ursa Major in Vedic lore. The six visible stars of the Pleiades are Krittika, the foster mothers of Murugan or Subramanya, a young Mars-like deity who became the general of the celestial army of the devas. One of Murugan's alternate names is Kartikeya, a reference to the Pleiades. Murugan grew six heads so he could look at his six foster mothers. Each head had a special virtue: wisdom, detachment, strength, fame, wealth, and divine powers. The Krittika are the wives of the Rishi (sages) stars of Ursa Major. There are plenty of ties between Mars and these sky figures in Hindu tradition. The Pleiades have a Mars-Moon association, too. The star Megrez (*delta Ursa Major* 1♍21) is the wise Rishi Atri who rules the other stars of the bear.

Weavers and spinners at the Celestial North Pole provide another association with Mars. The Weavers of Fate include Klotho, who spins the threads and Lakhesis, the apportioner of Lots who measures the threads and weaves them together. The threads are cut by Atropos, she who cannot be turned. Mars rules cutting instruments like scissors, knives, swords, and scalpels. The North Celestial Pole's association with the paths of the dead allude to the cutting of the thread of life.

Mars is a more convincing association for Ursa Major when it's characterized as a chariot or wagon. Mars signifies energy and speed. In contemporary astrology, combustion engine are attributed to Mars. The Major Arcana card VII. The Chariot is assigned to Mars in the Hermetic/Wirth attribution system of the late 19th century. The esoteric meaning of the card is an unstoppable force that propels events forward. The Greek view of the revolving cosmos was mechanistic. Ursa's Mars-attributed stars are the engine that powers the cosmic revolutions.

The star-planet color theory utterly fails here. **Dubhe** (alpha, 15♌29) is a yellow star. **Merak** (beta, 19♌43) is greenish white, **Phecda** (gamma, 0♍45) is topaz yellow, **Megrez** (delta, 1♍21) is pale yellow, **Mizar** (zeta 1, 15♍59) is a white-emerald binary, **Alcaid** (eta, 27♍13) is brilliant white.

Ursa Major and Minor are dry constellations more closely associated with strong winds than with rain storms. For viewers at 41° north latitude, these stars never sink beneath the horizon. Ursa Major and Minor are always visible in northern latitudes. The Big Dipper (Ursa Major) appears to shift from season to season as it rotates around the pole. In equatorial coastal regions, most stars appear to sink into the ocean, but the stars of the Bears never do. Mars, a hot and dry planet, is properly associated with a dry constellation.

References
[1] Allen, **Star-Names and their Meanings**, p 422
[2] ibid, p 424
[3] ibid, p 427
[4] ibid, p 433
[5] Pliny the Elder, **Natural History, A Selection**. Translation by John Healy. Penguin Books, 1991, pp 20-21 "Comets as portents."

Zodiacal Constellations

The Stars of Capricorn

The figure of Capricorn is a goat that's curled up in front with a fish's tail instead of a hind end. Ptolemy said that composite creatures are the "domain of Neptune." Extremely ancient legends speak of a time when composite creatures were common and roamed the earth. Perhaps these allude to humanity's earliest memories the evolutionary process. Or it could refer to an early awareness of aquatic mammals like dolphins and whales who reside in the realm of Neptune, lord of the oceans. All mythologies include complex entanglements between water deities, humans, and animals. Capricorn represents the evolutionary transition from water to land, and from primal instincts to conscious thought.

The Capricorn constellation is a dimpled triangle. The head and forelegs of the animal are nestled up for a winter-time rest. The aquatic tail points upward. Capricorn's stars are magnitude 3 or less, as reticent as natives of the sign can sometimes be. The current positions of the stars range from 4 to 24 Aquarius, and occupy declinations from -12 to -27.

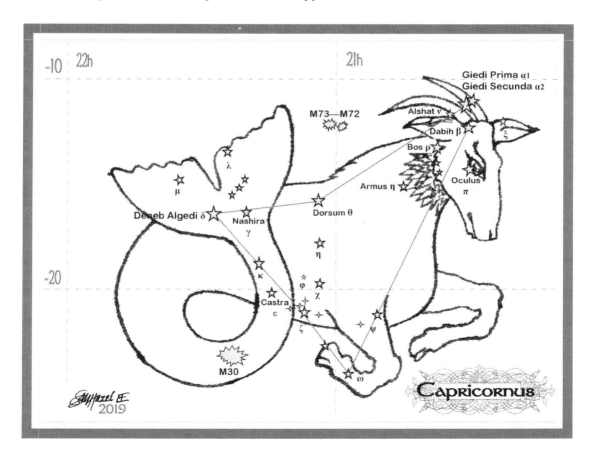

Manilius expressed the mixed nature of the Goat-Fish as fertile and sterile, and the position of the body as an image of dormant Nature resting while the earth is frozen. Capricorn was linked to the Goddess Vesta, the patroness of hearth fires. Natives of Capricorn may have interests and skills that depend on fire. This includes digging for metals and minerals, metallurgy and smithing, and working with furnaces and ovens. These are Mars-related professions and Mars exalts in Capricorn. Heat sources can be used to cook, melt, forge, purify, dry, desiccate, and preserve. Other traits include a focus on cold weather clothing, "men who shift their property, and minds swimming in a sea of change." (Manilius)

Hestia/Vesta was a quiet, unassuming goddess. She was offered two suitors, Apollo and Poseidon, but chose to remain unmarried so she could teach sacred rituals to humanity. The Vestal fires ensured the protection of a city as long as devotees kept the fires burning. Temples of Vesta were used for the storage of wills, and her priestesses witnessed the signing of these wills and attested to their veracity. Vestal priestesses had exceptionally high status and privileges within society. These privileges hinged on their reputation, which was eventually linked to sustaining virginity. The Vestal College was an exclusive group with a rigorous training period, initiations, and long-term commitments. Personal sacrifices were required to sustain membership, but were balanced with the special benefits of belonging, including the right to property acquisition and ownership, and the right to inherit and personally control wealth. Some of these traits, skills, and qualities are echoed by people with natal placements in Capricorn, the sign associated with responsibility and commitment.

The Goat's Head

The Goat-Fish is divided into three sections. The stars of each section are attributed to different planetary pairs. Ptolemy's book assigns the stars of the Goat's head to Venus with some Mars influence. Valens states that a person with planet contacts to the head stars are "a slave to Venus." The horns are marked by **Giedi 1 and 2**, sometimes referred to as **Algedi Prima** and **Secunda**. Al Giedi is from the Arabic *Al Jadii*, the goat. Giedi often is used to refer to the pair as they're quite close together. **Alshat** is in the horns. **Dabih** is at the base of the horn near **Bos**, which is usually depicted in the ear. **Oculus** is the eye star, and **Bos** is in the cheek.

Stars of the Goat's Head

χ (horn)	2 Aq 30	-12.37	Mag 5.9
Giedi Prima *alpha 1*	4 Aq 03	-12.27	Mag 4.6 horn
Giedi Secunda *alpha 2*	4 Aqu 06	-12.29	Mag 3.8 horn
Alshat *nu*	4 Aqu 42	-12.42	Mag 4.8 horn
Dabih *beta*	4 Aqu 03	-14.43	Mag 3.2 horn
Oculus *pi*	5 Aqu 00	-16.02	Mag 5.2 eye
Bos *rho*	5 Aqu 27	-17.45	Mag 5.0 neck
NCG 6903	3 Aq 36		head
omicron	5 Aq 13		
Youe *psi*	7 Aq 09	-25.16	Mag 4.14 breast/heart
tau	8 Aqu 18	-14.57	Mag 5.22 neck
ν, ω and #17 *omega*	7 Aq 40 and 8 Aq 11		knee/body

The Goat's Venus/Mars stars have benefits and liabilities. **Giedi** brings peculiar gains and losses but tends toward good luck. The darker side is the "horny goat" effect, a super-powered libido and desire nature that's driven by lust and greed. This could lead to love affairs that end in scandals and upsets. Venus-Mars stars start with Venusian love and desire and proceed toward martial conflict. The desire nature isn't limited to sexual conquests. It may be directed at material acquisitions, a drive for power, and even lust for knowledge and information. One example could be a person who prizes knowledge and studies intensely, then becomes a know-it-all or an intellectual snob. The Venus influence inspires generosity and hospitality, while the Mars influence alludes to editing people or things that have become obsolete, problematic, or even boring. Giedi receives the most descriptions in older fixed star references. The other stars of the Goat's head and neck share similar meanings and the Venus/Mars attribution.

The Goat's Venus-related instincts and tendencies are more pronounced as these stars precess through the first decan of Aquarius, the Face of Venus. This face corresponds to the Five of Swords, a card that signifies betrayals, disappointments, and efforts that don't turn out as planned. The planner has to go back to the drawing board. The price for the Venusian emotional investment is disappointment and sorrow. Venus, the lesser benefic, promises more than she can deliver. The overwhelming desires aroused by Venus are spoiled by the Mars influence as it wastes and damages the efforts and intentions. Another way of looking at it is that Venus is a here-and-now planet inclined to instant gratification, whereas Mars is the celestial general responsible for fulfilling strategic goals through well-crafted tactics. A lack of this necessary foresight, planning, and marshaling of resources may result in efforts that come to naught. The Five of Swords card may also represent a situation that's finished but not over, like when a relationship has ended but isn't really finished. People with star-contacts to the Goat's face take losses seriously and personally.

Back and Torso

The torso of the Goat contains **Dorsum** on the Goat's back. **Armus** is at the center of the body, the belly of the Goat with chi, #19, #20, and #24 (faint star clusters). The torso stars are assigned to Mercury with the influence of Saturn. The paired planet assignment leans toward gut instincts, hunches, and an ability to pick up on subtle signals. This includes body

Stars of the Goat's Belly and Back

#24, belly	11 Aqu 51	-25	Mag 4.5 belly
#19, #20	11 Aq 06 and 11 Aq 53		belly
Armus η/*eta*	13 Aqu 01	-19.40	Mag 4.9 belly
χ *chi*	13 Aq 17		belly
Dorsum θ/*theta*	14 Aqu 07	-17.02	Mag 4.2 back
Yen ζ *zeta*	16 Aq 56	-22.5	Mag 3.74 lower belly
Tai ι *iota*	17 Aq 41	-16.50	Mag 4.28 back/tail
ω *omega*	15 Aq 02		belly
#30	16 Aq 22		belly/tail
#36	17 Aq 35		belly/tail
M30 (globular cluster) 19 Aq 43		-23.11	Mag 7.5 under tail

language, the unspoken subtext or implications of a conversation, and allusions to things that aren't openly mentioned like the "elephant in the room" nobody wants to acknowledge. The belly stars influences range from pious abstinence to gluttony.

Mercury-Saturn stars promote the development of valuable practical skills. Mercury absorbs information like a sponge and Saturn adds the discipline and will to acquire mastery over time. These stars show the dichotomy of a pronounced instinctual nature and a pragmatic, practical outlook on work and skills. Rosenberg links these stars to distinctly secular interests like politics, philosophy, and theoretical or conceptual thinking. The Saturnian influence can increase irritability and grumpiness, and a propensity for being overloaded with responsibilities. People with planets conjunct these stars may work as custodians, curators, archivists, or guardians (Vesta-related jobs). As often happens with Saturn, those burdens may be thrust upon the individual by importuning circumstances.

6 of Swords

Six of Swords from the
Whispering Tarot

The second decan of Aquarius is the Face of Mercury. While Capricorn's Mercury-Saturn stars are precessing through Mercury's Face, the influence of these stars heighten the affinity to the inner-most planet. These stars inspire original thinking and relentless ambitions. The Face is attributed to the Six of Swords. This is a card of travel, memory, and skills. There are opportunities to demonstrate those skills to those who may have need of them. An employment interview is an apt illustration. It involves all sorts of Mercury-related things: the initial submission of a resume, phone calls or e-mails to set up an interview, and travel to a new location when the interview is conducted. The interviewee exchanges several types of information with the person conducting the interview: past work experiences, training and educational history, and more subtle things like personality and preferences. Some employers require various Saturnian tests as well, including background and credit reports, drug tests, and other (sometimes invasive) research into one's personal history. Exchanges are Mercury's specialty. Saturn is the list of requirements, standards, limits, baselines, and potential long-term prospects with the hopeful outcome of a stable employment situation.

The Mercury-Saturn attribution may manifest in other ways, too. Aquarius signifies groups, clubs, philanthropy and political affiliations. Mercury-related information exchanges and travel possibilities are funneled through Saturnian standards, requirements, and sociopolitical responsibilities and structures. Once the basic Mercury-type activities have been accomplished, Saturn offers benefits and refinements over the long-term through network building, seniority, and the possibility of being elected to an office on a group's board or steering committees. Event planning and fund-raising are high priorities. Mercury and Saturn imply selecting dates for the future on a calendar, a human construct for understanding and managing time (Saturn). Anticipated events require the Mercury-related announcements to members and the community, and selecting entertainment or programmed activities to raise the funds that help a group fulfill its mandate.

The image typically shown in the Six of Swords is a person or two riding in a boat with another person managing the oars or rudder. Sometimes the boat has a sail so its movement is assisted by the winds. Passengers bring memories of the past, what was accomplished (or not), and hopes and plans for the future. Although there are only one or two passengers, the card implies that everyone is in the same boat traveling through time and space together. It emphasizes commonalities, shared interests and goals, and an agenda for the future. The Goat's Heart stars are practical and hopeful, ambitious and intuitive, but occasionally melancholy and regretful.

The Tail Stars
The Goat's tail stars represent the fertile and watery segment of this constellation. The final three signs of the zodiac share connections to the weather typical of winter and early spring. The Goat huddles up to endure snow and ice and the deep chill of winter. The Water Bearer signals even more moisture, mixed between the snow and sleet that gives way to chilly rains as the Sun arrives in Pisces. The front half of the Goat is cold and dry, but the fishy tail is cold and wet.

The tail stars are attributed to Saturn and Jupiter. The named stars are **Castra**, **Nashira**, and **Deneb Algedi** (or Algiedi, both spellings seem acceptable). Kappa is mid-tail. Somewhat above the tip of the tail are two more stars, lambda and mu. The Chinese called this pair "the howling dogs," signifying dogs whose master has died. The dogs lay near the grave and howl until they die, too. A novel called **Greyfriar's Bobby** by Eleanor Atkinson (1912, made into a Disney film in 1961) tells essentially the same story.

The Saturn-Jupiter tail stars occupy the Moon-ruled third decan of Aquarius. Aquarius's ruler Saturn is dominant. In ancient astrology, Saturn was linked to the sea, to maritime professions, ships, and oceanic traveling. Ptolemy's description indicates that a person born under the tail stars would labor hard to maintain a ship, constantly risking danger and death in that profession. The *risk* of death isn't exactly the same as dying. Saturn is canny at calculating the odds of success or failure. A successful voyage could be highly profitable, a Jupiter factor that offsets the risks. No pain, no gain!

The theme of **Deneb Algedi** is extremes of luck and risk. The star is linked to exceptional wealth and fame but also the potential for substantial losses. As is common for Saturn-

Stars of the Goat's Tail

Castra ε *epsilon*	20 Aqu 29	-19.23	Mag 4.7 tail
Nashira γ *gamma*	22 Aqu 04	-16.34	Mag 3.8 tail fin
Deneb Algedi δ *delta*	23 Aqu 49	-16.02	Mag 3.0 tail fin
2135-147 κ *kappa*	21 Aqu 57		tail
Kuh (dog) μ *mu*	25 Aqu 50	-13.33	Mag 5.08 tip of tail
λ (dog) *lambda*	22 Aqu 59		tail
#42, #46 and ecliptic quasar PKS 2146-133 Capr			
	23 to 25 Aqu		tail
NGC 7158	27 Aqu 26	-11.36	triple star; tail fin

Jupiter stars, the person's ability to maintain integrity and honor are absolutely critical over the long-term. The star is linked to spirituality, religion, and the occult, and their contemporary cousins science, physics, and the capacity for discovery and invention. A natal contact to this star can lead to the individual occupying positions of authority and trust. Proper performance and pristine honesty generally yield karma cookies. Failure to maintain absolute integrity may lead to an ignominious downfall and lost reputation. Saturn demands responsibility, discipline and mastery all wrapped in a blanket of integrity and moral-ethical refinement. If those standards are violated, penalties are harsh.

The North Node, Venus, the IC and Saturn contact the back and tail stars of Capricorn in Gloria Steinem's natal chart. She took great risks early in her career as a journalist and author, assumed positions of responsibility and trust, ran profitable magazine enterprises, wrote news-making books, and became a national icon and spokeswoman for women's rights. On the few occasions where she's made statements that didn't ring true to her causes, the negative publicity against her was harsh.

Gloria Steinem
March 25, 1934
10:00 pm EST
Toledo, Ohio
Tropical-Placidus
True Node

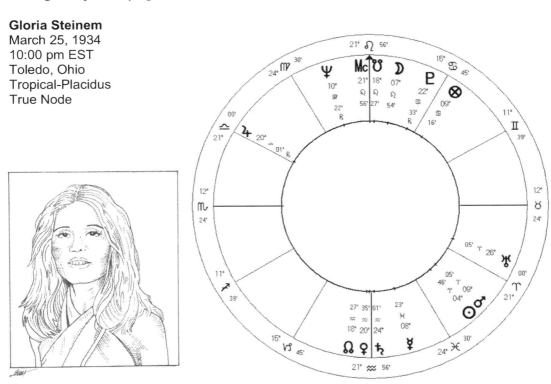

The Moon-ruled third decan of Aquarius is an oddity. It's attributed to the Seven of Swords. The rendering of this card varies from deck to deck. In the Waite-Smith deck, a man carrying four swords sneaks away from the scene, leaving three swords behind. The traditional meaning is "getting away with what you can carry" and/or "cut your losses and scamper." The card implies theft or perhaps quietly escaping from a bad situation before it gets worse.

The relationship between the Moon's Face and the Saturn-Jupiter attribution to the tail stars isn't obvious. A subtle connection can be conveyed by using a boat on the ocean as a metaphor. An experienced sailor reads signs in the sky, the stars, and the winds to forecast atmospheric disturbances. Perhaps he has that characteristic Saturnian ailment and his knees ache when the weather is about to change. The Moon always signifies circumstances in a state of flux. A storm or an ill-wind could be on the way. A smart sailor battens down the hatches and changes course to avoid sailing directly into a tempest. The implications aren't necessarily nefarious. Risks can result in gains or losses. The Moon-related ability to trust one's senses, read the signs, and listen to one's knees are survival skills that help a person land on the plus side of the risk balance sheet.

7 of Swords

Seven of Swords from the **Whispering Tarot**

A ship's captain and crew take on the responsibility (Saturn) to transport valuable cargo to sell for a profit (Jupiter), and possibly to return with yet more valuable goods to be sold and traded for yet more profits. Seafaring commerce is real enough, but "a voyage upon the waters" is a metaphor for traveling into a realm without known boundaries in conditions that could suddenly change from hospitable to exceptionally dangerous. The destination may or may not be known. Reaching it is only the first half of the job; the second half is returning intact with the goods and profits in hand.

This metaphor relates to all sorts of life circumstances. Deneb Algedi signifies inventors, industrialists, attorneys, councilors, and sometimes religious or spiritual leaders. Attaining a position is just the first hurdle. The individual with natal planets in the Goat's tail is under Saturn's thumb. Success is inextricably linked with pressure to finish the job or complete the process. Inventing something new is brilliant, but efforts don't end until that invention has been tested on the seas of uncertainty, found to be useful and necessary, put into production, shipped out to the collective, and had its profit potential proven through sales. For some natives of Deneb Algedi and the other tail stars, the process of creation, development, and sales may be an ongoing career feature.

Even after great successes, the inventor (attorney, industrialist, minister, etc) could hit snags. There could be an invention that seems promising but doesn't appeal to the public or doesn't perform as promised. There could be a client whose case is nearly impossible to settle satisfactorily, in which case, the attorney and client will have to walk away with what they can carry.

Rosenberg connects the tail stars with windfalls, lottery wins, and wild luck, but also with devastating storms and tempests, destructive fires, fogs that can precede wrecks and crack-ups on the rocks. The connection with fogs and mists is a significant hitch in the metaphor of a voyage. A person who has scored some big successes may feel invulnerable, blessed with the golden touch. But even such a person can make mistakes. From a position of great power and wealth, mistakes are a magnitude of order larger than a basic small-scale screw-ups. Hundreds of people could lose their jobs and livelihoods. A badly-made widget that's installed in a piece of critical technology could get people killed. An invention that fails to perform or sell is devastating to someone who's accustomed to success. A successful person can become cocky and sloppy. The possibility of fogged vision and blind spots increases unless the individual is humble, wary of pitfalls, and accepts good advice.

Saturn demands the application of meticulous attention to detail regardless of previous successes. Attention to detail might mean admitting that a new product is faulty or doesn't work as well as expected. The product might have to be withdrawn or recalled. Some compensation may have to be made. It takes great integrity and personal strength to admit to making an error of judgment, to apologize, and to make things right for those who were affected.

Strength of character is developed through coping with failures, by what is learned and by the tenacity shown in carrying forward in spite of it. Failure after a string of successes may present the most dire pitfall of all. It requires ruthless self-honesty and humble truthfulness toward others, and perhaps even the painful but necessary process of making amends. When people who have worked hard to attain success hit this pitfall, they are truly dropped into Saturn's realm. There can be blame, guilt, and regret – all facets of the Seven of Swords. They have to "walk away with what they can carry." The ideal in this case is to walk away with integrity intact, to find the courage and honor needed to make amends, and to have the strength of will to return to the drawing board to make corrections or start over. Beneath the tricky tarot imagery is the tempered steel of Saturn-Jupiter stars in the Moon's face: retaining dignity in all circumstances.

The final signs of the zodiac hold some of the sky's most difficult lessons. The third decan of Aquarius is the Moon's final Face, followed by the Saturn/Pisces decan. One can arrive at success with dignity and grace by remaining quiet, humble, and just as committed to the meticulous attention to detail that paved the route to the success.

The Moon is what the public sees. An example of this is found in the reaction of lottery and big prize winners. Those winners who smile and nod, and shake hands with the host or official in charge are most likely to be the people who handle that prize with good common sense. The winners who scream, yell, sob, cry, and spew emotions are less likely to manage their prize with good sense and necessary caution. The prize-giver doesn't have to regard the winner as an equal or as a peer. The winner is just a jerk with money who will return to being a jerk without money soon enough. They can be devoured by rapacious attorneys, relatives, televangelists, and other sorts of financial predators. The screaming and weeping winners lure all the sharks in the sea.

A screaming winner may not always be a fool, but it's more likely that a dignified winner will *not* be a fool. The Faces are like wardrobes for the planets that own them. What costume or outfit does the Moon wear in Aquarius, Saturn's favored sign in his airy triplicity? A Saturn-y Moon is an elderly lady, neatly dressed and coiffed. She carries a cane to steady her steps. She speaks like a retired English teacher. She maintains the dignity of wisdom and age. She is a matriarch or a community leader and knows where all the bodies are buried. She feels no obligation to share her secrets. Only her eyes may give away the thoughts racing behind the restrained facial expression. She never raises her voice to command obedience. The Crone Moon has come to terms with Saturn. She is his peer. She has accepted the passing of beauty and vigor in exchange for the dignity and wisdom of old age. She has mastered emotional control and the ability to appear unruffled no matter the circumstances.

The Goat's tail swishes back and forth, from one extreme to another. The grounded Goat's nature doesn't change, nor does the mandate of its ruler Saturn. Honor, integrity, honesty are traits upon which good reputations are built. It doesn't matter whether Tiberius is on the throne surrounded by his Sphinctrians or if popular reality shows lionize sloppy emotions, dishonor, and dysfunction. The core of a culture is ever reliant on individuals of talent, honor and integrity. Tiberius, his minions, and pop trends are only a speck in the eye of history. The adamant value of persons of integrity and honor hasn't diminished a bit since the days of Cincinnatus, Scipio Africanus, and Germanicus. Wells of corruption are evil precisely because they exist in opposition of honor, truth, and integrity. A civilization can't remain civilized if noble traits like honor and integrity are devalued.

The Goat's word is his bond. His projects and missions are his responsibility, and fulfilling a mandate is a serious commitment. Sloppy ethics and lax morality get no quarter because reputation is like virginity: once it is lost, it can't be regained. Philosopher Onora O'Neill's work emphasizes the importance of trust, consent and respect for autonomy in a just society. New Zealand-born philosopher Annette Baier wrote that trust is the key to morality. She emphasizes that trust is difficult when inequalities exist. Relationships hinge on trust. Not money, not fame, not love, not attention-getting skills, but *trust*. Trust is justified, or plausible, when one person knows the other person is able to fulfill their agreement. Capricorn is the sign that most aptly represents this intangible foundation of human relationships. Without integrity and honor, trust cannot survive.

Planets that occupy the Goat's tail present the critical choice between the ethical extremes of honor and corruption. This point sticks to the wall when considering that the tail stars have precessed to the degree of the Aquarius Moon in the US Sibley chart.

The Stars of Gemini

There are two methods for working with stars. One is to calculate parans: star risings, culminations and settings during the day for which a chart is being erected. The second method is to use the longitude or zodiacal degree of a fixed star to determine if radix planets or chart points form conjunctions. Both methods have much to offer in chart interpretation. The zodiacal longitude method is simpler and a good starting point for those who are new to fixed star lore.

Stars are sherpas of astrological lore. New meanings don't invalidate the old meanings, they're simply added to the star-Sherpa's backpack. Major bright stars have been given many names and meanings through the centuries. One bit of baggage that often goes unnoticed is the ancient planetary attributions to fixed stars. There are few clues about how to use them. Most stars have two planet attributions. A few constellations have a single planet assignment, like Hercules (Mercury) and Ursa Major (Mars). In a survey of 148 named fixed stars with magnitudes 1 to 5, only 15% (twenty-two stars) were assigned to a single planet. Stars with a single planet attribution offer unique insights into the rationale of star-planet affiliations. They also demonstrate the surprising utility of star-planet assignments as an interpretive tool.

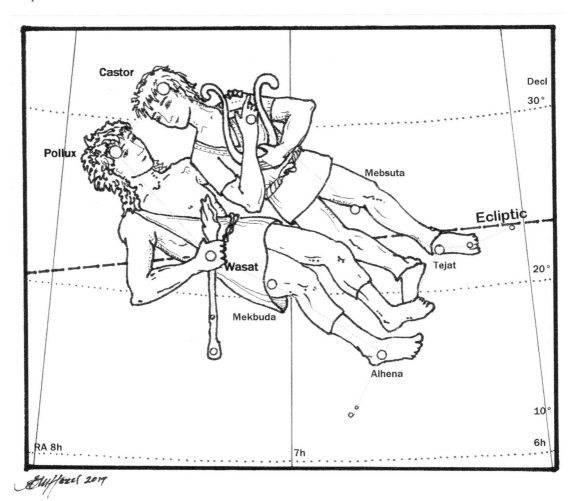

One of a Kind

Gemini, a double-bodied sign, is endowed with a singular feature: three of its stars have different single planet attributions. It is the only zodiac sign with this feature and a rarity among all constellations. Gemini occupies 20° of arc and has precessed entirely into tropical Cancer. All the stars except Castor are within the Via Solis.

Tejat and Alhena mark the feet of the Twins. Both are associated with Mercury and Venus. Alhena's meaning includes making a mark in the world, or being marked in some lasting way. [1] An exceptional example is the June 30, 1908 Tunguska strike with the Sun conjunct Alhena. The meteor created an eight hundred thirty square mile mark on the face of the earth. Tejat and Alhena give grace and talents, charm, popularity, and a variety of skills and traits commonly associated with a Gemini Sun-sign.

The Bright Stars of Gemini			
Star		**Longitude**	**Attribution**
Tejat Prior (Propus)	eta	3♋43	☿ ♀
Tejat Secunda	mu	5♋35	☿ ♀
Alhena	gamma	9♋23	☿ ♀
Mebsuta	epsilon	10♋13	☿ ♀
Wasat	delta	18♋48	♄
Castor	alpha	20♋31	☿
Pollux	beta	23♋30	♂

Wasat

Wasat, from *Al Wasat* "the middle," has a Saturn attribution. The name reflects the star's position on the ecliptic. [2] Wasat marks Pollux's right hand positioned at his waist. Meanings include expertise and useful skills, but being prone to hardships, compulsory changes, losses and sorrows. [3] Ptolemy's star-planet attributions in *Almagest* came from earlier sources generated well before Gemini's stars precessed into tropical Cancer. [4] The Sun rose with these stars *prior* to summer solstice, when diurnal sect planet power is at a peak. Diurnal Saturn is less malefic so the positive attributes of mastery and legacies are emphasized.

Natives of Wasat

The chart of John Forbes Nash has a fierce conjunction of Wasat, Pluto and Ascendant. These are closely parallel, with Pluto at +21°40', Ascendant at +22°21', and Wasat at +21°56'. Nash was a brilliant but very arrogant, egocentric mathematician. After developing the Game Theory at Princeton, he joined the faculty of MIT in 1951. In January 1958, just after his Saturn return, Nash's mental health eroded in a matter of weeks. He was relieved of his teaching duties in February. His wife Alicia had him committed and he was diagnosed with paranoid schizophrenia. Decades of illness followed. His wife divorced him, but later decided to allow him house space. This stable environment helped Nash gradually recover. He re-established an informal association with Princeton and became a senior research mathematician in 1995. After the 1960s, his Game Theory became invaluable to economists. Nash received several prizes, including the Nobel Prize in 1994. The 1998 biography by Sylvia Nasar, *A Brilliant Madness*, inspired a factual documentary by PBS in 2002. Ron Howard directed *A Beautiful Mind* (2001) starring Russell Crowe as Nash. Nash died on May 23, 2015. [5]

Nash's Wasat alignment makes the condition of natal Saturn and other Saturn associations crucial. It's also important to search for chart elements that counter-balance or mitigate the negative connotations.

Nash's Saturn and South Node in Sagittarius are the chart's bucket handle. Saturn conjuncts the sixth house cusp and Ras Algethi, a Mercury star in Hercules. The Kneeler climbs toward the summit of the celestial North Pole, but is linked to mythic underworld travelers Gilgamesh and Orpheus. [6] Ras Algethi confers single-minded dedication. The sixth house relates to potential health problems and to tools and items of utility. Nash's equations are abstract tools (Sagittarius) that use numbers (Saturn). Saturn-Ras Algethi signifies Nash's sheer genius and mental refinement, but also his years in the underworld struggling with schizophrenia, a disease of the head, as Ras Algethi is the star that marks the head of The Kneeling One

John Forbes Nash
June 13, 1928
7:00 am EST
Bluefield, WV
Topical-Placidus
True Node
RR: A

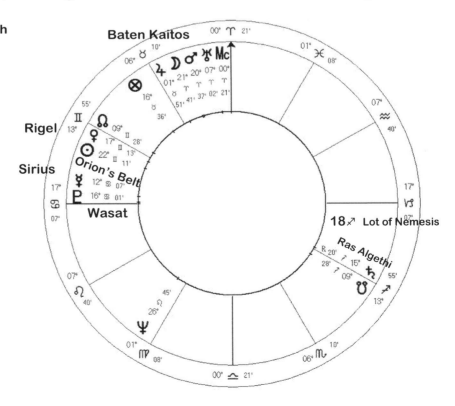

His Moon and Mars conjunct Baten Kaitos, the Belly of the Whale. This is another star with a sole Saturn attribution. Its meanings are dire and include periods of exile, forced emigration, lengthy torments and profound losses. Moon-Mars trine Saturn creates an escape hatch. The clue to mitigation is in the meaning of Saturn's Lot of Retribution or Nemesis (diurnal formula is Asc + PF – Saturn, nocturnal formula Asc + Saturn – PF) at 18 Sagittarius. Benefic aspects to this Lot offer better coping skills and a means of escape or release from problems. In charts with an exceptionally well-dignified Saturn, the person may become "a bird in a golden cage" (Saturn in Aquarius trines the Lot of Nemesis in the chart of Whitney Houston). Problems may be transformed into strengths or advantages over time. Nash's schizophrenia subsided and his work was recognized later in life.

Nash's chart contains mitigating star contacts, too. His Cancer Sun is conjunct the exceptionally fortunate stars of Orion's Belt. Venus conjuncts Rigel and Mercury conjuncts Sirius. Nash's chart is a turbulent storm of stellar energies that highlights his mathematical genius while simultaneously unleashing mental torment and a period of family and career exile. The Saturnian influences imply that recognition would occur late in life. Venus-Rigel signifies widely-circulated influential ideas that are applicable to collective circumstances (the stock market). Venus disposits his Part of Fortune in the eleventh house of awards and recognition.

Anne Frank was born one year after Nash with the same Wasat-Pluto occultation in her twelfth house. Saturn trine Neptune-Regulus emphasizes her noble philosophical nature, courage, and imagination. Anne's Jupiter-Neptune square coincides with the "Armada Square" between Regulus and the Hyades. [7] The Armada Square augurs calamities from unstoppable forces. The American edition of *Anne Frank: Diary of a Young Girl* was published by Doubleday on June 12, 1952, on what would have been her twenty-third birthday. It featured a 1939 photograph of Anne on the cover. Anne's Virgo Moon is conjunct Zosma, a star associated with victims. Francine Prose wrote that "...she is the most commonly recognized and easily recognizable victim of the Nazi campaign against the Jews, or of any genocide before or since." [8] She shares Nash's solar conjunction with the fortunate stars of Orion's Belt.

Author Arthur Miller's chart features a Wasat-Saturn-Midheaven conjunction. His Saturn has good connections: it receives his fifth house Aquarian Moon and trines Jupiter in Pisces in his sixth house. His first house Sun is conjunct Spica/Arcturus. Miller's books and plays (including *Death of a Salesman*, a Saturnian title!) are a notable legacy. His marriage to Marilyn Monroe was beset with nationally-reported tragedies. Miller was subpoenaed by the House UnAmerican Activities Committee in 1958. He was blacklisted and charged with contempt, but it was overturned on appeal. HUAC interrogations damaged one's reputation and career (tenth house matters) regardless of guilt or innocence. The supportive trine with reception from Jupiter, which exalts in Cancer, and the trine from the Lot of Nemesis at 9 Scorpio averted permanent career damage and helped him escape the harsh fate of other writers. Miller's plays often feature Wasat themes. The main characters struggle with issues of conscience, responsibility and estrangement. Some die or commit suicide. Miller left a substantial body of work, plays that continue to be performed and books that continue to be read. Saturn's best expression as a star attribution is an enduring legacy.

The Twin Stars

Castor (α, 20°♋31', +31 declination, Mag 1.6 binary, ☿) is the mortal son of Leda and Tyndarus. His twin brother Pollux (β, 23°♋30', +27, Mag 1.2, ♂) is the immortal son of Leda and Zeus. It's appropriate for the *lucida* or alpha star of this constellation to be associated with Mercury, Gemini's ruler. Over the centuries, Castor has dimmed somewhat. Pollux is now the brighter star. [9]

Castor the Horseman (aka Eques) gives a strong intellectual bent toward writing and law, along with creativity, travel, refinement, fame and success. Castor natives possess a firm moral center that may find an outlet through social criticism and satire. Difficult aspects to a natal Castor contact can result in mischief and violence. [10] The native's life journey may be like a ride on a high-strung bucking bronco, with sporadic circumstances that unseat the rider.

Pollux is the pugilist or fighter. This star's meanings include cruelty, harsh judgments, and tyranny. Natives may be cunning, crafty, and audacious, but may gain eminence and renown. One's work and studies may include travel or emigration. For some it may indicate periods of torment, struggles with creative efforts, and being deceived by others. [11]

Castor and Pollux offer gifts with warnings attached. Exceptional skills can be used for either good or evil. Immortality (i.e. being part of the collective memory) is possible, but one's name may be attached from anything from fame to infamy.

A definitive link to the planet associations of Castor and Pollux is found in the ancient geomantic figures. Albus and Rubeus are identical in shape with Rubeus is inverted. Albus is called "The White Head" and is associated with Mercury/Gemini. The figure's meanings include clarity of thought, intelligence, experience, wisdom, and good judgment. It symbolizes a pale or fair complexion, and is a positive figure for new ventures. Rubeus is associated with Mars/Scorpio. It's called "The Red Head" and signifies rashness, a passionate nature, fiery temper, and accidents. It's a warning sign that hidden issues will rise to the surface. Other meanings include vices, the color red, and blood. [12] The geomantic figures confirm that the colors of these two stars are linked to the planetary assignments. Castor's binary stars are both white, ergo the White Head. Pollux is an orange -red star, the Red Head. The Twin stars are unusual in this respect. Star-planet attributions are rarely related to color.

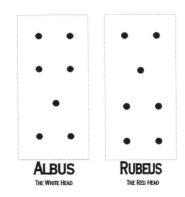

ALBUS
The White Head

RUBEUS
The Red Head

Pollux, The Red Head

Charts with natal conjunctions to Pollux include: Irving Stone (Sun); Julian Assange (Mercury); Mary McCarthy (Neptune); Gloria Steinem, Lady Antonia Fraser, and Bill Moyers (Pluto). They're writers, journalists, and information dispersers.

Irving Stone was the author of meticulously researched, best-selling fictionalized biographies about historic individuals who had turbulent lives with much contention. Stone traveled a great deal for research.

Assange became notorious for his Wikileaks website. He exemplifies the crafty and audacious nature of Pollux and Rubeus by bringing hidden material into public view. He embodies the paradox of the Twins by being either a hero or a traitor. Assange relocated to avoid prosecution.

Mary McCarthy's most famous book is *The Group* (1963), a fictional tale Vassar students who proceed into lives of glory and scandal. McCarthy's **Pollux-Neptune** energies seep into her tragic characters. McCarthy had a longstanding enmity with writer Lillian Hellman. Contention centered on Hellman's association with the American Communist Party, which came about through her relationship with Dashiell Hammett. McCarthy's attacks cast a long shadow over the second half of Hellman's life. Poisonous attacks exemplify Pollux-Neptune. McCarthy's reputation was diminished by her relentless character assassination.

Gloria Steinem's eighth house **Pollux-Pluto** is the focal point of a T-square with Jupiter and Uranus. Her journalistic career began with incisive critiques of the male-dominated status quo, including an exposé on the exploitative Playboy empire. Steinem is a relentless fighter in the war for women's rights. Her later career includes extensive lecture tours and books such as *The Revolution Within* and a biography of Marilyn Monroe.

Lady Antonia Fraser is known for her definitive biographies of monarchs. Her twelfth house **Pollux-Pluto** sextiles her third house Jupiter, the significator of royalty. Pollux-Pluto is expressed through the turbulent lives of the individuals she chooses to write about, and her deep, obsessive research into every detail of these lives. Fraser's biographies include exact event dates and times extruded from primary resources, so her books are a bonanza for astrologers.

Bill Moyers is an investigative journalist. His sixth house **Pollux-Pluto** trines his Scorpio Midheaven. Saturn in Aquarius rises in his first house with a tight square to his Midheaven. Moyers is fearless about exposing corruption in government and industry through his reports and critiques.

These Pollux natives share their intense focus on spreading information, along with a capacity for digging deep for good dirt and exposing skeletons in closets. There's a spectrum of information utility, from scholarly or knowledge-sharing purposes to deliberately provocative revelations. More specific delineations of how-and-why can be gleaned through the specific planet contacting Pollux and aspect relationships in the natal chart.

Castor, The White Head

Many Castor natives have created substantial legacies. Remarkably consistent traits include determination, courage, risk-taking, and career-related travels.

Castor-Sun natives include Nikola Tesla and virtuoso pianist Van Cliburn. Both were highly talented individuals with quirky and neurotic yet refined personalities. Both traveled extensively in their careers. A seventh house **Castor-Moon** conjunction is featured in the chart of Eleanor Roosevelt. She was a speaker, writer, and indefatigable minority advocate who was always on the road. The Moon is a significator of "the people" in mundane astrology. Few individuals have ever shown as much concern about the well-being of the common people as Mrs. Roosevelt.

A **Castor-Mercury** conjunction is featured in the chart of Dr. John Dee, the most enigmatic figure of the English Renaissance. Mercury is conjunct Jupiter, trine Neptune, and shares a mutual antiscion conjunction with Uranus. Dee wrote several books and made extensive trips to Europe to obtain manuscripts. His personal book index is invaluable to researchers. Dee's interest in secret codes, astrology, magic, and scrying for angelic communications with Edward Kelley yielded enduring legacies. He was a skilled cartographer and advised New World explorers. Dee's Castor-Mercury highlights his lifelong dedication to gaining knowledge, expanding the boundaries of communication, and multi-disciplinary intellectual pursuits. [13]

Dr John Dee
July 13, 1527 OS
4:02 pm LMT
Wimbledon, England
Tropical-Placidus
True Node
RR: B (from bio "The
Queen's Conjuror")

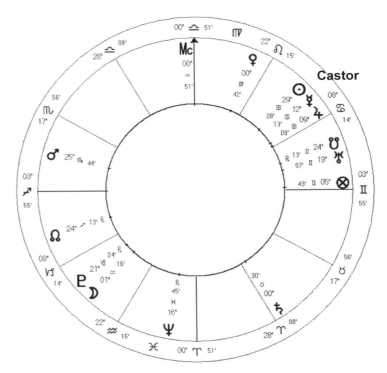

Castor-Venus conjunctions appear in the charts of occultist Oswald Wirth and film star Judy Garland. Wirth was a Swiss occultist who, with Stanislas de Guaita, developed the esoteric *Le Tarot des Bohemiens* and attribution system presented in his book, *Tarot of the Magicians* (1927). Castor-Venus is in Judy Garland's first house. Mercury is linked to child prodigies, and the Mercury association to Castor sometimes reflects this. Garland's phenomenal talents as symbolized by Castor-Venus are without question, but Venus receives no helpful Ptolemaic aspects or other forms of support in the chart. The lack of contacts may also explain why her talents remained intact while her life and health eroded.

The story of Katherine Goble Johnson is featured in the non-fiction book and film *Hidden Figures*. [14] Katherine was born with an unaspected **Castor-Mars** conjunction with Mars in fall. In and of itself, this suggests exceptional talents with few viable outlets. Castor-Mars receives excellent (if sneaky) support through a mutual antiscion conjunction with Jupiter-Aldebaran, a Mars-attributed Royal star. Jupiter trines Venus in Libra. Katherine was a child prodigy with a preternatural grasp of abstract math and geometry. After being hired by

NASA as a "West computer," Katherine was quickly diverted into a special projects division. Her intellect, charm, charisma and avid curiosity helped her overcome gender and racial barriers. She calculated the space capsule re-entry trajectories for NASA's Mercury and Apollo missions, literally determining the bull's eye in the sky (Aldebaran) for rockets (Mars) descending (Mars in fall).

Mars Rx-Saturn Rx-Castor are in the chart of Dolly Parton, who launched her singing-songwriting career in her teens. Saturn in Cancer rules and opposes her natal Capricorn Sun, Mercury and Venus; these form a T-square with Jupiter in Libra. Saturn disposits Mercury, creating an unusual star-attribution reception with Saturn's conjunction to a Mercury-attributed star. Mars Rx, ruler of her third house, signifies her career as a singer-songwriter. It also rules her eighth house, the source of massive royalties from cover renditions of her songs. Behind Dolly's charm, humor and beauty lies the mind of a sharp businesswoman who wrangled her way to the top of the competitive, male-dominated country music business. Saturn-Mars-Castor emphasizes toughness, endurance, travels, and her extensive musical legacy.

Castor-Jupiter contacts are tricky in spite of (or because of) Jupiter's exaltation in Cancer. Professional success is possible, but there's danger of excess and imbalance when it's not well integrated into the chart. A difficult Mercury placement exacerbates the instability. James Barrie, playwright and author of *Peter Pan*, has Castor-Jupiter in a T-square with Mercury in Aries and Mars in Capricorn. His iconic fictional character has become synonymous with a refusal to embrace maturity. His chart is full of difficult squares and oppositions. Barrie's life was fraught with troubles.

Janis Joplin is another **Castor-Jupiter** native. (*see chart, pg 66*) Fifth house Jupiter is retrograde and with the Moon; both planets are unaspected. Her talents were fueled by Cancerian emotion, but her romantic life was characterized by frustrations and disappointments. Her Mercury is retrograde and in opposition to Pluto. Heaven's Gate leader Marshall Applewhite had angular **Castor-Jupiter-Pluto** square Uranus and in opposition to Saturn. Mercury and Neptune form a grand trine with the Midheaven. His delusional ideas were ultimately deadly to his followers.

Bruce Willis has tenth house **Castor-Jupiter** trine Saturn. Mercury trines his Midheaven and Nodal axes. Willis transforms these placements into a "lone cowboy" combination. Castor-Jupiter excesses are channeled into physically dynamic but emotionally stunted film characters with romantic and family turmoil. Saturn appears to restrain the Castor-Jupiter contact, compartmentalizing these energies into his professional work.

Actor Tim Curry has a **Castor-Saturn** contact. Saturn is at 22° north declination and in joy in the twelfth house. It sextiles Venus in Taurus (elaborate costumes and music) and squares Jupiter in Libra (operatic and tragic figures). Curry has Pluto rising in Leo trine his Aries Midheaven, a get-away-with-anything aspect he shares with Monty Python alumnus Eric Idle. Curry has a unique ability to portray shadow-figures in stories laden with taboo plot devices. Curry's Prince of the Underworld character kidnaps and falls in love with a young princess in *Legend*. In *The Rocky Horror Picture Show*, Dr. Frankenfurter entraps a newlywed couple, Bob and Janet, and seduces both of them. Saturn signifies imprisonment.

Two natives of **Castor-Uranus**, Nicholas Culpeper and Michael Moore, demonstrate the social criticism facet of Castor. Culpeper was a doctor, astrologer and herbalist. Castor-Uranus trines his tenth house Venus in Scorpio and sextiles a Saturn-Pluto conjunction in Taurus. Culpeper rebelled against the greedy and dangerous medical practices of his time. He provided cheap and free services to patients because "no man deserved to starve to pay an insulting, insolent physician." Social disorder provided a narrow window of opportunity for his books. His peers were unable to censor him or prevent publication. Culpeper served as an anti-royalist battle surgeon during the English Civil War. His best-known book, *The English Physician*, now called *The Complete Herbal*, has been continuously in print since 1653. He died of tuberculosis three months after the book's completion in 1654. The book's herbal lore became a springboard for the avaricious modern pharmaceutical industry. [15]

Michael Moore's films are a laundry list of probing inquiries into government corruption and political misbehavior. He was an advocate for his hometown, Flint, Michigan, long before the drinking water became toxic. Uranus-Castor are conjunct the South Node in Moore's twelfth house, forming a nodal T-square with Mercury and the Part of Fortune in Aries. Moore gleefully kicks over political apple carts without regrets or apologies, but he draws fire for his exposés.

Jacques Yves Cousteau's career embodies his natal **Castor-Neptune** with Mars in his tenth house. Cousteau single-handedly made the public aware of the beauty and grandeur of life beneath the ocean's waves through a popular TV series. He pioneered methods of filming underwater, a very Neptunian kind of activity.

Pluto made a lengthy conjunction to Castor in 1931-1932. The first **Castor-Pluto** representative, however, is from the Pluto's Cancer transit during the Renaissance. Marsilio Ficino was a noted translator and author. His *Three Books on Life* (1489) offered medical and astrological advice. *Book III: On Obtaining life from the heavens* went a step further by outlining astrological talismanic practices. "The first 'self-help' book of its kind, it gained immense popularity, running to thirty editions by 1647." [16] Precession places Ficino's Castor -Pluto at 12° Cancer in opposition to his Capricorn Moon. He was compelled to invent self-help methods for his own health problems! Ficino was questioned by the Inquisition and forced to apologize after his book was published. Castor-Pluto alludes to periods of deep despair and his risky occult leanings.

Notable **Castor-Pluto** natives of 1931-1932 include actor Leonard Nimoy, whose televised fictional travels to "where no man had gone before" as Mr. Spock on **Star Trek** and death-to-life journey in the film series are an apt yet quirky expression of Castor-Pluto in opposition to Saturn. Robert Anton Wilson was the co-author of *The Illuminati* ("a fairy-tale for paranoids"). His books and essays feature radical thinking, social and scientific criticism, taboo topics, and extreme skepticism about government institutions. His Pluto-Castor opposes the Sun and Saturn in Capricorn.

Clive Davis has natal **Castor-Pluto** square Uranus in Aries. His life path is notable for sudden shifts and successful risk-taking. Davis was orphaned as a teenager. He worked his way through a law degree from Harvard. At age 28 (1960) he made a career leap to Columbia Records and became president of CBS Records by 1966. After being fired for misappropriation of funds, he founded Arista Records. Although he has no musical training, Davis built recording empires by spotting and nurturing talent. [17] His grand stellium in Aries with Moon, Mars, Sun, Uranus, and Mercury, attests to his indefatigable energy and enthusiasm, while his Castor-Pluto connection describes his ability to transform raw talent into top-rated music acts. Davis, now in his eighties, shows no signs of slowing down. He revealed his bisexuality in his 2013 autobiography *Soundtrack of My Life*. Davis has received numerous industry awards and is a major supporter of NYU.

Conclusion

Star-planet contacts in a nativity prompt an examination of the planet(s) attributed to that star. Contacts with a single-planet star place a greater emphasis on the attributed planet. That planet's condition and contacts in the natal chart help determine the particular facet of the star's meanings that will manifest. A lack of close, helpful Ptolemaic aspects to a planet-star contact is a warning flag. Antiscia and joys should be included in the analysis repertoire. A planet in extremes of dignity–exaltation or fall–can signify excesses related to the star's meaning, or challenges finding an outlet for talents. Planet attributions to stars are an interpretive tool that merit study and consideration.

References

1. Bernadette Brady, **Brady's Book of Fixed Stars**, Samuel Weiser, Inc., 1998, pp 249-51; Bernadette Brady, **Star and Planet Combinations**, The Wessex Astrologer, 2008, pp 145-147 and pp 196-199. Vivian Robson, **Fixed Stars and Constellations**, Samuel Weiser, Inc., 1984, pp 126-127. Reinhold Ebertin, **Fixed Stars and Their Interpretation**, AFA, 1971, pg 38.

2. Richard Hinckley Allen, **Star-Names and Their Meanings**, G. E. Stechert, 1899, p 234.

3. Robson, *ibid*, p 216.

4. James H Holden, AFA Conference August 2010, key note address. Mr Holden vociferously stated that Claudius Ptolemy was an encyclopedist who was paid to gather astrological information for a client. Sections of his books are copied from other ancient writers. The star-planet associations came from another source; Ptolemy didn't invent them.

5. John Forbes Nash biographical information, see Encyclopaedia Britannica entry: https://www.britannica.com/biography/John-Nash; Wikipedia entry: https://en.wikipedia.org/wiki/John_Forbes_Nash_Jr. The PBS documentary, *A Brilliant Mind*, can be seen at: https://www.youtube.com/watch?v=oM1SflhJDoc

6. Allen, *ibid*, pp 238-9.

7. see page 37, The Armada Square—Saturn-Hyades square Jupiter-Regulus.

8. Francine Prose, **Anne Frank: The Book, the Life, the Afterlife**, HarperCollins, 2009, pg 89.

9. Allen, *ibid*, pp 232.

10. Robson, *ibid*, pp 154-156; Brady 1998, *ibid*, pp 248-249; Brady 2008, *ibid*, pp 145-147; Ebertin, *ibid*, pp 40-41; Allen, ibid, pp 230-233.

11. Robson, ibid, pp 185-187; Brady 1998, *ibid*, pp 248-249; Brady 2008, *ibid*, pp 196-199; Ebertin, *ibid*, pp 41-42; Allen, ibid, pp 233-234.

12. Elizabeth Hazel, **Geomantic Divination**, Kozmic Kitchen Press, 2013, pg 2.

13. Benjamin Woolley, **The Queen's Conjurer**, Henry Holt and Company, 2001.

14. Margot Lee Shetterly, **Hidden Figures**, William Morrow, 2016.

15. Nicholas Culpepper biographical information, see Wikipedia: https://en.wikipedia.org/wiki/Nicholas_Culpeper; Dylan Warren Davis "Nicholas Culpeper, Herbalist of the People," *The Traditional Astrologer* magazine, Issue 5, Summer 1994, at http://www.skyscript.co.uk/culpeper.html

16. **Western Esoteric Masters Series: Marsilio Ficino**, edited and introduced by Angela Voss. North Atlantic Books, 2006, pg 41.

17. Jason Hollander, "The Man with the Platinum Ears," *NYU Alumni Magazine,* 2007. https://www.nyu.edu/alumni.magazine/issue17/17_FEA_Davis.html

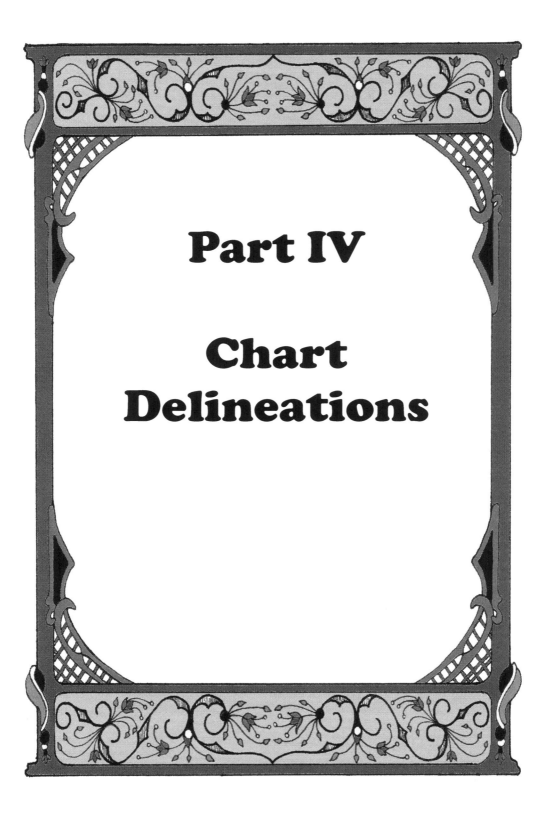

Part IV

Chart
Delineations

Introduction to Part IV

The four charts presented here have been road-tested during fixed star lectures. The delineations illustrate in-depth views of natal planet-star contacts. Much like the essays and articles in Part III, the chart delineations are intended to help readers learn to work more effectively with their own charts and client's charts by demonstrating:

- how particular planets work as conduits for stellar energies
- how different planets highlight different facets of star-meanings, and
- how star-planet attributions assist in delineating natal planet-star contacts

Poets cultivate their channels of inspiration and use sophisticated imagery to present their thoughts and feelings. The best poems resonate on a collective level, which suggests that the source of inspiration that poets tap into has a broad universal source. One might tie it to Jung's collective unconscious, but this is a book about the stars. The constellations are a cosmic library filled with timeless human experiences, stories and plots, character motivations and outcomes.

The poets whose charts are delineated in this section all have natal Saturn connected to a major star. Saturn rules poetic and compositional forms as well as the significator of the refinement and mastery gained through disciplined long-term efforts. As the outer-most visible planet it's the Lord of the Gate to the outer sphere of the stars in the pre-Copernican cosmos. These poets had an astounding gift for plumbing the depths of their souls for inspiration. In that process, they touched upon imagery linked to their natal planet-star contacts with breathtaking precision. Souls are made of star-stuff! The greatest poets can stretch their minds past Saturn's esoteric boundaries into their personal contacts to the stellar library and return filled with liminal and chthonic visions. Yes, I know—it's intense! And as you read through their personal histories and chart delineations, you'll see what it cost them to engage in this soul-plumbing process. Nothing is ever free with Saturn.

Whether these collective images are contained within the mind as a collective unconscious or as an external constellational library upon which specific star-points are imprinted at the moment birth, I leave for the reader to decide. It may be that certain individuals are blessed with the ability to tap into their interior and exterior-natal sources as creative well-springs. Perhaps they are the same thing understood differently by people in separate disciplines. Jung harnessed mythology, but star lore is specific to an individual's chart. No guessing is required. Astrology reduces projection bias because the astrologer reads and interprets what's in the chart instead of performing extemporaneous Jungian myth-related interpretations of a client's emotional revelations and dream content.

When it comes to the deepest feelings, mystic or spiritual experiences, words often fail. Skilled poets come the closest to expressing the inexpressible. In doing so, great poets are capable of giving the most precise expressions to their natal star energies. Some poetic quotes are used to demonstrate this point.

7

The Poets

Arthur Rimbaud

Born October 20, 1854 (NS), 6:00 am LMT, Charleville-Mézières, France
Fixed stars for the following charts are at earlier degrees because of precession

Personal History

Jean Nicholas Arthur Rimbaud was the son of Captain Rimbaud, a French soldier stationed at Charleville near the Belgian border. He married Vitalie Cuif, the daughter of a prosperous farmer. Captain Rimbaud deserted the family because he couldn't get along with his wife. Vitalie was strict, severe, religious, bigoted, and a constant fault-finder. Arthur, the second son, was a neatly-groomed, pious and studious child. He became intrigued with poetry in his early teens. By the time he was sixteen, he was in full rebellion against Vitalie's repressive parenting style. He let his hair get shaggy, stopped bathing, wore dirty, raggedy clothing, started smoking a pipe, spitting, and using vulgar language. He ran off to Paris and witnessed the horrors of the Franco-Prussian war that spread across France after July 1870. The Germans bombed and then occupied Mézières-Charleville. When Arthur came back home, he started sending letters and poems to publishers and famous poets in Paris.

He repeatedly ran away from home but was compelled to return. A fateful turn of events occurred when Paul Verlaine, another poet, took an interest in his writing. Verlaine was an older man with a very pregnant young wife. He sent Rimbaud a train ticket to Paris in the autumn of 1871. They embarked on a scandalous sexual relationship heavily lubricated with booze and drugs. The pair scorched their way through the absinthe and hashish parlors of Paris, and wandered back and forth between London and Brussels. All the while, Rimbaud was producing amazing poetry.

Rimbaud was working on his final series of poems "A Season in Hell," when the relationship went sour. Verlaine shot Arthur in the hand in a moment of madness. Verlaine was arrested and jailed for eighteen months. Rimbaud went home, finished his poems, sent them off to be published, and went on a long walking tour of Europe. He joined the Dutch Foreign Legion and was shipped to Java. He ended up in Africa exporting gold, frankincense and ivory from an unexplored desert region. Rimbaud wrote occasional reports and observations about the area that were sent back to France and published in newspapers.

Health problems surfaced when Arthur reached his mid-30s. He returned to France for medical care. He was diagnosed with an osteocarcinoma in his knee. Doctors amputated his lower leg, but it was too late. Arthur Rimbaud died on November 10, 1891 in Marseille at age 37.

Verlaine collected Rimbaud's letters and poetry and got it published. Rimbaud's five years of poetry writing (from 1870-1875) profoundly changed the art form. It inspired the Symbolists, Decadents, Dadists, and Surrealists, as well as having a major impact on American poets like Allen Ginsberg, T. S. Eliot, Henry Miller, Frank O'Hara, John Ashbery, Jim Morrison (who produced books of poetry while singing for The Doors), Bob Dylan, and others.

Birth Chart Analysis

Arthur Rimbaud's life exemplifies the Wild Child-Wild Ride square between Achernar and Rigel. His Ascendant rises with a cluster of powerful stars: **Caphir** and **Spica** (Virgo), and **Arcturus** and **Nekkar** (alpha and beta Boötes). These stars give exceptional talent, the potential to attract patronage, fame and fortune, but also the potential to choose unworthy friends and cause one's own problems. He was born just before sunrise, so his Libra Sun occupies the first house and applies to an out-of-sign opposition to Pluto. This aspect reflects his transformative impact on others, but also his volcanic nature – he erupted into a teen rebellion, erupted into an obsessive outpouring of poetry, then abandoned it entirely and bounced around Europe, Asia and Africa for the next fifteen years. He was so dynamic that he pushed other peoples' wants and desires to the side in order to fulfill his own, as he left Verlaine humiliated and imprisoned in Brussels! Sun-Pluto can indicate a powerful sexual appeal infused with danger or risk. Homosexuality was illegal and Verlaine was impris-

Arthur Rimbaud
October 20, 1854 NS
6:00 am LMT
Charleville Mèziéres,
France
Tropical-Placidus
True Node
RR: AA

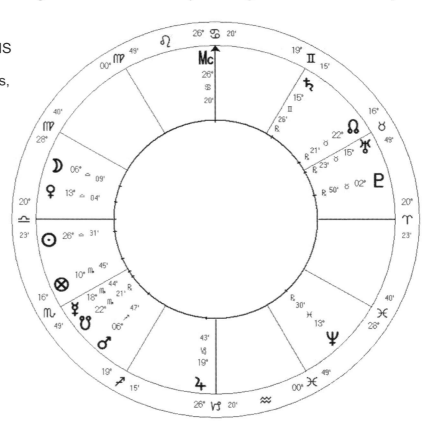

oned on charges of sodomy (much like Oscar Wilde some years later). Sun-Pluto describes the potently obsessive impact of his poetry. Henry Miller described the effect of Rimbaud's poems as "pure dynamite." [1] The mind-bending effect of his poems stems from the wild mixture of the sublime and refined (Sun in Libra) with the filthy, disgusting, and offensive (Pluto in Taurus with the head stars of Aries).

The Sun rose with the stars of Boötes and conjuncts **Izar**, the star on the right elbow. This is the arm that holds the magical staff. The Boötes constellation rises in the autumn like a jack-in-the-box. Rimbaud's entire oeuvre was a fast and furious production, and he never wrote poetry again. Pluto Rx was conjunct **Mesarthim** and **Sheratan**, the alpha and beta stars of Aries. These are highly aggressive Mars-Saturn stars. Mars and Saturn are in a loose opposition in the natal chart. His teen rebellion coincided with a regional war, and he had a use-'em-and-loose-'em attitude toward relationships. He was a force of nature. Few could resist him and no one could hold him when he decided it was time to leave.

Sunrise charts are of particular interest if there are planets rising before the Sun. Rimbaud has the Moon and Venus rising in the twelfth house. They act as *doryphories*, spear-bearers marching ahead of the Sun. Different ancient writers give a range of definitions for doryphories; I prefer using planets that aren't combust and rise before the Sun to fulfill the task of announcing what the Sun is going to do. Case in point: oriental Venus in rulership in Libra infused Rimbaud with an idealistic nature and great talent in the arts. He wrote: "**the poet is a Parnassian, in love with ideal beauty.**" [2] Morning star Venus is daring, eager for novel experiences, and can be quite fearless in youth. Venus trines Saturn in Gemini, the planet that exalts in Libra. This is a significant aspect for artistic innovations: Venus symbolizes the contents, Saturn symbolizes the shape or form; "**I searched continually to find the place and the formula.**" [3] His early works reflect traditional poetic forms but eventually he abandoned them. Arthur's shift to prose poetry and his development of new forms are two of his greatest accomplishments.

The fourth-quarter Moon rises with **Diadem**, the pearl-star in the crown of Coma Berenices. This star signifies recognition and acclaim, although the link to eighth house Saturn suggests posthumous fame. The Moon sextiles Mars in Sagittarius in the second house. This aspect signifies his highly rhythmic and aggressively innovative use of language. His poems feature color and sensory metaphors. Mars is conjunct **Antares**, the heart of the Scorpion. Antares is anti-Ares or anti-Mars, so this is an inflammatory combination. Rimbaud was brutally unsentimental. He burned bridges when he tired of situations, and he appeared to do so without regret. He willfully destroyed poetic conventions and created new ones. Antares contacts can signify hidden terminal diseases. Mars is disposited by Jupiter in Capricorn, the sign linked to the knees, and Jupiter rules the sixth house of illness.

The Sun and Mercury both have oppositions to outer planets. Evening star Mercury follows the Sun in Scorpio in the second house. It's conjunct **Zuben Elschemali** and in opposition to Uranus. This star brings the assessment and judgment skills he applied to his poetry early in life, and to his business interests as an exporter in Africa. He had a singular aptitude for deciding what was appropriate for himself at lightning speed and making abrupt breaks and changes with little concern for its impact on others. This repeats the theme of his Sun-Pluto opposition. Uranus is conjunct the eighth house cusp, emphasizing the publication of his poetry after his death. The Mercury-Uranus opposition also represents his attitude toward the creative process. Rimbaud sought a state of internal mental chaos and the destruction of all inner barriers in order to force visions to the surface so they could be spun into poetry. The Mercury-Uranus opposition straddles the Nodal Axis in the fixed signs Scorpio/Taurus, emphasizing how his creative theories and poetry exerted an incredible influence on writers for an exceptionally sustained period of time.

Neptune occupies the fifth house and bisects the Mercury-Uranus opposition with a trine-sextile. Rimbaud dissolved the conventions of poetic meters and rhymes when he shifted to prose poetry. Jupiter, the planet that rules the third house of writing, also is linked to the Mercury-Uranus and nodal oppositions with a trine-sextile. Zuben Elschemali is attributed to Jupiter-Mercury, so Mercury's conjunction to the star combined with his natal Mercury-Jupiter sextile super-fuels the star's meanings and its scope for expression. Jupiter is conjunct **Sulaphat**, a star in poetic and musical Lyra. It reiterates the theme of lasting posthumous fame. Apollo placed the Lyre in the sky after the death of Orpheus, the only singer-poet who ever beat Apollo in an artistic contest. The stars of Lyra allude to immortality when combined with other extraordinary chart connections.

In the famous "Vision Letters" Rimbaud wrote to George Izambard on May 13 and to Paul Demeny on May 15, 1871, he says that in order to be truly creative, "[t]he problem is to attain the unknown by disorganizing all the senses. The suffering is immense..." In the second letter he expanded on this notion:

> "For *I* is an *other*...I am a spectator at the flowering of my thought: I watch it, I listen to it...The first task of the man who wants to be a poet is to study his own awareness of himself; in its entirety; he seeks out his soul, he inspects it, he tests it, he learns it...But the problem is to make the soul into a monster...A Poet makes himself a visionary through a long, boundless, and systematized *disorganization of all the senses*. All forms of love, of suffering, of madness, he searches himself, he exhausts within himself all poisons, and preserves their quintessences...He attains the unknown, and if, demented, he finally loses the understanding of his visions, he will at least have seen them!...The poet, therefore, is truly the thief of fire." [4]

Mercury, the king of thieves, exchanges an opposition (dynamic conflict) with the amorally chaotic and creative Uranus. Uranus is sometimes linked to Prometheus, the Titan who stole fire from the gods to share with humanity, although Mercury is perfectly capable of pulling the heist. Uranus confers the ability to dissociate from one's own thoughts and feelings while Mercury observes them and takes notes. Taurus and Scorpio are tough enough to endure the strain of the prolonged suffering and madness this process requires. He was seventeen when he wrote these letters. Mercury represents the purity of the *puer*, the young prodigy. Young Arthur expressed the meaning of his own natal Mercury-Uranus opposition with astonishing precision!

In mid-May 1871, Venus and Jupiter were conjunct in the late degrees of Gemini making powerful combined contacts to **Betelgeuze** and **Polaris**, the star of navigation. The Moon was conjunct **Achernar** (his Neptune), Mercury was retrograding over **Caput Algol**, and the Sun was conjunct **Capulus**, the sword of Perseus and his natal North Node. One might summarize his experience of these aspects as: if I'm going to walk the path of a poet and seek the ultimate vision, I must chop off the head of reason!

The Wild Child-Wild Ride square between **Achernar and Rigel** imposes an uneasy destiny in this chart. Neptune is conjunct **Achernar**, the source of the River Eridanus. [5] It signifies the potential to gain wisdom through travels. Saturn is conjunct **Rigel**, Orion's foot at the whirlpool of current events, emerging trends, and socio-cultural movements rising to collective awareness. Saturn and Neptune are symbolic opposites: Saturn has distinct limits; Neptune has no boundaries. Where Saturn imposes structure and form, Neptune is amorphous and tends to dissipate solidity. People with natal conjunctions to both Achernar and Rigel may spend many years occupied with extraordinary wandering on zig-zagging paths that eventually lead to discovery. It is never easy and can hold potential dangers like rocks hidden under the churning river's current.

The poem that perfectly encapsulates Rimbaud's Wild-Ride Saturn-Neptune square is titled *The Drunken Boat*. It is one of his most famous early poems. It opens with "I drifted on a river I could not control." The poem relates a dizzying array of beautiful, bizarre, and horrible visions that appear as he's dragged along by the current. The sixth stanza reads:

> Now I drift through the Poem of the Sea;
> This gruel of stars mirrors the milky sky,
> Devours green azures, ecstatic flotsam,
> Drowned men, pale and thoughtful, sometimes drift by.

Near the end of the poem, the poet's willingness to absorb more visions and experiences wanes and he begs for release:

> True, I've cried too much; I am heartsick at dawn,
> The moon is bitter and the sun is sour...
> Love burns me; I am swollen and slow.
> Let my keel break! Oh, let me sink in the sea! [6]

Rimbaud was a Wild Child and his life was a Wild Ride. But he wasn't a stereotypical dreamy poet, he was a man of action. When he lost touch with his teenage poetic vision, he abandoned it and traveled in search of other curiosities and eventually became a legendary explorer in Africa. He's the prototype of an artistic radical who predated the Beatnik and Hippie movements, the sexual and gay liberation movements, and the psychedelic movement by nearly a century.

End Notes

1. Arthur Rimbaud. **Complete Works**. translated by Paul Schmidt. Harper Perennial/ Modern Classics, 1975. Excerpt from Henry Miller, *The Time of the Assassins*, 1946. Appendix, p 23.
2. ibid, Rimbaud letter to Theodore de Banville, May 24, 1870, p 38. The poets of France were called Parnassians, an allusion to attaining the heights of Mount Parnassus.
3. ibid, Introduction, p xiv.
4. ibid, pp 113-117.
5. Neptune recently transited Achernar in 2018-2019. The work of famous individuals is often revived during Neptune returns to their natal charts. Consider, too, the impact on children born with a Neptune-Achernar contact during 2019. The Wild Ride square with Neptune-Achernar was activated by Mars, Venus, and the Moon conjunct Rigel in 2019.

6. Rimbaud, pg 136 and 139.

Additional Material
Arthur Rimbaud by Enid Starkie is considered the definitive biography
Total Eclipse (Warner, 112 min, released Nov 3, 1995) directed by Agnieszka Holland, starring Leonardo DiCaprio as Rimbaud and David Thewlis as Verlaine. The film depicts Rimbaud's poetic period and his turbulent relationship with Verlaine. It shows Rimbaud's poetic fervor, his obnoxious behavior and filthy life style, and the late 19th century environment he inhabited. Borrow it from the library or stream the film, as one viewing is enough.

Federico Garcia Lorca
Born June 5, 1889, 12:01 am LMT, Fuente Obejuna, Spain

Personal History
Federicao del Sagrado Corazón de Jesús Garcia Lorca was an immensely talented and extremely handsome man from a wealthy family. His literary talents surfaced during his teen years. He was also an accomplished pianist and artist. He studied law, literature and composition at the University of Granada (1915). His friend, the composer Manuel de Falla, imparted an abiding love of Spanish folklore, Andalusian flamenco, and *cante jondos* (deep songs). Federico wrote, "The melody begins, an undulant, endless melody. [It] loses itself horizontally, escapes from our hands as we see it withdraw from us toward a point of common longing and perfect passion." **[1]** He wrote his first book, *Impressions and Landscapes* (1918), after touring northern Spain with a university professor.

Garcia Lorca moved to Madrid in 1919 to attend the progressive Residencia de Estudiantes. He was drawn into a group of *avante guarde* artists that included Salvador Dali and Luis Buñuel. This loose association of Spanish poets, artists and musicians became known as the Generation of '27. They introduced symbolism, futurism and surrealism into Spanish literature and arts. Federico wrote his first play, *The Butterfly's Evil Spell*, in 1920. It's about an impossible romance between a cockroach and a butterfly surrounded by a cast of other insects. The first performance was a flop. The play was laughed off the stage. Federico was humiliated and didn't write another play until 1927. He returned to college to complete degrees in law and philosophy.

Libro de poemas was published in 1921. This poetry collection centered on spirituality, isolation, and nature. In 1922 he helped Manuel de Falla produce the *Concurso de Cante Jondo* festival to feature flamenco performances. He began work on another series of poems that was eventually published as *Poema del Cante Jondo* (Poem of the Deep Song) in 1931. Another series of poems from this period, *Suites*, wasn't published until 1983. Garcia Lorco joined de Falla for a second project. They adapted an Andalusian story for a script and li-

bretto titled *The Girl that Waters the Basil and the Inquisitive Prince.* This children's musical was produced in 1923.

Canciones (Songs) was published in 1927, followed by an exhibit of his drawings at the Galeries Dalmau in Barcelona from June 25 to July 2, 1927. His literary and artistic work of this period featured a blend of Andalusian motifs and Cubist influences. *Romamcero Gitano* (Gypsy Ballads) was published in 1928 and became some of his best-loved poetry. Garcia Lorca described it as "gypsies, horses, archangels, planets, its Jewish and Roman breezes, rivers, crimes, the everyday touch of the smuggler and the celestial note of the naked children of Córdoba." Federico was drawn back to theater and wrote a farce called *The Shoemaker's Prodigious Wife* in 1926, although it wasn't produced until the early 1930s. A second play called *Mariana Pineda* was produced to great acclaim in 1927 and featured sets by Salvador Dali.

Garcia Lorca became deeply and passionately involved with Dali for about three years (1925-28), although the artist rejected his sexual advances. He became romantically involved with sculptor Emilio Adadren Perojo. Both relationships faltered after the success of Federico's *Romamcero Gitano*. He fell into a pit of dark depression that was in part fueled by anguish about his homosexuality. His public success was at sharp odds with his inner torment.

He needed a change of pace and place. His family arranged for Federico to travel to the United States in 1929. He spent most of his time in New York City and enrolled at Columbia University to study English. He was impressed with the melting pot of jazz and blues evolving in Spanish Harlem and African American neighborhoods. Garcia Lorca was in New York City during the 1929 stock market crash. His thoughts and literary output took a sharp turn from folklore to anti-capitalistic politics.

A liberal Second Spanish Republic was established around the time that Garcia Lorca returned to Spain in 1930. Garcia Lorca co-founded La Barraca (The Shack), a government-sponsored student theatrical troupe that performed Spanish classics and his original plays in remote, impoverished areas of Spain. He wrote and directed a trilogy of rural plays: *Blood Wedding; Yerma;* and *The House of Bernarda Alba* during the tours. These plays challenged the Spanish class structure, the roles of women in society, social rules, and taboo sexual issues. Garcia Lorca made no effort to hide his liberal political views or his homosexuality.

Garcia Lorca went to Buenos Aires to direct the Argentine premiere of *Blood Wedding* in 1933. He also gave lectures on his theories of artistic inspiration. He posited that great art depends on an awareness of death, a connection with nature, and venturing beyond the limitations of reason. The leap beyond the constraints of reason echoes the sentiments found in Arthur Rimbaud's Vision Letters. His last poetic work was a return to traditional forms, *Sonetos de amor oscuro* (Sonnets of Dark Love). Documents found later reveal that the poems were written for Juan Ramirez de Lucas, a nineteen-year old with whom Garcia Lorca hoped to emigrate to Mexico. These poems remained hidden until 1983-84, when the collection was published from the drafts. No final manuscript has been located. It is some of his most moving and surreal image-laden poetry, the work of a mature master poet.

The Spanish Civil War erupted in the mid-1930s after the assassination of monarchist Jose Calvo Sotelo. The nation was in chaos. Granada had no mayor for months. Franco's troops went through the countryside murdering helpless citizens and destroying communities. Falange (fascist) forces occupied the area in and around Granada.

Garcia Lorca had friends on both sides of the conflict. His brother-in-law took the position of mayor of Granada and was assassinated within the week. Nationalist troops arrested Federico on August 18, 1936. On August 19, 1936, he was summarily executed with three other men at a place known as Fuente Grande (Great Spring) on the road between Alfacar and Viznar. The Franco-era report from July 9, 1965 describes him as "a socialist...freemason belonging to the Alhambra lodge, [who engaged in] homosexual and abnormal practices." The 1936 dossier on the execution compiled at Franco's request hasn't been found.

Controversy over the reason for Federico Garcia Lorca's brutal execution continues. It may have been prompted by his relationships and friendships with non-fascist citizens or his sexual orientation. His death may have been part of a campaign to eliminate supporters of the Leftist Popular Front. Garcia Lorca was 38 years old. His body was never found. Franco banned his works and refused to allow any investigation into his death. Many of his works were published posthumously outside of Spain. Garcia Lorca's works weren't published in Spain until after Franco's death in 1953. An investigation into his death was initiated in 2008. Excavations at likely burial sites yielded nothing. Additional excavations in 2016 had the same results.

Federico Garcia's poems, books, and plays circulated widely through Europe and America and had a huge impact on the arts during the 1940s and 1950s. His poems were set to music, his plays were performed, and his written works were translated into several languages. Many artistic works were either directly inspired by his work, or dedicated to his memory. Osvaldo Golijov, a Brazilian composer, was commissioned by the Boston Symphony Orchestra to compose an opera for the Tanglewood Music Center. The libretto was written by David Henry Hwang. *Ainadamar* [from an Arabic word that means "the fountain of tears"] depicts events on the day of Garcia Lorca's execution. It premiered at Tanglewood on August 10, 2003. The opera's music is infused with flamenco, rumba, folk, bel canto, and popular genres.

The family's summer home became a museum that opened in 1995. There are readings of his works on the anniversary of his death. His niece, Laura Garcia Lorca, sponsors celebrations and directs the Fundacion Federico Garcia Lorca, which funds the annual celebrations and preserves his documents and literary trust.

Chart Analysis

Garcia Lorca's birth chart features the three things to seek when incorporating fixed stars into a natal chart: a star conjunct the Ascendant, a heliacal rising star, and a star on the Midheaven.

His Ascendant at 3 Pisces is conjunct **Fomalhaut**. This Royal Watcher star is the Queen Star that loosely opposes Regulus, the King Star. Fomalhaut is the star that marks the mouth of the Southern Fish, Pisces Australinus. It's a Venus-Mercury star that confers abundant talents, charm, and beauty. Garcia Lorca was an exceptionally handsome man who exuded a great deal of charisma.

His Sun and Pluto at 14 Gemini are conjunct **Rigel**. A star may be a heliacal rising star for some days before or after birth, and big, magnitude 1 stars close to the ecliptic are especially potent. Rigel is the foot of Orion in the Whirlpool (*see pg 77*). Rigel is a star that emphasizes expression and the need to contribute to the contemporary cultural. "Fly from my throat, you voice of burning ice,/yet don't abandon me here in the wild/where flesh and sky mate without bearing fruit." [*Sonnet of Dark Love*, trans Scott Tucker]

Garcia Lorca was a member of The Generation of '27 movement that transformed the artistic and cultural life of Spain. Rigel signifies involvement in the whirl of groups, cultural movements, and/or anything at the cutting edge of arts and science. Rigel natives are seen and talked about by others when there's a strong natal chart contact. The Sun, Pluto and Rigel

Federico Garcia Lorca
June 5, 1898 NS
12:01 am LMT
Fuente Obejuna, Spain
Tropical-Placidus
True Node
RR: AA

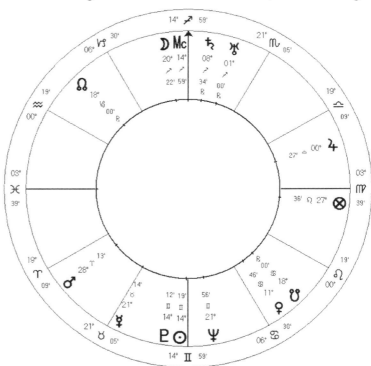

are in the third house only a few minutes past the IC. Garcia Lorca was intrinsically connected to the arts movement in Spain, and Pluto relates to the transformation of Spain's artistic culture.

Pluto can inspire very dark, vengeful feelings in others and it relates to the destruction and devastation of war. The war showed up quite literally on his doorstep (the IC) and Garcia Lorca was killed without explanation. The fourth house is the resting place of the body, but his remains have never been located. What happened? The Sun-Pluto-Rigel tell us that his body was probably taken by soldiers (Pluto) and tossed along the side of a road (third house and Gemini) near a stream or ditch (Rigel). It was then obliterated (Pluto) by wild animals and insects. He had a powerful intuition about his tragic death: "Then I realized I had been murdered./They looked for me in cafes, cemeteries and churches/....but they did not find me./They never found me? No. they never found me." [from "The Fable and Round of the Three Friends" from *Poet in New York*, 1929] A visceral awareness of death was one of his focal qualities for artistic inspiration and his fascination with death appears repeatedly in his poetry. "Little eagles I said/where is my grave-/In my tail said the sun/On my throat said the moon." [*Of the Dark Doves*, trans. Sarah Arvio]

Garcia Lorca's Midheaven at 14 Sagittarius is conjunct **Ras Algethi**, the head of The Kneeler. His Moon is nearby at 20 Sagittarius conjunct **Maasym** (lambda Hercules at 18 Sag) and **Ras Alhague** (Ophiuchus/Venus-Saturn). The tragic nature of his Moon-star contacts are evident in his love poetry: "Moon came to the forge/in her petticoat of nard*/The boy looks and looks/the boy looks at the Moon/In the turbulent air." [*Ballad of the Moon Moon*, trans Sarah Arvio. *Nard is spikenard.] His love poems give the object of desire an unattainable quality. Apropos of Ras Alhague, the head of the snake charmer-alchemist, the objects in his poems are transformed into bizarre substances and different colors. "If you are the gold I dive for on the reef,/if you are my cross and stigma running red,/if I am dog and slave to lord and master,/don't count up my poor gain and spend it all,/don't decorate the dark drift of your river/with the once-green bounty of my brilliant fall." [*Sonnet of Sweet Lament* from *Sonnets of Dark Love*, trans Scott Tucker]

Ras Algethi is in a star opposition with Rigel. Where Rigel connects to the trends, emerging inventions and discoveries of one's era, Ras Algethi signifies enormous devotion and dedication to a cause, the desire to make things perfect, self-improvement, and even the desire for soul evolution. Federico Garcia Lorca personifies the opposition between Rigel and Ras Algethi. He participated in a cultural artistic movement that brought him into contact with many other artists and talented people in Spain and elsewhere through his extensive travels. What he witnessed and experienced was channeled into his own poems, plays, paintings, and books. Yet he was continually striving to find a perfect love and to devise the perfect formula for expressing his innermost feelings through poetry.

In every chart, the Sun is always in opposition to the Earth. Astrologers never bother to plot the glyph for the Earth [⊕] into charts presumably because we know it's there. In this chart, the Sun-Earth opposition and the MC-IC opposition straddle the Rigel-Ras Algethi opposition. Garcia Lorca was a sponge. He absorbed a myriad of influences from his environment, rattled it around in his soul-closet and squeezed it out again as something new and wonderful – a poem, a play, a book. He was dedicated to his theatrical efforts, too. His troupe performed for people in impoverished, remote locations with no modern conveniences. He was a rich young man and no one was demanding this effort from him. That's the influence of Ras Algethi. He was so dedicated and believed so much in the importance of sharing plays with rural audiences that he traveled for several months with his troupe while living in the most primitive conditions.

The theatrical tours exemplify the general traits of Orion and Hercules. Orion is the brute, crude and unlearned. It relates to the audiences to whom the plays were presented, the simply farmers and herders of rural and remote Spain. Garcia Lorca inhabited the role of The Kneeler by offering a unique artistic experience to these people. Rural and remote people might be simple, but they aren't stupid. Garcia Lorca knew they would benefit from the experience and perhaps be inspired by it. He must have discovered (as I have through decades of performing) to never underestimate your audience.

Other star contacts in his chart include Venus-**Sirius**, Mars-**Mirach** (Andromeda/Venus), Saturn-**Antares** (Scorpio, a second Royal Watcher star); Uranus-**Acrab**; and Neptune-**Alnilam** (Orion's Belt, quite fortunate). Garcia Lorca repeatedly mention dogs (Sirius) in connection with love (Venus) in his poems. "All night long, in the orchard/my eyes, like two dogs./All night long, quinces/of poison, flowing./Sometimes the wind is a tulip of fear,/a sick tulip/daybreak of winter/A wall of difficult dreams/divides me from the dead." [*Gacela of the Remembrance of Love*, trans. James Wright]

References
[1] Alex Ross, *Ainadamar: Golijov's Deep Song*. Liner notes from the recording of the revised version of **Ainadamar** performed by the Santa Fe Opera on July 20, 2005. Deutsche Grammophon, 2006, p 5.
[2] Garcia Lorca poetry quotes are from The Poetry Foundation at
    https://www.poetryfoundation.org/poets/federico-garcia-lorca

Biographical Information
https://www.biography.com/writer/federico-garcia-lorca
https://www.britannica.com/biography/Federico-Garcia-Lorca
https://en.wikipedia.org/wiki/Federico_Garc%C3%ADa_Lorca

John Ronald Reuel Tolkien

Born January 3, 1892 NS, 10:00 pm, Bloemfontein, South Africa. RR: C

Personal History

J. R. R. Tolkien (pronounced *tol-keen*) was a highly prolific author and poet who worked as a professor of the English language and literature at Oxford. He was born during the Neptune-Pluto conjunction in Gemini, as were many of the Great Generation that lived through two world wars and the massive leaps in technology that characterized the first half of the twentieth century.

The Neptune-Pluto conjunction was close to **Aldebaran**, the eye of the Bull, and the **Hyades**, a cluster of stars in the Bull's neck. Aldebaran is an aggressive red Mars or Jupiter-Mars star that augurs both success and potential violence. The lengthy two-year conjunction of Neptune, Pluto and Aldebaran made an indelible generational thumbprint on people born from 1892 to 1894 (part of the Great Generation). They lived through global wars, political and social-cultural upheavals. As with all Royal Watcher stars, maintaining one's integrity and using power properly are critical life tests. Many died in battle or in bombings during World War I, or subsequently from the Spanish influenza pandemic. The Russian Revolution resulted in yet more casualties. The years after World War I were intensely creative and fun for some, but marred by political unrest and transformation as ideas about socialism, communism, and anarchy penetrated mainstream awareness. Monarchies fell and were replaced with either dictators or democracies. China's emperor was overthrown and the nation lurched through decades of civil war, famine, and rebellions that ended with Mao. A different kind of disaster struck when the stock market crashed in 1929 and led to a Great Depression, a polio epidemic, and Dust Bowl famine that lingered through the 1930s, followed by the second World War.

The Hyades signify spring rains and water. The star cluster is named for the daughters of Atlas who shed tears of sorrow for their fallen brother. The Great Generation suffered a great many sorrows and shed a river of tears, but there were also many opportunities for greatness and renown through providing leadership, invention, the development of automotive and aerospace technologies, telecommunications, or the radio, music recording and film arts that burgeoned through the first half of the century, and mass-produced consumer products that were accompanied by a parallel boom in advertising.

Tolkien is one of the focal literary contributors of this generation. His parents Arthur and Mabel Tolkien relocated to South Africa for Arthur's work as a bank manager. Mabel took her two sons back to England for a visit but Arthur died while they were gone. They lived with various relatives and the boys were home-schooled by Mabel, who converted her family to Catholicism. Mabel died prematurely and the family priest, Father Francis Xavier Morgan, became boys' guardian. Author Louisa May Alcott's chart shares Tolkien's first house Saturn square fourth house Mercury aspect; she too lost her mother early and became responsible for her siblings and brilliant but impoverished father. [1]

Ronald and his brother Hilary became foster children and resided in various homes. They attended King Edward's School in Birmingham. Ronald grew interested in inventing languages. Ronald and his three best school friends formed a semi-secret society called TCBS, the Tea Club and Barrovian Society. This meeting of young minds stimulated his interest in poetry. He was accepted into Exeter College, Oxford on a scholarship in classics. He transferred to English language and literature in 1913 and graduated in 1915 with first-class honors.

Another orphan, Emily Bratt, lived in the same boarding house with the Tolkien boys. Ronald and Emily fell in love in 1909, but Father Morgan discouraged a relationship with a non-Catholic. He forbade all contact until Ronald was 21 years old. Ronald obeyed this prohibition and didn't see Emily for three years. They became engaged in 1913 and married on March 22, 1916.

Ronald didn't immediately join the army when the war started. He completed his college degree in July 1915 and was commissioned as a second lieutenant in the Lancashire Fusiliers. After eleven months of training and a few months with his new bride, he was shipped to France in July 1916. Tolkien was at the Western Front in various actions including the Battle of the Somme. Soldiers spent months in filthy, lice-infested trenches shooting at Germans in filthy trenches fifty yards away. It was long, bloody stalemate. The Germans started using mustard gas, a poisonous vapor that caused death, blindness and other injuries upon exposure. Tolkien caught trench fever and was shipped back to England. Two of Ronald's TCBS friends died and his battalion was almost wiped out after his departure.

During his recovery, he started to work on material that would eventually become a part of the lore of Middle Earth. His goal was to create a mythology for England to replace the indigenous lore that was lost during the lengthy Roman occupation. His first job after leaving the army was providing the etymology for words with Germanic origin for the *Oxford English Dictionary*. He was a professor at the University of Leeds from 1920 to 1925. He wrote *A Middle English Vocabulary* and co-authored a definitive translation of *Sir Gawain and the Green Knight*. He also translated *Pearl* and *Sir Orfeo*.

He then became the Rawlinson and Bosworth Professor of Anglo-Saxon and Fellow of Pembroke College, Oxford (1925 – 1945). Tolkien did a significant translation of *Beowulf*. This old Anglo-Saxon poem was one of his literary touchstones. His children's tale, **The Hobbit**, was published in 1937. He followed up with work on **The Lord of the Rings**. After World War II, he became the Merton Professor of English Language and Literature and Fellow of Merton college, Oxford (1945 – 1959). **The Lord of the Rings** was completed in 1948. It was published as a trilogy by Allen-Unwin from 1954-55.

Tolkien never suspected how popular his Middle Earth books would become. Being regarded as a celebrity and pop icon was a shock. Attention became so intense that Ronald and Edith relocated to Bournemouth after his retirement to restore their privacy. Edith enjoyed being a society hostess but Ronald missed his literary friends. Throughout their long lives together, Ronald and Edith cherished their life with their four children. They were both orphans, their love was severely thwarted before they could reunite and marry, and most of Ronald's friends were killed in the first World War. With so many early losses, their intense devotion to family and tight emotional bonds are understandable. After Edith died in November 1971, Ronald moved back to Oxford. He died on September 2, 1973 at age 81.

Publications

Tolkien wrote **The Hobbit** as a story for his children. It came to the attention of an editor at George Allen and Unwin in 1936 and was published the next year. Sales were good enough that the publisher requested a sequel. It took several years for him to produce **The Lord of the Rings**, which was published as three volumes in 1954 and 1955. His copious Middle Earth background material was later organized by his son Christopher Tolkien (Ronald's literary executor) and Guy Gavriel Kay and published as **The Silmarillion** in 1977. Christopher organized Ronald's scattered Middle Earth writings into a twelve-volume set, **The History of Middle-earth**, that was published from 1983 to 1996.

Christopher mined Ronald's college course materials for more books. **The Legend of Sigurd and Gudrun** is a long narrative poem in alliterative verse that reconstructs the Völsung saga and legend of the Niflungs, with notes and commentaries. Another work is **The Fall of Arthur** (2013) another original narrative poem imitating the epic style of *Beowulf*. **Beowulf: A Translation and Commentary** was finally published in 2014. The 200 pages of commentary included in the book were the basis of his acclaimed 1936 lecture on the subject. **The Story of Kullervo** is Tolkien's retelling of a 19th century Finnish poem from material assembled when he was a college student in 1915.

Tolkien's oeuvre includes dozens of poems in addition to the poetry presented in **The Hobbit**, **The Lord of the Rings**, and **The Silmarillion**. What's striking about many of these poetic works is his integration of ancient bardic meter and alliteration techniques. His specialized knowledge of ancient Northern languages influenced his distinctive writing style, as he avoided using words with Latin and Greek roots where possible. It's rumored that the editors at Allen-Unwin were afraid to edit his manuscripts. Anyone with the least shred of self-preservation instinct wouldn't want to get into an editorial battle with a sitting professor of the English Language at Oxford! But Tolkien's invented languages caused typographical problems. Misspellings were corrected in a subsequent edition. Tolkien saw the necessity and took the opportunity to add the valuable Appendices to **The Return of the King**.

Chart Analysis

Tolkien's chart is unique for its exceptional number of contacts with major stars. Charts laden with star contacts seem to result in much more fateful and fated lives. A greater number of fixed star contacts requires the individual to fulfill a particular role in society. The person's life follows constellational mythic themes or story lines that echo his or her star-planet contacts. Like Rimbaud, Tolkien's interest in poetry and language took hold at a young age. Oddly enough, there was a bit of a fad for invented languages in the early 20th century, so the idea wasn't original to Tolkien. What he did that was exceptionally original was inventing languages that integrated bits and pieces of ancient Finnish, Icelandic, German, and Anglo-Saxon. At least one biographer has suggested that he developed the lore of Middle Earth simply so he'd have people to use his invented languages.

The significator of language and linguistic skills is Mercury. Language is used and exchanged through the third and ninth houses. Tolkien's **Mercury Rx** at 0° Capricorn Rx is in a partile square to **Saturn** at 0° Libra. Saturn is exalted and receives Mercury. Mercury rules the first and tenth houses, so it's the chart ruler.

Saturn is conjunct the **Galactic North Pole of the Milky Way** at 29° Virgo, the intersection of the ecliptic and Earth's equator at 0° Libra, and the **Super Galactic Center** at 1° Libra.

Mercury Rx is particularly prominent as it's near the **Galactic Center** at 27° Sagittarius. The GC produces intense X-ray and infrared emissions that allegedly influence the subconscious and super-conscious mind, perhaps linking individuals who have natal contacts to the GC to alien or divine sources of knowledge (*alien* and *divine* could be the same thing). The contacts of **Mercury** and **Saturn** to celestial crossroads and galactic centers implies a high degree of interconnection with an exceptional aptitude for inspired thinking, the integration of highly complex ideas and story threads, and his singular propensity for creating imaginary worlds laced with magic and quests of the highest magnitude.

Mercury Rx is between **Spiculum** (Mars-Moon) and **Polis** (mu Sagittarius, Jupiter-Mars). **Spiculum** is a nebular cluster with a stellar T-association of young stars. The celestial South Pole is associated with a Titan called Crius the Inquirer who was the husband of the Moon Goddess Phoebe. The intersection of the ecliptic and Galactic Equator is at 23° South declination with the nearby **Spiculum** cluster. Tolkien's Mercury Rx is at 20° South, close to par-

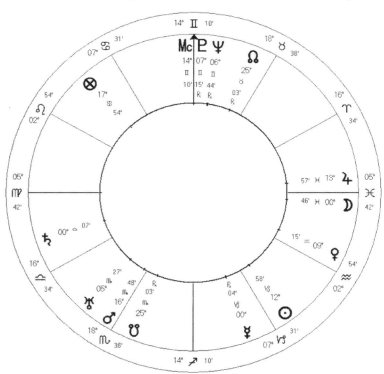

J. R. R. Tolkien
January 3, 1892 NS
10:00 pm
Bloemfontein,
South Africa
Tropical-Placidus
True Node
RR: C

allel this crucial celestial zone. Spiculum is attributed to Mars-Moon, as are all visible nebula. Mars-Moon stars are typically delineated as eye problems and there is some truth to this. A consistent effect of nebulae contacts is family sorrows, abrupt or early deaths, and turbulent family dramas. Tolkien surely had his share of those with his early loss of his parents followed the by the loss of so many of his friends.

His chart is nocturnal: Mercury is the nocturnal triplicity lord of air signs, and it squares the diurnal air triplicity lord Saturn. As the primary triplicity lord of this element, Mercury signifies conditions in the early part of his life - a period of extreme personal losses. Saturn signifies conditions during his middle years: a period of quiet domesticity and stable, long-term employment in a scholarly field, with additional work translating ancient poems. Translating old poems reeks of Saturn-Mercury, doesn't it? As does teaching ancient dead languages to young people in a university setting.

Saturn and Mercury Rx are both at celestial crossroads, with Mercury at the Capricorn Gate. These positions resonate with phrases used in Bilbo's poem:

> Still round the corner there may wait
> A new road or a secret gate
> And though I oft have passed them by
> A day will come at last when I
> Shall take the hidden paths that run
> West of the Moon, East of the Sun. [2]

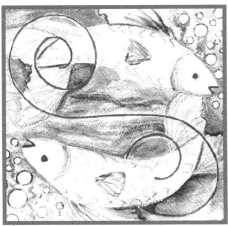

"Hidden paths" and "secret gate" describe the Paths of the Dead and the Capricorn Gate used for soul travel. The phrase "around the corner" is significant, too: the Sun turns at the solstice point, and indeed the word *solstice* means sun [*sol*] turning [*stice*]. The cardinal direction West appears continually in his writings. His Moon and Jupiter are both at the western axis of his chart. The forbidden lands to the West of Middle Earth are only accessible by sailing the waters (Pisces).

The relationship between Crius (GC/Spiculum) and Phoebe is significant as Tolkien's Mercury sextiles his **Moon** at 0° Pisces. This signifies a deep and profound romantic connection. His Moon is conjunct the lucky Royal Watcher star **Fomalhaut** and **Sadalmelek** (alpha Aquarius, Saturn-Mercury). **Moon/Sadalmelek** is super-powered by his natal **Saturn-Mercury** connection and the **Moon's** contact with **Mercury**. Ronald's Solar Return for 1909, the year he met Emily, and the transits on his wedding day share chart contacts. His 1909 Solar Return has transiting Jupiter in opposition to his powerful natal 7th house Jupiter, the sign's ruler. The SR ASC was conjunct his natal Uranus, with SR Venus conjunct his IC and SR Moon conjunct his MC.

Ronald and Edith's marriage was charmed. On the day of their wedding, the Moon was conjunct natal Uranus, Mercury conjunct natal Jupiter, and Venus trine his Sun. Tolkien's progressed Moon and Mercury were conjunct and trine transiting Venus; transiting Mercury was conjunct his progressed Venus and natal Jupiter and trine the transiting Moon in Scorpio; and the transiting Sun was conjunct his Venus. The marriage chart is magical, but the newly-married couple had a lot of strikes against them! Ronald was still a student without a job and with little in the way of job prospects. Pluto formed a T-square with his natal Mercury-Saturn square, so the couple weren't able to remain together for long after their marriage. Edith took a huge risk when she married him, as he had already been commissioned as an officer and was heading off to war. Many soldiers fighting on the front lines had already returned either dead or severely damaged. He survived the war and returned to her, and they settled into a happy family life.

Inner Wheel -
JRR Tolkien natal chart

Outer Wheel -
Tolkien-Bratt marriage
March 22, 1916,
Oxford, England
(time set for noon UT)

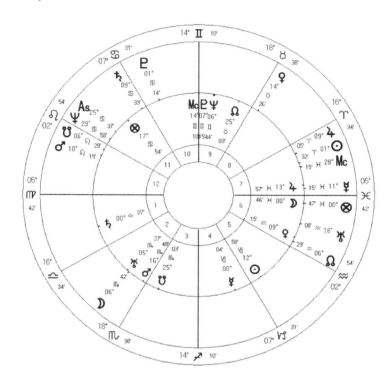

Tolkien's Capricorn **Sun** is conjunct the fortunate stars **Vega** (alpha Lyra) and **Manubrium** (om Sagittarius). **Vega** bestows great talents and exceptional skills, particularly poetry, and is also known as "Talyn Arthur." Vega resonates with his interest in Arthurian legends and other ancient epics that were the bedrock of inspiration for his Middle Earth books. This star gives oratorical skills and charisma. Tolkien spent decades giving lectures to college students. **Manubrium** is a star in the Centaur's body that offers benefits from travels, a strong affinity for education and learning, and significant and enduring friendships. He experienced that through the Inklings, a group of fellow writers who encouraged him to finish and submit **The Hobbit** for publication.

His **Venus** is approaching conjunctions to **Albali** (epsilon Aquarius, Saturn-Mercury), a star in the Water Bearer's arm that gives charm and skills; and **Armus** (eta Capricorn, Mercury-Saturn), a star in the Goat's body associated with mastering skills and crafts, great attention to detail, and a strong constitution. Both stars are more beneficial because of his natal Mercury-Saturn contact.

Mars is conjunct **Zuben Hakrabi** and **Zuben Elschemali**, stars of the Northern Scale of Libra that signify honors and distinction, benefits from literature, speaking skills, and education. Efforts produce lasting results and contributions to society. This star is linked to changing things from bad to good; the powers of good overcoming evil is a major theme of **LotR**.

Jupiter is in rulership in Pisces and angular. It's conjunct **Achernar** and **Ankaa** (alpha Phoenix) and squares the **Midheaven and Rigel** at 14 Gemini. Once again the Wild Ride-Wild Child square is active in a poet's chart. Where Rimbaud quite literally wandered the world, Tolkien delegated the adventures and wanderings to his fictional characters. **The Silmarillion** and **The Hobbit/LotR** feature mass migrations and epic quests requiring long journeys. The Fellowship even spends part of their journey boating down a long river. All of the stars of the river Eridanus are attributed to Saturn except for Achernar, the source of the river, which is attributed to Jupiter. Achernar grants well-earned wisdom, success, and strong spiritual faith (Jupiter is a significator of wisdom). Jupiter is conjunct a very fine Jupiter star, making it all the more beneficial and prosperous. Tolkien's childhood and tour of duty were quite enough of a wild ride for this studious, scholarly young man, and he happily settled into a quiet existence as a college professor with a growing family. **LotR** features a 'wild child' living by a river though: Tom Bombadil. He's called the First Man and is apparently immortal. The hobbits benefit greatly from Bombadil's aid when they landed in trouble at the beginning of their journey. Tom Bombadil is a **Jupiter/Achernar** character, possessing great wisdom but little desire for material wealth.

Ankaa is the Phoenix star. Immortality is a major theme in the Middle Earth saga. Jealousy of elven immortality drives humans to violate divine laws. The immortal Elves withdraw into private enclaves and minimize interactions with humans and other races of Middle Earth, and eventually leave it. Two of the most important romances of Middle Earth involve Elven women who have to give up their immortality to be with human men (Luthien and Beren, and Arwen and Aragorn). Tolkien addresses all of the issues surrounding immortality. As one of the top authors of the 20th century, Tolkien earned his immortality.

J. R. R. Tolkien's most unusual natal combination is **Uranus** at 5° Scorpio 27' (-12°53') conjunct and parallel **Khambalia** (5° Scorpio 26'/-12°52'). This Mercury-Mars star is located in Virgo's left foot. It's not a big magnitude star, but Tolkien's **Uranus** certainly was plugged into it! Khambalia is nick-named "Merlin's Star" and is associated with occult skills, great dexterity and eloquence. His chart has two stellar ties to the Arthurian legends (the other is Vega), but this star in particular emphasizes wizards. A coven of wizards is sent by the Valar to keep order in Middle Earth after the fall of Numenor. The group is called the *Istari*. (I-*star*-i—get it?) Only three of the five are specifically mentioned in the books: Mithrandir, aka Gandalf the Grey; Saruman; and Radagast. Gandalf has become a mainstream pop icon.

With wizards running around, dragons are a necessity. His **Ascendant** is conjunct **Thuban**, the alpha star of Draco the dragon. The Mesopotamians associated **Thuban** with heavenly judges since the star is the pivot of the constellation. It's associated with danger and diseases, but also with vigilance and guarding treasure hoards, whether material or spiritual. Smaug the dragon guarded the great hoard of the dwarves in the Lonely Mountain. But what was the real treasure in Tolkien's books? It's what the hobbits prize most – good food, a pipe and mug of beer shared with family and friends at the end of a day, plenty of feasts and parties, and cozy hobbit burrows scattered through a verdant, unspoiled countryside.

"Wizard Wondering"

Mercury's square to Saturn and the contacts these two planets make to the galactic crossroads yield an inventor and builder of worlds. The Winter Solstice point is the portal of the gods as well as human souls. A natal Mercury retrograde gave Tolkien a glimpse of realities unseen by others. The solstitial portals are analyzed in Section III. J.R.R. Tolkien is one example of how a natal contact to the energies of a soul portal can manifest in a birth chart. His fictional characters constantly mention stars, too. The Elves have a singular love of starlight and their lore includes star legends. This is no accident. Plenty of myths are astronomical in nature, passing down ancient peoples' wisdom about the sky. Having read all the northern European ancient epics and having translated a number of them, Tolkien had singularly excellent access to this body of lore and recognized the extent of sky lore contained in them.

Consider the import of that in context of Tolkien's copious fixed star contacts and the idea of fatedness. He was destined to be a great story-teller and teacher. **The Silmarillion** is not read nearly as often as his other Middle Earth books, but it contains the kind of epic writing found in the Kalevala, the Norse Eddas, the Mahabarata, and the Burgundian Nibelung sagas. It begins with a cosmogony of exquisite beauty that was *written in English*. It's the only substantial cosmogony originally written in that language! Cultural pantheons all share origin stories, legends about how the cosmos was created and how the gods were born. Tolkien knew enough about the ancient cosmogonies to follow most of the rules of what they contain, too. Not perfectly, but close enough. If star-planet contacts program people to fulfill certain roles in the world (and the lore of fixed stars contacts suggest that they do), his particular natal picture augured a person perfectly suited to continue the great bardic tradition into the twentieth century, a time when that tradition was most likely to be lost to humanity, but when humanity most needed it.

When critics dismiss Tolkien's books (and they do), they're missing the nature of the contribution and what it signifies. No one has done any celestial housekeeping in two thousand years. I gripe about this a lot. It used to be the business of priests and storytellers to update constellations and make sure that the figures around the equinoctial and solstitial points were relevant to the lives and deaths of their peoples. If humanity loses touch with the cosmos, it loses something integral to its existence on Earth. If people can't see what's beautiful in the sky, it becomes more challenging to see what's beautiful on Earth and within our souls. Our souls are made of star stuff, and that is not a link that should be severed in the collective consciousness.

The machine-minds of Sauron and Saruman transformed the poetic, star-loving Elves into Orcs. The love of beauty and nature is stripped away; Orcs simply serve, grovel, suffer and fight. Their lives have no joy, only cruelty and bestiality. How much humanity has been stripped away by technology? How much has greed, selfishness, and the demand for more and more productivity stripped away all that is good and sweet in life? Tolkien was keenly aware, even by the middle of the twentieth century, of how badly mechanization and technology ruined people. The Elves depart Middle Earth never to return, and the Age of Men begins. Their lore, their poetry, and their love of Middle Earth is lost forever. Orcs are bred to serve despotic masters, not to live lives filled with health and joy.

The aeon shift is upon us – the old gods are dying, and new gods will be created. Old lore will fade and new will be created. Small people can do great things, though. They can overcome tyranny through courage and fortitude in spite of all odds. Individuals can choose to embrace their inner courage and defy all that is orcish, all that is evil and destructive. What else is free will for, if not to empower people to choose freedom, love and peace rather than war and hate? Tolkien's epics are a reminder of this at the turning of a new age, a time when people are always most in danger of losing that choice.

References
Tolkien's birth data from *The Mountain Astrologer*, June-July 2009 issue, p 59.

[1] Louisa May Alcott born November 29, 1832, 12:30 am LMT, Germantown
      (Philadelphia County), Pennsylvania, RR: AA (from ADB)
[2] Tolkien Gateway contributors, "Upon The Hearth The Fire Is Red," Frodo's slightly altered version of the stanza found in "The Grey Havens" in **Return of the King**.
Tolkien Gateway, http://tolkiengateway.net/w/index.php?
title=Upon_The_Hearth_The_Fire_Is_Red&oldid=309570 (accessed April 15, 2020).

Biographical Material
https://www.tolkiensociety.org/author/biography/
https://en.wikipedia.org/wiki/J._R._R._Tolkien

Allen Ginsberg

Born June 3 1926, 1:55 am EDT, Newark, NJ (RR: AA)

Personal History

Ginsberg's childhood was fraught with trauma and difficulty. His mother Naomi suffered from episodes of paranoid schizophrenia and spent a lot of time in institutions. Allen was close to Naomi so her absences were painful periods of abandonment. Political quarrels added additional stress into the household. Naomi and her sister were communists and his father was a socialist. Their affiliations weren't illegal or all that unusual in the 1920s or 1930s as ideas about socialism and communism were circulating freely, especially on the East Coast. [1]

Allen's strange journey into poetry started after he was accepted at Columbia University during WWII. He got involved with Lucien Carr, a rowdy rebel who introduced him to Jack Kerouac, Neal Cassady, and William Burroughs. They shared the notion of a "New Vision" for American literature. These young men were fellow outsiders and nonconformists during the McCarthy era. Jazz clubs, colleges and coffee shops were the primary nexus of anti-establishment ideas that boiled to the surface in America over the next decade. Carr murdered an older professor, David Kammerer, and claimed the stabbing was self-defense against a sexual predator. He served only a few months for manslaughter. He asked Allen to write a deposition for his trial but refused to use Allen's piece, "The Night in Question." Allen decided to recycle the essay for one of his college classes. Because of the shocking nature of the incident, Allen was forced to decide whether to withdraw the paper or be expelled. He graduated with a bachelor of arts from Columbia in 1948.

Ginsberg met Gregory Corso at the Pony Stable Bar and was immediately drawn to the poet. He introduced Corso to his circle of friends, and eventually they traveled together. Ginsberg was briefly involved with Elise Nada Cowen, aka "Beat Alice," a Barnard College student steeped in the poetry of Ezra Pound and T. S. Eliot. He befriended the Beat poet Joyce Johnson.

While living in an apartment in Harlem in 1948, he had a waking vision triggered by reading William Blake's poetry. He called it his "Blake Vision." It lasted for several days. He felt connected with the universe and experienced the unity of all things. His visions were a profound, life-changing experience.

Ginsberg joined the San Francisco Renaissance in the early 1950s. He obtained a job as a market researcher. He met Peter Orlovsky in 1954. They fell in love and remained life-long partners. William Carlos Williams became his mentor, and he befriended the literary critic and anarchist poet Kenneth Rexroth. He co-founded the *Beatitude Poetry Magazine*. He helped organize the *Six Poets at Six Gallery* poetry reading event held on October 7, 1955 at 8:00 pm in San Francisco. It was an epic event that brought east and west coast Beat poets together. Ginsberg shared excerpts from his poem *Howl*. Jack Kerouac described the event in his book *Dharma Bums*.

Albert Ferlinghetti, the owner of City Lights Bookstore, arranged for *HOWL* to be published through the Pocket Poet Series printed in England by Villiers in 1956. The first shipment arrived without incident, but part of a second printing was stopped by US Customs on March 25, 1957. The use of profanity and graphic descriptions of hetero- and homosexual activity created a censorship problem. Ferlinghetti got the ACLU involved just before he and store clerk Shigeyoshi Murao were arrested on obscenity charges. [2]

Event invitation

Judge Clayton W. Horn adhered to the standards set in the Supreme Court decision in *Roth v United States*, [3] which had been handed down four months before the *HOWL* trial. It provided an important new censorship standard: *unless a book is entirely lacking in social importance, it cannot be held obscene*. The prosecution and defense called expert witnesses to testify about the poem's value and social importance or lack of it. *HOWL*'s vindication was a landmark First Amendment/free speech case, a critical step on the long, arduous path to the Supreme Court decision that overturned most censorship laws in 1964.

Ginsberg wisely skedaddled before the arrests. He and Peter arrived in Paris, France in September 1957 and found housing in a shabby Parisian building called The Beat Hotel. Ginsberg, Orlovsky, Corso, Kerouac, and Burroughs joined photographer Harold Chapman and others "on the run from US middle class society." [4] It was a hyper-productive developmental period, a crucible for the Beat resistance movement. The Beat Hotel's residents created a cooperative, collaborative environment. Corso produced important poetry. Ginsberg helped Burroughs type the manuscript of *Naked Lunch*. Chapman documented the hotel's activities with photographs. When his mother died in an insane asylum, Ginsberg spent three days at the Cafe Le Select at Montparnass writing *Kaddish*, one of his best poems. Artist-activist-poet Jean Jacque Lebel introduced the American Beat Hotel residents to French surrealists Andre Breton, Marcel Duchamp and Péret. Later Lebel translated *HOWL* into French. Ginsberg left his mark on France. During the May 1968 general strike, quotes from *HOWL* were painted on the walls of Parisian buildings.

Allen believed his friends were geniuses and that their literary works were crucial to the development of American society. He launched an intense letter-writing campaign, visited editors, and used his marketing experience to promote their work. He connected with Maurice Girodias, the owner of Olympia Press, who finally agreed to publish *Naked Lunch*. Excerpts from the book were reprinted in the university publication *Chicago Review* in the Autumn 1958 issue and triggered another censorship case. The magazine's editors were fired and the publication was closed. Irving Rosenthal started *Big Table Magazine* in order to continue publishing excerpts from *Naked Lunch*.

Allen and Peter traveled extensively in India in 1962 to 1963. Allen became fascinated with mantra chanting. They arrived in Great Britain in May 1965. Allen joined with Barbara Rubin to organize and participate in the International Poetry Incarnation at the Royal Albert Hall on June 11, 1965. Seven thousand people attended, and the event had a significant impact on British poetry and culture. The event was filmed by Peter Whitehead and later released as the documentary *Wholly Communion*.

When he returned to the US, Allen had a chance encounter with Chōgyam Trumgpa Rinpoche when they tried to catch the same cab. Another life-long friendship was formed. Ginsberg's huge network of friends made him a link between the Beatnik and Hippie movements. He was acquainted with Timothy Leary, Ken Kesey, Bob Dylan, Hunter S. Thompson, Patti Smith, Phil Ochs, members of The Clash, and the Dalai Lama. Allen played a significant role in establishing A. C. Bhaktivedanta Swami Pradhupada, the founder of the Hare Krishna movement, in the US. Allen donated time, money and material to help the Swami get published, found his first temple, and promote his movement.

Ginsberg was an intrinsic participant in several protest movements through the 1960s–1970s, including anti-Vietnam War protests, free speech and drug legalization activism. In 1964, Allen co-authored "*A Letter to New York City against Free Speech Suppression by the NYC Police.*" The letter was necessitated and inspired by Lenny Bruce's pending obscenity trial. New York City cops, egged on by Frank Hogan, the hyper-conservative Catholic prosecutor, were harassing artists and writers. Lenny Bruce was a thorn in the prosecutor's side because one of his comedy routines satirized the Catholic Church's venality. The letter was signed by an astounding number of famous artists and writers. It was printed in the *New York Times* in June 1964. By late June 1964, the Supreme Court had virtually eliminated censorship, but the New York judges refused to drop the charges against Lenny. They convicted him and gave him a sentence of three months in a work house (which he never served since California refused to extradite him).

Allen was at the Human Be-In at the San Francisco Golden Gate Park and co-signed the anti-war manifesto "*A Call to Resist Illegitimate Authority*" in 1967. He was at the turbulent Democratic National Convention in Chicago in 1968. He co-organized Mantra-Rock-Dance at the Avalon Ballroom in San Francisco on January 29, 1967 at 8:00 pm. He joined the Black Panther rally at Yale University in 1970.

Allen met Alfred W. McCoy at a rally in New Haven to free Black Panther leader Huey P. Newton. He became involved with McCoy's work on his book, **The Politics of Heroin in Southeast Asia** (Harper and Row, 1972), an exposé of the CIA's drug trade in Burma, Thailand and Laos. The book's revelations were mostly ignored but later found to be true. Ginsberg actually challenged CIA director Richard Helms on the issue of CIA drug trade. He wrote an open letter to Senator Clifford P Hansen demanding an investigation. Hansen refused. But Ginsberg wouldn't let the issue rest! He spoke about it on the Dick Cavett Show and soon after published his poem entitled *CIA Dope/Calypso* (1972). Allen helped the US public become aware of the misdeeds of its most secret spy agency.

He was a key figure in the gay rights movement, too. This is significant as he was one of the few homosexuals who "came out of the closet" during the 1950s. He spoke about it openly on Dick Cavett's and William Buckley's TV interview shows, calling himself a "faggot individualist." He admitted how painful it was to come out to Kerouac, who was sympathetic. He and Peter Orlovsky made a permanent vow of "celestial heavenly earthly immortal fidelity" when Allen was 28 and Peter was about 21. Allen said, "I think it's the clinging of an identity that gives rise to homophobia, the clinging to the heterosexual identity, it's the clinging to a homosexual identity as a fixed solidified thing that gives people a sense of guilt or anger that is projected. But it is the attempt to solidify an identity and make it, force it on others, whether you're Pat Robertson or Jesse Helms, or the Pope, or the Ayatollah (Khomeini), or some gay guy that is so angry at his parents and angry at himself that he has to scream out angrily that he's gay and challenge everybody in front of their face, instead of seducing them, or instead of just being whatever self there is apparent at the moment". [5]

During the 1970s his health faltered. He had high blood pressure and suffered two mini-strokes. He eventually had to reduce his energetic activism and globe trotting. Poetry continued to flow and *Fall of America*, a collection of his poems, won the 1974 National Book Award. Allen was inducted into the American Academy and Institute of Arts and Letters in 1979, and won the Robert Frost Medal in 1986. He was a Pulitzer finalist in 1995 for *Cosmopolitan Greetings: Poems 1986-1992*. Ginsberg settled down with Peter and took a teaching position at Brooklyn College.

Allen Ginsberg died on April 5, 1997 at age 70 in the East Village in New York City. He is memorialized as the Father of Free Literature in America. J. D. McClatchy, editor of Yale Review, wrote an obituary for the *New York Times*. He claimed that while Kerouac better reflected Rimbaud's authentic self expression with the "quicksilver mind of America's only literary virtuoso," Allen Ginsberg was "the best-known American poet of his generation, as much a social force as a literary phenomenon." [6]

Chart Analysis

Ginsberg's **Ascendant and Mars** are conjunct **Markab**. First house **Uranus** is conjunct **Scheat**. Pegasus is a bucking bronco and most of its stars are attributed Mars-Mercury. These stars are associated with potentially fatal accidents, fires, explosions, all kinds of disasters and the resulting injuries or death. The secondary Mercury attribution implies modes of travel, carelessness and inattention (particularly of young people), and the speed at which accidents can take place.

Markab-Ascendant-Mars shows the potential for a lot of danger! Riding on a bucking bronco isn't impossible if a person figures out a way to channel the star's erratic and unpredictable energies, providing he lives long enough to do so. Young Allen left for college in full rebellion and ripe for serious Mars-Markab problems. Kammerer's murder was followed by a terrible car accident and eight months of incarceration in a mental institution (a plea deal to avoid prison for being in a stolen car with stolen goods). He could have died but people with Jupiter in the twelfth house often have good angels watching over them. Mars eventually cools down when it's in its own watery triplicity. People with a watery Mars usually become more cautious after a few close calls force them manage their passions and develop better judgment skills. Mars-Markab fares best when individuals channel the martial energy into helping others and improving society. The life-threatening situations faded when Ginsberg moved to Paris, although he constantly flirted with danger for a few decades by tweaking the establishment's nose.

Ginsberg learned to channel his Pegasus star conjunctions by becoming "a Johnny-on-the-

Allen Ginsberg
June 3, 1926
1:55 am EDT
Newark, New Jersey
Tropical-Placidus
True Node
RR: AA
(Helen Weaver)

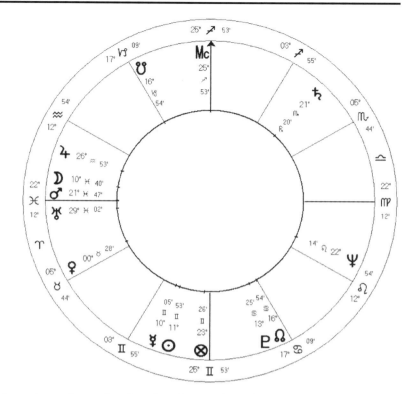

spot, and an arbiter and champion of creative freedom." [7] His active years have a pattern of constant movement and adventurous involvement in counter-culture and protest movements. He embraced his inner bucking bronco. The **Uranus-Scheat** conjunction doubles down on Pegasus significations. Allen had an intellectual fascination with rebellious ideas and the ability to devise innovative methods for challenging authority. He had a first-hand sublime visionary experience that lifted him to the peak of cosmic awareness, after which his consciousness flowered in diverse ways. William Blake's Uranus-MC are conjunct Markab, and his Moon conjunct Canopus. The 18th century visionary Blake shares these two star contacts with Ginsberg.

Venus rises in Taurus conjunct **Stella Mira**, a Saturn star. Mira shares the horrible significations of other Cetus stars – forced emigration, upheavals and losses, and periods of exile. Venus in rulership charms Mira into friendlier forms of expression. Allen's years of exile were a learning experience. He traveled with friends and made yet more new friends (Venus), and organized another big literary event before his return to the United States. The result was a highly productive experience (Taurus).

Venus-Mira functioned through Ginsberg's organizational efforts and the publication of his poetry collections. He organized multi-disciplinary arts gatherings and protest events that changed the culture. Where ever he went, he made friends! He facilitated group cooperation and offered guidance for producing culture-changing events that created a burst of attention-getting light at that location. Stella Mira shifts from magnitude 3 to 10, shining brightly and then subsiding. When the objective was completed and the light subsided, Ginsberg pursued another big project somewhere else with another group of people.

Stella Mira is "the beautiful star," an extremely variable star in the Southern Hemisphere that was discovered during the 1700s when courageous European explorers were circumnavigating the Earth for the first time. Ginsberg's sporadic public appearances and publications reflect Mira's attributes in a positive way as he united people with a brief but focused purpose. Venus in Taurus is the hostess that nurtures her guests with sweetness and abundance. Ginsberg's abundance was his skill for eliciting artistic and revolutionary cooperation. These events left a permanent impression in the ambient culture. Fixed signs give indelible results.

Ginsberg's **Sun and Mercury** are conjunct **Aldebaran** the Bull's Eye. This power-house heliacal rising star is merged with the significator of writing, Mercury, in Gemini in the third house. Aldebaran is a Mars (or Jupiter-Mars) star, and Ginsberg has Mars rising. He channeled that Mars energy by having specific societal targets that he challenged with his poetry and protests, and by being energetic! Over time this had a deleterious impact on his health through circulatory problems that were, at least in part, triggered by long-term stress and overwork. The Sun rules his sixth house of health, and his twelfth house Moon squares the Sun and Mercury. His health problems were hidden (twelfth house) until his mini-strokes. He also had bad vision requiring thick glasses. The Sun and Moon are significators of the eyes, and a Sun-Moon square can sometimes signify vision problems. It doesn't help that the Sun is conjunct a star that marks the *eye* of the Bull. If the rulers of the first or sixth house are conjunct fixed stars, note the bodily location if constellational figure is a human or animal. The person is likely to have health issues with that area of the body.

Ginsberg's **Pluto** at 12° Cancer is conjunct **Canopus**. Canopus is close to Sirius by longitudinal degree but there's a palpable difference in how these stars manifest. Canopus encourages extensive travels and learning, whereas Sirius is a territorial home-body. Pluto crossed over these two stars for a few years during the mid-1920s, as well as the Sun in US Sibley chart. Tremendous social changes were taking place in America: a dramatic population shift from rural farming communities to urban life and manufacturing jobs; and access to modern conveniences like electricity, plumbing, telephones, and radios. Women got the vote and pushed toward better work opportunities and less restrictive clothing. The Beat generation were hyper-conscious of the harm caused by over-crowded, urban, technological servitude, industrial blight, and pollution.

Canopus is the pilot steering the ship on a journey to the underworld. *HOWL* shares that quality. Just as Dante conducts readers through the levels of Hell in his *Inferno*, Ginsberg guides his readers through the soul-crushing depersonalization of modernization, technology, and urban filth. Allen traveled deeply into his mind to dredge up the feelings, inspirations, and existential angst that fueled his poetic soul. Pluto suggests that this was a painful process, but Pluto's darkness is best countered by bringing the pain into the light and acknowledging it. *HOWL* begins: "I saw the best minds of my generation destroyed by madness, starving hysterical naked,/dragging themselves through the negro streets at dawn looking for an angry fix,/angelheaded hipsters burning for the ancient heavenly connection to the starry dynamo in the/machinery of night.../who chained themselves to subways for the endless ride from Battery to holy Bronx on/benzedrine until the noise of wheels and children brought them down shuddering mouth-wracked and battered bleak of brain all drained of brilliance in the drear light of Zoo..." [8]

Pluto-Canopus underscores Ginsberg's role as a pilot for the counter-culture movements that transformed America from the late 1950s through the 1970s. His Pisces Moon trines Pluto in Cancer. Ginsberg's leadership style was one of nurturing and creating strong emotional bonds with others to foster effective cooperation by co-authoring, co-founding, and co-producing. He didn't seem to want or need to be glorified as a fearless leader so much as he wanted objectives to be met and resistance to change overcome. After he had made more than his share of journeys, he settled in and turned into a teacher, sharing the wisdom he'd gained through his many adventures with younger people.

Canopus is a Saturn-Jupiter star. His Saturn receives and squares Jupiter in Aquarius. Acquiring wisdom and learning takes time. Saturn signifies his slow path to mastery and personal authority, and the secondary Jupiter attribution symbolizes how he generously shared his wisdom and accumulated experiences with others.

His **Midheaven** is conjunct **Aculeus** and the Scorpion's stinger stars. Aculeus is linked to attacks and character assassination, and as a Mars-Moon star-nebula it's associated with family difficulties. The tenth house represents the mother in traditional astrology. His mother was severely afflicted with mental illness and believed she was being attacked. Midheaven ruler Jupiter occupies the twelfth house and his mother was institutionalized on multiple occasions. His Part of Fortune opposes the MC. The PF (Lot of the Moon) tends to be regarded as "lucky," but in ancient writings it was the place where available resources in the environment are most easily accessible. His mother's mental illness and her political beliefs were something heavily accessed in Ginsberg's poetry and hands-on involvement in organizing anti-establishment activities. His work sometimes reflects the anguish of his mother's illness and absences. Allen wrote the poem *Kaddish* after Naomi's death. "The telephone rang at 3 A.M. - Emergency — she'd gone mad — Naomi hiding under the bed screaming/ bugs of Mussolini — Help! Louis! Buba! Fascists! Death! - the landlady frightened- old fag attendant/screaming back at her...Her big leg crouched to her breast, hand outstretched Keep Away, wool dress on her thighs, fur coat/dragged under the bed — she barricaded herself under bedspring with suitcases." [9]

Great poetry requires disordering of the soul and the draining of all poisons, as Rimbaud suggested many years earlier. You gotta live the blues to sing the blues. It goes without saying that J Edgar Hoover's FBI tracked Ginsberg closely. Nixon and conservatives regarded him as a public enemy, so his reputation was under constant attack by the right wing. Ginsberg's erratic movements from place to place helped him avoid trouble.

Saturn is at 21° Scorpio Rx conjunct **Unukalhai** (Saturn-Mars), the head or neck of the serpent held by Ophiuchus. This is *not* a user-friendly star as it signifies intrigues, poisons and various dangers. Mars and Saturn are malefics, the hard planets. It can't be understated how important it is that Ginsberg had Mars conjunct a Mars-Mercury star and Saturn conjunct a Saturn star. The trine between Mars and Saturn directs, harnesses, and controls this energy. Apropos of Unukalhai, Ginsberg used drugs and fought for drug legalization. Mars is a warrior! But he also was singularly able to channel the "poisons" and sorrows of his early life into a remarkable body of poetry over time (Saturn). He wasn't defined by his wounds; he used them as an elixir of creativity and source of inspiration. He fought against government suppression of sexual freedoms, against a pointless foreign war, and against authoritarian censorship of ideas, art, music and writing.

Saturn-Unukalhai squares **Jupiter-Gienah**, the wing star of the Swan connected to fame, vast distribution and record sales. His Mars-Saturn trine reflects his writing method, poetic forms and content. Early in his career, Allen adopted Keroac's "spontaneous prose" concept, allowing hidden subconscious material (Scorpio-eighth house) to rise from his soul without conscious restrictions (Mars-1st house). Allen was much more willing to edit and revise than Kerouac, representing the tempering and controlling energies of Saturn. The Saturn-Unukalhai/Jupiter-Gienah square is representative of the influences that swirl through Ginsberg's poems: modernism; romanticism; jazz; Judiaism; Kagyu Buddhism; the French surrealist poets Antonin Artaud, Jean Genet, and Andre Breton; and the work of earlier visionary poets that William Blake, Walt Whitman, Federico Garcia Lorca, and William Carlos Williams. Like Rimbaud and Garcia Lorca, Ginsberg packs his poetry with potent visual imagery. He drew inspiration from Paul Cezanne's paintings, from which he derived the concept of the "eyeball kick" - placing two starkly dissimilar images in close proximity. Shades of Aldebaran, the Bull's Eye! Merging styles and techniques from the past with new material is a Jupiter-Saturn function. Rather than spewing poison, Saturn-Unukalhai in Ginsberg's chart is about potion-blending, taking an unusually eclectic jumble of ideas and transforming them into a poetic rallying call for his generation.

Mars-Markab demands immense freedom to ride the unpredictable surges of creativity. One might tend to see this eighth house Saturn as a bad placement, but Rimbaud has the same thing—an eighth house Saturn trine to a planet near the Ascendant (Venus). The same artistic delineation holds true for both charts. Saturn provides the form, but in Ginsberg's chart, Mars-Markab supplies the poetic contents. The eighth house is associated with the occult. Occult simply means *hidden*. A poet delves deeply to find his inner alchemical gold. It's an extremely private and tortuous process, a lonely journey to the center of the soul and then back out again. In both charts, Saturn provides the mental and emotional stability that kept these poets on track and helped them complete their long works. Eighth house planets can give great fortitude and resilience!

Giovanni Battista Tiepolo "Seated Figure of Time"
circa 1760. The Met Collection (public domain)

Saturn is sometimes depicted as Father Time carrying a scythe in old illustrations. Poems may begin as an outpouring of the unconscious contents into words on paper, but great poems are more like swords – tempered and hammered into the desired shape. In the ancient world, blacksmiths (a Mars profession) were considered magical. Some did spells or chants as they hammered weapons and tools on the anvil. Mars in Pisces overflows with words and feelings, and Saturn in Scorpio eliminates the excess and trims them into shape. Mars receives Saturn in Scorpio, so this was a harmonious process for Ginsberg. His poems are weapons for cutting through the barriers of social resistance to change. Contrast that with Rimbaud's Venus-Saturn: his poetic output ended up revitalizing a specialized form of beauty. His oriental Venus (also in rulership) signifies renewal and invention.

Ginsberg's **Moon** has a special connection with **Skat**, a fortunate star in the shin of the Water Bearer that signifies mysticism, lasting happiness, help and good luck from good friends and overall good fortune. The Moon-Skat contact set Ginsberg's internal compass. Instead of being bogged down by sorrows and misery (his other planet-star connections are incredibly difficult ones), he chose to explore the world, made an amazing number of great friends he kept for life, and shared his life experiences and spiritual discoveries with others. The Beatnik movement channeled Eastern mysticism, Buddhism and Taoism into American culture. Ginsberg wasn't satisfied with second-hand knowledge. He went to India and absorbed the culture and their religious lifestyles first hand.

The Moon occupies the twelfth house, which generally signifies confinement and isolation. Pisces needs for solitude and time away from peoples' demands. The Moon-Pluto trine suggests that Allen's need for solitude was intense at times. But Pisces Moon folks also love socializing with others, sharing ideas and activities, and being where the action is. Allen's singular ability to bring people together for specific purposes was preternatural. He had the rare instinctual sense that power shared is power gained, a very atypical viewpoint for a white male during his time period. It's a collective attitude derived, in part, from his mother's communistic theories.

Allen wasn't a communist but he did ascribe to some of its tenants. He recognized the white old boys' hierarchical power structure controlling the government, laws, and economy as the enemy of anyone who wasn't a part of that insular power structure. Gloria Steinem explicates more about the movement against hierarchical power structures in her book *Revolution from Within*. [10] People whose choices were being politically repressed in the 1950s and 1960s were well aware that the insular political and religious power structures were the source of the repression. They experimented with alternative group power structures within their counter-culture movements. Hippie communal living was one expression of this desire to break away from hierarchies.

The Fifth Sacred Thing also explores alternative collective power structures. Starhawk quotes Beat poet Diane de Prima's ideas about how social choices for sustainability can be implemented within a collectivized power structure. [11,12] It's quite possible that people will revisit and renew their views of power structures as Pluto transits Aquarius. The Beatniks, Hippies and women's movement did some good work re-imagining and experimenting with methods for power-sharing but never got it to stick.

Poetry IS revolutionary. Rimbaud experienced it as a revolution within the soul while behaving like an obnoxious brat toward his elders. Poets from Ovid to William Blake, Lord Byron, Garcia Lorca and Allen Ginsberg used it as a call for revolution against the restrictive societies in which they lived. A great deal of attention is placed on the causes of protests and counter-cultural movements of the mid-twentieth century, yet insufficient attention is given to the issues surrounding power that were being discussed at the time, as well the alternatives to hierarchical power structures that were developed through those discussions. If political and social revolutions don't succeed in dramatically transforming the repressive power and social structures that are at the root of the problems, those problems are revisited during subsequent Saturn-Pluto conjunctions that occur every 34 to 36 years.

Let's return to Pegasus and its crucial role in Ginsberg's chart. Analysts of myths sometimes become focused on one part of a story while ignoring another. The Medusa myth gets tossed around a lot but few bother to include the crucial details of her story's ending. When Perseus beheaded Medusa, Chrysaor and Pegasus sprang from her body fully formed. They were the offspring of her unwilling union with Poseidon-Neptune. There are almost no ancient mythic references to Chrysaor, the golden warrior, but a few things can be tickled out of his name. When you orient a shiny material, like gold or a mirror, toward the sun or a significant light source, the reflection can blind one's opponent. Reflections of light can be used to signal to one's allies. Gold is the incorruptible metal linked to the Sun, the light of life itself. Being good isn't enough; good must always fight against evil. Patriarchal cultures have ob-

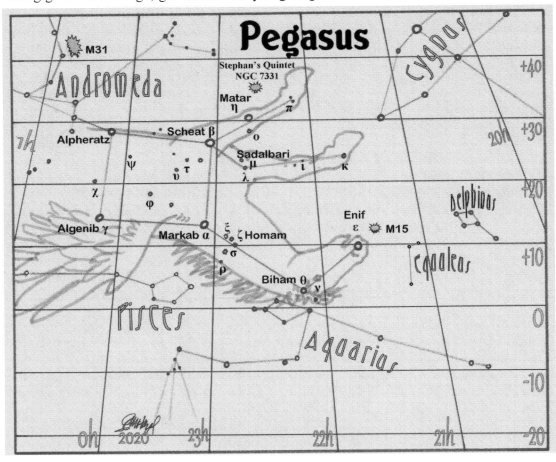

sessed about "the perfect warrior" for centuries. The Spartans were entirely dedicated to the quest for martial perfection and that quest continues. How many contemporary films are there about scientists trying to create the perfect soldier? It always backfires when the warrior goes rogue. Well, of course! Chrysaor is the son of Poseidon, one of the trickiest, most subversive and underhanded gods in the Greek pantheon. The apple doesn't fall far from the tree. If you get a perfect warrior you'll never be able to control him!

Chrysaor's twin brother Pegasus, the famous winged horse, is featured in various myths. The winged horse was untamable and couldn't be ridden. Athena, goddess of wisdom and skills, gave a magical bridle to Bellerophon. He mounted Pegasus and attempted to fly the horse to Olympus. Zeus struck the boy off the horse's back, and then placed Pegasus in the sky as a constellation. What does this myth suggest? The gods are not at home to visitors! Humans cannot be gods, although they sometimes want to be or act like it. On a more subtle level, though, Bellerophon was challenging the Olympian power structure and got flicked away like an annoying bug for his troubles. His hurtling force met an immovable object.

This is an apt description of the challenges faced by the Beatniks, the Hippies, the Women's Liberation movement, the Civil Rights movement, the Gay Liberation movement, and the anti-war protestors during the 1960s and 1970s. The government was *not* going to yield. Protesters were characterized as public enemies. J. Edgar Hoover and the FBI collected mountainous files of information on them. The more the government and bastions of conservatism resisted change, the more violent the protests became. It escalated to the point where President Nixon ordered the Ohio National Guard to respond to a protest against the bombing of Cambodia at Kent State University on May 4, 1970. It was a peaceful protest and the students were unarmed. Four students were shot dead. Neil Young immortalized the horrific incident in a song called *Ohio*. The violence escalated. Groups like the Weathermen, the Black Panthers and others started arming themselves and bombing selected targets, with some dubious assistance from a little tome called **The Anarchist's Cookbook**. [13] Women burned their bras and draft-dodgers burned their draft cards. Progress came in slow steps. Congress produced legislation to ensure civil rights and equal opportunity. The Supreme Court overturned restrictions on women participating in the economy and decided that women should have a right to choose to have an abortion. The Vietnam War ended in 1973 when US troops abandoned the South Vietnamese people to the predations the Viet-Cong army. The power structure, however, remained unchanged.

None of these were perfect or final solutions! But perhaps this helps underscore the importance of a person like Ginsberg riding the Winged Horse and challenging the monolithic power structure. When a chart is so intensely focused on Pegasus, one might want to take a peek at Daddy Dearest Neptune to see what that planet is doing. Well, what do you know? It's in opposition to Jupiter, the bug-flicker himself, and in a T-square with Jupiter and Saturn. The Saturn-Neptune square is a sign of dissolving structures. Ginsberg's T-square gains incredible potency with planets in fixed signs. Ginsberg shares a Saturn-Neptune square with Rimbaud.

Fixed signs symbolize things that are very difficult to change, especially once they slide into a state of static entropy. After World War II ended in 1945 and soldiers returned home, the United States settled into a lengthy Cold War with the USSR. The white Anglo-Saxon Protestants (WASPs) exerted rigid control on public opinion and mores. There was exceptionally strong pressure to conform to expectations—get a wife and a job, have kids and work, buy a house and a car, and don't cause trouble or breed dissent. The most egregious offense was associating with communists! The Congressional House UnAmerican Activities Committee (HUAC) conducted years of investigations into the Soviet infiltration of American institutions and businesses. Individuals merely suspected of flirting with anything deemed "unAmerican" were labeled as a subversive and ostracized. Writers in particular were blacklisted and shunned.

Ginsberg was a young adult during this period—a young adult discovering that he was gay. The suppression of homosexuality was especially intense and vile. Suppression was applied to any form of recreational drug use, interest in Eastern religions, or any kind of speech or writings that didn't kow-tow to the dominant WASP ethical code. So Ginsberg, with his Jewish background, had several strikes against him in the tight-laced tightie-whitie ambient culture. Mounting Pegasus and striking a blows for freedom was his choice. He could have just as easily self-destructed as other non-conformists did, including John Coltrane and Miles Davis who were both born in 1926. Ginsberg's buddy Jack Kerouac, born in 1922, had natal conjunctions to Markab and Scheat and died young from severe alcoholism. Another more recent example of a Winged Horse rider is Kurt Cobain with Venus and Saturn in Pisces conjunct Pegasus stars Scheat and Matar. His ride ended badly. These are not easy stars!

Ginsberg is singular example of a Pegasus rider who managed to ride the bucking winged bronco with grace. The difference is in the total natal star-planet picture. Ginsberg's Mars-Ascendant-Markab trine to Saturn provided control and moderation: he learned painful lessons about the importance of risk assessment from dangerous incidents in his youth. He learned to express his dissatisfaction with the ruling authorities in a peaceful enough manner to avoid being arrested or shot (like Garcia Lorca, who may well have expressed anti-fascist sentiments to the wrong person at the wrong time). Perhaps individuals who learn to master Pegasus stars eventually become Chrysaor, the golden warrior whose reflected light blinds the adversary.

During the latter part of his life, Ginsberg received recognition for his work through prizes and awards for his poetry. He was endlessly controversial but ended up as a culture hero. Not all of the social issues he worked to change were changed during his lifetime. Some of the issues only had a patina of change as American discovered in the 2010s. But Ginsberg was deft enough and sufficiently leveraged his network of diverse and multi-disciplinary friends to heave these issues into the public view. Things can only be changed when there's awareness of a problem, and not before.

References

1. Biographical information is drawn from numerous sources including Edward de Grazia, **Girls Lean Back Everywhere: The Law of Obscenity and the Assault on Genius**. Random House, 1992. Chapter 17 (pp 327-338) provides details of Ginsberg's personal history. Wiki biography at: https://en.wikipedia.org/wiki/Allen_Ginsberg

2. de Grazia, Chapter 17 (pp 327-338). de Grazia is a first amendment attorney. This book offers an in-depth description of the *HOWL* trial. Note that the publisher was on trial, not the author. It wasn't illegal to write obscene material, but it was illegal to print and distribute it.

Publishers were the real heroes in the censorship battles. By the time the *HOWL* trial took place, Ginsberg was in Tangiers. Also see *HOWL*, a film that depicts this legal battle. James Franco portrays Allen Ginsberg.

3. de Grazia, Ch 15 and Ch 16, pp 273 – 325. *Roth v United States*, case 254 U.S. 475 (1957), was a crucial censorship case that challenged the constitutionality of the 1873 Comstock Law, which allowed the US Postal Service to censor materials sent through the mail. Roth was a sleazy publisher who operated under dozens of business names to evade detection by Post Office censors when shipping publications with pornography and writings of dubious provenance (he also neglected to secure copyrights and pay royalties) to subscribers. Although his case resulted in the Comstock Law being overturned, he was still guilty of some of the other charges against him and spent five years in jail. "Doubts centered on the breadth and vagueness of the [Comstock] law's coverage and purposes, but there was also a growing appreciation that such laws allowed an undemocratic and paternalistic governmental supervision of literary and artistic expression and taste...Comstock flunked the review." (ibid, p 308) The Supreme Court's *Roth* decision shifted the burden of proof from the defendant to the prosecution. This set the stage for *HOWL*'s relatively speedy legal vindication.

4. *The Beat Hotel* (2011) documentary directed by Alan Govenar.

5. quotes from the film *The Life and Times of Allen Ginsberg* by Jerry Aronson, transcription at https://allenginsberg.org/2017/06/gay-pride/

6. McClatchy is quoted by Willborn Hampton in his obit, "Allen Ginsberg, Master Poet of Beat Generation, Dies at 79" *New York Times*, April 6, 1997.

7. p 3. de Grazia, p 329.

8. *HOWL* quote from The Poetry Foundation, www.poetryfoundation.org.

9. *Kaddish* quote from The Poetry Foundation, www.poetryfoundation.org

10. Gloria Steinem, **Revolution from Within: A Book of Self-Esteem.** Little, Brown and Company 1992. "Instead of defining power as domination, it is being redefined as self-determination." (p188) "If people regard themselves as part of nature...they tend toward a communal, circular paradigm that is modeled on the cycles of birth-growth-death-and-rebirth. If they measure progress by their conquering of nature, they create a hierarchical paradigm...As Marilyn French wrote in *Beyond Power*, her historian's diagnosis of patriarchy: "No really profound sense of human equality can ever emerge from a philosophy rooted in a stance of human superiority over nature."" (pg 290)

11. Starhawk, **The Fifth Sacred Thing**. Bantam Books, 1993. "The Five Criteria of True Wealth: Usefulness, Sustainability (must generate or save as much energy as it consumes and doesn't depend on nonrenewable resources), Beauty, Healing for the earth, or at least not being destructive. Nurturing for the spirit." [paraphrased from pg 275] On patriarchal power: "Once this drive for power-over and domination appeared on the planet, it became a force that no one could escape for more than a breathing space. For either we submit, and it triumphs, or we mobilize to fight against it, diverting our energies and resources and transforming ourselves into what we do not want to be. It's like a virus, mindlessly destructive, yet we cannot eradicate it without changing our own internal balance." [a few paragraphs down] "[T]he poet Diane di Prima wrote a line that comes back to me now: 'The only war that counts is the war against the imagination.'...All war is first waged in the imagination, first conducted to limit our dreams and visions, to make us accept within ourselves its terms,

to believe that our only choices are those that it lays before us. If we let the terms of force describe the terrain of our battle, we will lose." [page 238]

12. de Grazia, p 329. Diane de Prima was a Beat poet who founded the New York Poets Theater and the Poets Press. She edited and published, with poet-playwright LeRoi Jones (Amiri Baraka) and later Alan Marlowe, a literary newsletter/journal called *Floating Bear*, whose publication of Baraka and William Burroughs led to the editors' arrest by the FBI in 1961 for sending obscenity through the mail. She wrote **Memoirs of a Beatnik** in 1969; republished as **Last Gas of San Francisco** in 1988.

13. William Powell, **The Anarchist Cookbook**. Lyle Stuart, 1971. (still in print)

Additional Material

Life and Times of Allen Ginsberg, 1994 documentary directed by Jerry Aronson

The Source, 1999 documentary directed by Chuck Workam investigating the cultural significans of the Beatniks

Howl, 2010 film directed by Rob Epstein and Jeffrey Friedman, starring James Franco as Ginsberg. The film depicts the *HOWL* censorship charges and obscenity trial in 1956-57.

E Hazel '07

Index of Constellational Images and Charts

About the Author and Artist

Elizabeth Hazel is an astrologer, tarotist, rune-reader, author and lecturer. She started studying tarot and astrology during the 1970s and began to offer consultations in the early 1980s.

Liz started writing about tarot and metaphysical topics during the 1990s. She providing many articles for the International Tarot Society, the American Tarot Association, and Llewellyn annuals.

Her book **Tarot Decoded: Using and Understanding Correspondences and Dignities** was published in 2004 (Red Wheel/Weiser). She spent several years creating the art work for **The Whispering Tarot** deck and book, which was published in 2008.

Liz is a long-time board member of SMARRT (Southeast Michigan Astrologers Research Round Table), the Ann Arbor chapter of NCGR. She has been co-president of the group since 2016. Her astrological activities include lecture presentations at the Great Lakes Astrology Conferences (GLAC), United Astrology Conference (UAC 2018), the Midwest School of Astrology, Kepler College, the Toledo Astrology group, and other area gatherings.

Her interests include gardening, perfumery, art and music. Liz has performed as a singer and pianist in a wide variety of genres including musical theater, professional choirs, rock bands, and as a soloist in numerous forums. She lives in Toledo, Ohio with her beloved and much-spoiled kitties. She offers private consultations.

Contact Liz through her website at www.kozmickitchenpress.com.

About the Contributing Author

Michael Munkasey earned two Degrees in Engineering. After serving in the military , including a tour in Vietnam, he worked for over 30 years as a computer information scientist in the medical and transportation industries in Systems Design, Data Base Design and Maintenance.

Michael began studying astrology in 1969. In 2008 he received the UAC Regulus Award for Discovery, Innovation and Research.

He holds Professional Astrologer's Certifications from all US organizations. Michael is a founding member of Kepler College and served on the Board of NCGR for over 22 years.

Michael's books include **House Keywords and More ...** [AFA, 2018]; and **Midpoints: Unleashing the Power of the Planets** [ACS Publications, 2018]. He is working on a massive fixed star research project that will be published in the near future.

Michael lives with his partner Billie Black in a rural over-55 community in the northern part of San Diego County, California, USA.

BOOKS BY ELIZABETH HAZEL

Tarot Decoded: Understanding and Using Correspondences and Dignities (Red Wheel/Weiser, 2004) paperback and e-book

***

PRIVATE PRINTINGS

The Whispering Tarot signed limited edition (900), 2008 ($25)
The Whispering Tarot: Softly Spoken Secrets book ($16)
Little Book of Fixed Stars, first edition 2017 ($15)
Geomantic Divination, 2013 ($10)
Lady Vala's Little Book of Mantras, 3rd edition 2014 ($9)
Lady Vala's Little Book of Sabbats, 3rd edition 2014 ($10.50)
(contact the author for purchase, some titles have limited availability)

COMING SOON FROM KOZMIC KITCHEN PRESS

The Advanced Tarot-Astrology Series:
The Twelve-House Spread: Uses and Variations
Attributions in Naked Splendor (follow-up to Tarot Decoded)

Astrological texts:
Antiscia: Secrets in the Mirror
Metaphysical Cosmos
The Evolution of Chiron
Lady Asteroids Vesta and Ceres: A New Perspective
Lady Asteroids Pallas Athena and Juno: A New Perspective

KOZMIC KITCHEN PRESS

www.kozmickitchenpress.com

Made in the USA
Coppell, TX
31 October 2024

39409877R00092